ONE MAN'S JUDAISM

ONE MAN'S JUDAISM

by

Emanuel Rackman

Philosophical Library

New York

in association with
Jewish Education Committee

To Ruth

Would that like her
my life, more than my words,
were fulfillment of the values
that are our heritage!

PREFACE

The teaching of Judaism has been my vocation for a long time. A number of congregants and pupils have led me to believe that what I have had to say helped them the better to understand and appreciate their religious heritage—especially its legal treasures. For that reason I occasionally did burst forth into print to share my views with a wider group. What I should really do now is systematize my philosophy of Judaism and clearly delineate my methodology. But I am still questing—my final answers are few. And the best I can do is organize and update what I have already published in the hope that others may glean from my meager fruit how exciting and edifying the enterprise was for me personally and how beckoning the literature is for more creative spirits.

The essays are not arranged in the order in which they were published. What I did instead was to organize them in sections and to connect them with brief introductions.

Almost ten years ago I used a number of the essays as background papers in a series of seminars I conducted for Jewish case and group workers under the auspices of the Jewish Education Committee of the Federation of Jewish Philanthropies of the City of New York. The seminars were part of the Jewish Orientation and Training Seminar co-sponsored by J.E.C.'s Department of Adult Education and the New York Metropolitan Section of the National Jewish Welfare Board. Dr. Leon A. Feldman was most gracious in publishing them in a volume entitled "Jewish Values for Modern Man." Dr. Leonard Rosenfeld, who presently directs the manifold activities of the Jewish Education Committee, encouraged me to enlarge and republish the volume and my present effort is very much a response to his stimulus and goading. I am most grateful to him.

Acknowledgments

The author expresses his profound gratitude to the following publishers and periodicals who permitted the reprinting of most of the essays contained herein: Atherton Press, Columbia University Press, Commentary, Hadassah Magazine, Jewish Chronicle (London), Jewish Heritage, Jewish Horizon, Judaism, Menorah Journal, New York University Law Review, Tradition, Yeshiva University Press, and Young Israel Viewpoint.

The author also wants to express his deep appreciation to Fifth Avenue Synagogue in New York, whose spiritual leader he presently is, for helping to make possible the publication of this volume and to its ritual director, Mr. David Finkelstein, for his careful reading of the proofs.

CONTENTS

SECTION ONE
One Man's Judaism

SECTION TWO
The Scope of the Law

SECTION THREE
God and Man

SECTION FOUR
The Law's Methodology

SECTION FIVE
Israel's Sancta

SECTION SIX
The Contemporary Scene

ONE MAN'S JUDAISM

SECTION ONE

ONE MAN'S JUDAISM

Introductory Note

My readers are entitled to know how I define Judaism and what I consider its basic doctrines.

Later sections will elaborate upon many of the positions articulated in the introductory chapters but some general statements, albeit brief ones, are called for.

Chapter One

JUDAISM—A TRADITIONALIST'S DEFINITION

Jews crave name changes not only for themselves but also for their faith. Reform Judaism prefers to be called "liberal." Conservative Judaism would rather be known as "historic" and Orthodox Judaism wants no descriptive adjective whatever. It insists that there is but one Judaism and giving it a first name would make it appear that other interpretations are equally valid and legitimate.

Even at the risk of being dubbed "intolerant," I too insist that there is but one authentic Judaism, while other approaches are error, distortion, heresy, or even pretense. Nonetheless, I admit that within the range of the authentic there is an enormous latitude in practice and interpretation. Judaism has never had a fixed philosophy, nor even one inflexible approach to law. There have always been, and will continue to be, many different modes of Jewish thought and conduct, and every generation does introduce a great

3

measure of innovation. There is still no hierarchy of authority; on the other hand, until the Messiah comes, the rabbinic groups seem to multiply and reflect ideological, geographical, and ethnic differences. How does one reconcile this diversity with an insistence that there is but one Judaism?

To resolve the paradox, one would do well to conceive of Judaism neither as a religion nor as a faith. If it is regarded as a faith, then Jews who are its devotees must be considered a community of believers. But not all Jews believe in God. And Orthodoxy, even more fervently than Conservative and Reform Judaism, refuses to exclude Jewish atheists from the fold. Furthermore, religions usually permit their adherents to exercise some choice—to be or not to be a member of the fellowship or a communicant of the church, visible or invisible. But Judaism gives Jews no choice. It recognizes neither resignation, withdrawal, renunciation, nor even apostasy as effective means to shed one's Jewishness.

Judaism as a Legal Order

For these reasons it is more accurate to conceive of Judaism as a legal order rather than a religion or faith. The anomalies thus become intelligible. A legal order presumes a constituency which is bound by a pyramid or hierarchy of norms which may apply to creed as well as practice, and definitely applies to the very process by which the norms themselves are derived and concretized. The legal order best known to us is the state. In our day an international legal order is also striving to be born. But Judaism always was, and still is, an international legal order for Jews. Moreover, upon careful analysis, it appears that every legal order is founded upon one basic norm. In the case of a political entity, the basic norm is usually the lawmaking power of the sovereign. From this norm most others are derived. In the case of Israel, the basic norm is God's covenant with His people.

4

Within the legal order there is diversity. However, existence of diversity does not mean that there is a multiplicity of legal orders. The freedom permitted is always proscribed. One can violate the norms—often with impunity. One can even defy the basic norm. But if the legal order grants no release from its grip, one has no legal power to make his exit. One may be deemed wicked, a sinner, a traitor, but the legal norms are not his to make. The legal order itself ordains how new norms shall come into being. One may have a voice in the process, but even a majority can rarely change the norms that are basic.

In this way Judaism can regard even a Jewish atheist as a Jew. As a legal order, Judaism has norms applicable to the non-observant, the agnostic, and the apostate—all of whom it continues to regard as subject to the legal order. Generations ago they might have been punished or excommunicated but they were never placed beyond the law. (Today we are not even permitted to act disdainfully toward them.) Their conduct and their thought may violate the norms of the legal order itself, but they remain Jews. There is but one Judaism and one Jewry. Even the guardians of the legal order may err (the legal order provides for such errors). But the legal order and its processes are supreme. One lives within them—perfectly or imperfectly —but one can never leave them except pursuant to the norms themselves.

Basic Tenets

What are the basic norms of the legal order that is Judaism?

God chose Abraham and his seed to give them a land and a law. The covenant—reconfirmed several times in the lives of the patriarchs and in the wilderness en route from Egypt to Canaan—is forever binding on us. Three basic dogmas of Jewish theology derive from the Covenant. First, God is personal—He intervenes in the lives of individuals and nations. Second, He chose a particular people. Third,

He and His people are forever bound by the provisions of the Torah.

Any interpretation of Judaism which does not involve commitment to these three facts as historical occurrences deviates so far from the preponderant weight of the tradition as to constitute a new faith.

(1) A Personal Omnipotent God

Jews may conceive of God differently. Their philosophies and theologies may be hewn from different sources. But all must believe that God is aware of individuals and nations whose Creator, rather than whose creature, He is. He does permit the exercise of free will so that He is not the sole author of history. Man also writes many a chapter of his own biography, as well as substantial parts of the annals of his people. But God, who is personal, knows what is happening, participates in events, and is the ultimate judge of all that is done. Moreover, as He is omniscient, so He is omnipotent.

The relationship between God and His people is a personal one. God can and does answer prayer. Even if one gives miracles a naturalistic interpretation—regarding them as occurrences within the frame of natural law so that only their remarkable coincidence with our need of the hour constitutes their miraculous character—a Jew must believe that God can perform and has performed miracles. According to the tradition, prayer is meaningless unless one has faith that God can and does intervene in nature to answer our supplications. That is why for Jews prayer is not merely an occasion for introspection and a stimulus to self-improvement. It is a confrontation of God by man. Moreover, God's miraculous intervention in nature will reach its climax when He sends the Messiah, establishes universal justice, resurrects the dead, and even divests the beasts of their evil propensities. Nature itself will reflect His perfection. For the Jew this is not only poetry. It is his commit-

6

ment. He stakes his life on the moral and logical necessity that a benign God must do no less.

Interestingly enough, it is not the Jew who doubts that this can happen who is regarded as the heretic. The heretic is he who denies that it can ever come to pass. This is a denial of God's omnipotence and infinite righteousness. To doubt is natural; to deny is sin.

(2) Revelation

Especially did God intervene to redeem His people from Egypt, the affirmation of which fact is a prelude to prayer. The most important intervention in nature, however, was in connection with Revelation. Jews may differ as to the exact form in which Revelation took place and the exact manner in which Torah was committed to writing. But all must believe that the Torah is God's will made manifest to His people. Jews, and non-Jews too, may have a voice in the fulfillment of that will in history, but the Torah—whose validity is the basic norm of the legal order of Judaism—ordains how that fulfillment shall occur.

(3) The Chosen People

The chosenness of the Jews flows from the fact that God redeemed them from bondage and gave them the Torah that they might become a holy people and a kingdom of priests. Whether or not they had a mission as such to the non-Jewish world remains debatable. Perhaps their achievement for humanity was to be only an incident of their service to God. What is not debatable is that there exists a special relationship between them and God pursuant to the Covenant.

(4) The Covenant

The Covenant pertains to every aspect of life—man's relationship to God, to his fellow, to his self, to the animal kingdom, to the very universe itself. It contains norms for war and peace, for family and nation, for time and even outer space. It is hard to visualize any system of norms that is more extensive than those of the Torah. However, the system was to be a dynamic one. Changes always occurred in the circumstances of Jews. Therefore, with the Written Law there was also transmitted from Moses an oral tradition. The oral tradition was the fulcrum controlling the Law's development so that it might cope with change.

Development of Jewish Law

In some instances the oral tradition represented the common law of the people. In other instances, it represented new interpretation. In the main, it was a method, a process, whereby Revelation was kept viable—and progressive.

Yet, who would be vested with this power to create law? Man had become God's partner in creation. The commandments to be fruitful and multiply and conquer the earth and all its hosts had made him such a partner. The Jew also became God's partner in expanding the Torah, God's will. Priests and judges, saints and sages, played their part. The process was an intricate one. It called for commitment to the basic norms and a profound understanding of the art and technique of fathoming God's will. In a legal order, not every wise or good man can be a final arbiter of what is right and wrong. There is a judicial process, eloquently described in our times by the late U.S. Supreme Court Justice Benjamin Cardozo, which one masters only after decades of preoccupation with the law. Similarly, the process was not a simple one for Jews. But God and His people in history were constantly creating, within the frame of the immutable law, new insights, new rules,

8

new directives. In the crucible from which the new interpretations emerged there were many fuels—the will of the
people, the challenges of the hour, the authorities of the
past, the imagination of poets, the yearning of saints, the
passion of prophets. During the millennia some Jews denied
that the creative process was legitimate—the Sadducees
and the Karaites, for example. Others denied that it had
any limitations—such as Reform Jews. Still others—Reconstructionists—denied one or more of the basic norms. Orthodoxy continued to make its fathoming of the process,
and its creativity within it, the core of Jewish life, and
differed with right-wing Conservative Judaism principally
in that the latter permitted many who are not committed to
the basic norms to have a major voice in directing the
destiny of the Covenant.

Modern Challenges and Adjustments

In the last few centuries the Law has faced its greatest
challenge. No earlier period of Jewish history saw more
fundamental changes in every phase of human existence.
From modern science and philosophy there came such a
plethora of challenges to the basic norms of Judaism that
the overwhelming majority of Jewish writers assumed that
the foundations of Judaism had crumbled. Jewish political,
social, and economic life also underwent such a revolution
that the very structure of the Jewish community in which
the Law might have been operative disintegrated. Everyone
could do as he pleased. Congregations became completely
autonomous. Rabbis lost their authority. Philosophies of
assimilation, secularism, even hedonism, enjoyed as much
respect in the Jewish community as philosophies of religion.

In the face of these trials, the guardians of the Law did
make manifest some readiness to be creative in meeting
new situations. For example, while the omnipresence of the
automobile has moved no Orthodox rabbi to permit its use
on the Sabbath, the emergence of the electric dishwasher
did evoke a very liberal decision permitting its use for both

9

dairy and meat dishes at different times, with specifications as to what must be done in the intervals between such uses. Similarly, while Orthodoxy dare not countenance any change in the incidence of the Sabbath day in spite of the pressure within the United Nations for calendar reform which will affect its fixity, Orthodoxy has given de jure recognition to the international date line for the purpose of computing when the Sabbath shall be observed on both sides of that longitude. Orthodoxy has also been exceedingly liberal in the matter of the adoption of non-Jewish children. And there is almost complete unanimity that a child conceived by artificial insemination even from a donor other than the husband is legitimate, though rabbis differ on the propriety of resorting to this method of procreation.

The threat to survival, however, has been so great that the natural tendency has been to resist revolution with counter-revolution and introduce a virtual "freeze" in the dynamism of the Law. Codes which were never intended to be final oracles became more immutable than the Bible, and customs, even forms of dress, which were hardly Jewish in origin, were canonized because they coincided in time with the "freeze." Within the ranks of Orthodoxy, this has been the basis for grave differences of opinion, and authorities respected for their learning and commitment to the Law still take different positions vis-à-vis the Jewish situation in the modern age.

One school has argued, for example, that the devout and the observant should insulate themselves against all contact with dissenters. While they concede that in ancient times Pharisees and Sadducees sat in the same Sanhedrin, the danger to the Law in the nineteenth and twentieth centuries seems to them to require more drastic measures. Another school is more respectful of the historic dogma involving the oneness as well as the chosenness of the Jewish people.

One school became anti-Zionist in the sense that they banned any co-operation with Zionists who were heretics. Another school saw in Zionism the beginning of the Messianic era and even sought to explain why in such an era

10

one must expect a higher incidence of deviationist behavior.

However, the failure to exploit the Law's potential to meet new situations wrought its greatest havoc in connection with Jewish family law. The result is that in the State of Israel, where the rabbinate remains in control of matters of personal status, there is far more liberalism than in the Diaspora, where the need for creativity is much greater. Because the Orthodox rabbinate in the Diaspora, as custodians of the Law, has only a minority of loyalists supporting it, all energies are expended on the dikes, to prevent breakthroughs, and all proposals for remedial measures are looked upon critically.

Yet, by the same token, this "freeze" of the modern age has saved from obsolescence much that is basic in Judaism. The Sabbath, for example, would long ago have lost its meaning and value but for the resistance of the traditionalists. Even the innovators are recognizing the folly of their license with the tradition, and ancestral forms and techniques are being refurbished for the greater bliss of beleaguered moderns. Psychiatrists too are now helping to give the Sabbath new significance in the face of that hedonistic philosophy in whose name they once whittled away all of its prohibitions.

Moreover, the deterioration of Jewish moral standards has also led to renewed interest in the tradition. In Israel, such interest has been due to the sense of alarm created by the increase in juvenile delinquency, while in America, a similar interest has developed as a result of the increase of sexual promiscuity and marital infidelity.

Goal of the Mitzvot

To strengthen one's faith and live by it is the goal of the mitzvot. Though some call this "supernaturalism," a traditionalist must maintain that without the possibility for transcending the natural in history one has no authentic Judaism. If anything, it is Judaism's unique hope that the supernatural will invade the natural and endow it with the perfection and the goodness which are God's.

11

In accomplishing this purpose the Jewish people are God's instrument. He decided to use the Jews and they consented to be used. For that purpose they entered into the Covenant with Him. A legal order was created. It was to be a legal order with its disciplines and its freedoms, its rights and its duties. The lowliest and the greatest had their roles to play. The confrontations with God were to be continuous—at least continuously sought. He is the Sovereign and we are His subjects. These words of the traditional liturgy are not figures of speech alone; they state the basic norm of our chosenness and our continued existence as a people.

Essentially the Law as codified in the Shulhan Aruch of Rabbis Karo and Isserles is the guide for Jewish practice in the synagogue and in the home. Dietary laws are to be observed as prescribed in this code. The order and manner of prayer are also set forth there. The strictest Sabbath and festival observance is ordained as well as a multitude of commandments applicable to man's behavior from the cradle to the grave, from the character of his business deportment to the time and manner of his sexual intercourse. No summary can possibly be made of the volumes of regulation that flow from the Covenant.

Wide Applicability of Jewish Law

The devotees of Jewish law are disturbed, however, that the Law is now commonly regarded as relevant to only a few areas of human life—Sabbath, festivals, food, and family. We must remember that considerably more of the sheer literary abundance of the Law deals with state and nation, agriculture and commerce, capital and labor, speech and thought. There is hardly a theme in philosophy, political science, economics, sociology, and psychology upon which the Law does not touch. Within the legal order which Judaism is, for example, there are prescriptions with regard to politics and the state—with regard to popularly elected legislatures, the use of proportional representation, and graduated income taxation in accordance with one's ability to pay. In the administration of criminal law, capital punishment is frowned upon. The accused always enjoys an absolute immunity against self-incrimination, far beyond the protection of the Fifth Amendment of the Federal Constitution of the United States. Because of Judaism's sanctification of human life, euthanasia is not permitted.

While the state's power to take life is strictly circumscribed, Jewish law gives the state much broader control of economic affairs than constitutional provisions in the United States permit. Prices can be fixed by duly constituted authorities. Accumulations of wealth can be limited, and testators do not have much choice as to what will happen with their fortunes after their death. To be supported by the state is a right: one can claim state help by judicial proceeding. The dignity of labor is vouchsafed. Workers may organize and strike; however, the public weal is of paramount importance. This is only a sampling of the extent to which the Covenant is applicable to every phase of human life.

Israel and Zionism

The traditionalist's approach to the philosophy and program of Zionism differs radically from that of other Jewish groups. For Abba Hillel Silver's Zionism, Theodor Herzl may have provided the rationale, and for Mordecai Kaplan's Zionism it may have been Ahad Ha'am. For the traditionalist the principal purpose of a return to Zion is that the whole of the Law may once again be fulfilled in practice.

To understand this approach to Zionism, one must first appreciate the fact that, in the words of Rabbi Abraham Kook, we have but two overall values in life, the sacred and secular. In our own era, Rabbi Kook says, we so suffer from an exaggerated overemphasis on the secular that it spreads over the entire breadth of life and darkens the sacred light within us.

"It is understood that if this movement (Zionism) were secular by nature, the elimination of the sacred from its values would not have affected it. . . . But since the source and foundation of the movement and our entire national rebirth come, in truth, from the sacredness of the holy of holies . . . its secular content is not suitable for it and does not measure up to its quality or character and, therefore, we feel weakness in all the parts and branches of our movement . . ."

It is especially painful that the basic law of the State of Israel continues to be essentially Ottoman, British, and French. What is more, several mentors of Israel's legislation carefully avoid historic Jewish jurisprudence even as there are frequent pronouncements by some of Israel's legal experts that Jewish law is inadequate for the purpose. This is one of the basic differences between the approach of Orthodoxy to the existence of a Jewish state and the approach of non-Orthodox Jews.

There are Jews who want no part of the State—and even refuse its ration cards. They regard it as a sin to hasten the appearance of the Messiah. The number of this group is shrinking. Even Agudat Yisrael, the political party which never joined the World Zionist movement, joined in the coalition government of the new state, participates in elections, and has its representatives in the legislature helping to collect its taxes and enact its laws. But together with the other religious parties it is committed to the fashioning of the State in accordance with the principles and mandates of Torah.

Issues Confronting the Traditionalists

In the United States, Orthodox Jews are not well organized. While the Conservative and Reform movements each have one rabbinical body and one seminary for their training as well as one union of their congregations, Ortho-

14

doxy has many of each. Oldest of all its seminaries is the Rabbi Isaac Elchanan Theological Seminary affiliated with Yeshiva University, which ordains each year the greatest number of rabbis. However, there are now scores of institutions specializing in the teaching of the Law, and there exists among them no coordination whatsoever, even in such matters as curriculum or fund-raising. Many of the congregations are affiliated with the Union of Jewish Orthodox Congregations of America, but others are affiliated with the National Council of Young Israel and Yeshiva University Synagogue Council. Many affiliate with no national body and are even proprietary in nature. The Union of Orthodox Rabbis of the United States and Canada is the oldest rabbinical group, while the Rabbinical Council of America is the largest. In addition, there are the Rabbinical Alliance of America, the Hitahdut ha-Rabbonim Haredim, the Agudat ha-Admorim, and the Council of Refugee Rabbis. These, too, coordinate little with each other and cooperate less. The lack of unity is patent. Nonetheless, while it makes for institutional weakness, it speaks for exceptional commitment. Differences in ideology and method are taken very seriously. The mood of "anything goes" is anathema.

In European countries and in Israel greater unity prevails. Indeed, wherever the state gives some semblance of support to the legal order which is Judaism there is less anarchy. That is why the United Synagogue of England—with Parliamentary recognition—does have considerable control over matters of kashrut, marriage, divorce, conversion, and even religious education. In Israel, too, through the rabbinical courts and the chief rabbinate the same goals are achieved. In the United States, however, neither the Jewish community is formally constituted—as many Reconstructionists would like to see it—nor is the legal order which is Judaism formally recognized.

The great challenge which the traditionalists face is that the legal order of Judaism is accepted only by a minority, while for the majority Judaism becomes like other religions —a creed with some rituals. Their future in America depends upon their ability to mobilize more devotees of the Law in every generation so that the legal order which it is will be applicable to many.

None can gainsay that the Law and its guardians have many problems. But their faith is eternal that the written and oral tradition have all the answers.

Chapter Two

THE CONDITION OF MY BELIEF

Judaism I have defined. However, some personal addenda are warranted. A group may share a common faith but every thinking individual must lay claim to that faith by some nuance of mind or will which makes it his *own*, his *personal*, commitment. To take title to property one must usually perform some act with respect to it. Shall one do less when becoming possessed of, or obsessed with, one's spiritual heritage? And in this chapter I bare a part of my soul.

Faith, Doubt and Autonomy

Perhaps, like Socrates, I corrupt youth but I do teach that Judaism encourages questioning even as it enjoins faith and commitment. A Jew dare not live with absolute certainty, not only because certainty is the hallmark of the fanatic and Judaism abhors fanaticism, but also because doubt is good for the human soul, its humility, and consequently its greater potential ultimately to discover its Creator.

This point the Bible conveys—according to Maimonides —when it tells of God's refusal to let Moses see anything but His back. God's back, needless to say, is not physical, nor can it be, without violent distortion of the meanings of words, God's negative attributes or the effects of His being

17

rather than His essence as cause. It signifies, rather, the absence of face-to-face encounter. Recognition from the rear does not yield more than a relative amount of certainty and that is the maximum we humans can expect vis-à-vis God. God may have had His own reasons for denying us certainty with regard to His existence and nature. One reason apparent to us is that man's certainty with regard to anything is poison to his soul. Who knows this better than moderns who have had to cope with dogmatic Fascists, Communists, and even scientists?

Yet, though I remain a creature of doubts, I believe not only that God is, but that He revealed His will to man, to Jews and non-Jews alike. My belief is quite different from, let us say, the beliefs of Hobbes and Locke with respect to the social contract. To them it mattered not whether a contract had ever in fact been consummated. What mattered rather was the precise terms of the contract as spelled out from the hypotheses which were basic to their philosophical structures. In my commitment, what matters is the fact that God did actually contact man—patriarchs and prophets—and covenant with them. How he did it will continue to be the subject of both conjecture and interpretation, but that He did it in history is the crucial point for me. As creation is a fact for me, though I cannot describe the how, so is revelation a fact, though its precise manner eludes me.

The most definitive record of God's encounters with man is contained in the Pentateuch. Much of it may have been written by people in different times, but at one point in history God not only made the people of Israel aware of His immediacy but caused Moses to write the eternal evidence of the covenant between Him and His people. Even the rabbis in the Talmud did not agree on the how. But all agreed that the record was divine and they cherished it beyond description, even as they cherished a manner of exegesis which Moses simultaneously transmitted to his colleagues and disciples. In their ongoing relationship with God they sought to fathom the meanings—apparent and concealed—of every word and letter of His revelation. And that quest has not yet ended. Even as He willed that man be His partner in the conquest of the earth, so He willed that man proclaim His holiness and help history ultimately to vanquish nature. For this purpose the Law was given.

Not all the commandments are applicable to all persons, places, or periods. Nor are all of equal importance. The written and oral traditions provide the norms for their hierarchical evaluation, but each commandment has its purpose even when its rationale cannot be explicated in purely humanist categories. The least that the least important of them must do is to make the observant conscious of God's will in all that he does—even in such trivial affairs as buying a garment or having a haircut. In inter-personal and communal relationships, the Law is even utilitarian in emphasis, and where God and man's perfectibility are concerned, the teleology is unmistakable. Even its deontological character serves the teleology.

The Jew who has not made the Law the principal preoccupation of his life may not be able to make his own decisions with regard to it. On some matters everyone must submit to authority lest anarchy be the state of the Jewish community, and the people qua people fail to fulfill their mission. Thus, for example, it is imperative in connection with the fixing of the calendar that the will of the Sanhedrin be imposed on dissenters. On most matters, however, the Jew who has mastered the Law can engage in the quest himself. He must be honest with God and himself and seek to ascertain God's will, not his own. That is why consultation with others is a desideratum. But Moses prayed that the entire congregation might consist of prophets. In periods of overwhelming Jewish illiteracy—as when the Hasidic movement emerged and today—there was and is an undue amount of unquestioning reliance upon "Rebbes" or so-called Gedolim (great men). I regard this phenomenon as unfortunate. When Jews become more knowledgeable in their Jewishness, I hope they will recapture in their personal lives a great amount of autonomy, interpreting and applying cherished source materials even as they continue to rely

19

on centralized authority in most matters affecting persons other than themselves.

Our Chosenness

My belief that God chose Abraham and his seed for the covenant is no warrant for any feeling of superiority over my fellow men. Abraham, according to the record, was selected because God recognized him to be one who would transmit to his posterity a sense of mission with regard to justice and righteousness. His seed had only the merit of the fathers—especially Abraham's. In Abraham's case, the merit was not that of Terah. Certainly neither Moses in Deuteronomy nor the prophets anywhere were enamored of Israel's virtue. Yet my existence has been ennobled because of the mission I have inherited and which I seek to fulfill. I cannot impose it on anyone other than my children—but anyone who wants to share it is free to do so. Even as a Jew, I cannot volunteer to share the burden of the priests— I cannot volunteer for their special role. My burden is heavy enough and I fall short of its accomplishment. Therefore, I will not attempt to persuade non-Jews to join me, but if they seek it, my burden is available to them in the same measure as it is to me. Perhaps they should be content to achieve excellence with regard to the seven Noahide laws (which are actually many more than seven, since one of them covers the entire gamut of what we call "justice"). But I must be the "commando" in God's service and attain holiness vis-à-vis God and man. That various theories of national and racial superiority derive from a Jewish idea troubles me. But I cannot abandon a conviction because of its perversion by others, any more than I would outlaw sex because some men practice sodomy.

Our Separateness

The first mandate to Abraham involving his "chosenness" was a command that was paradoxical: to withdraw from his surroundings that he might bless them. This became the model for Jewish existence. It did not necessarily spell exile—one does not have to wander to bless. But it did make for separateness and alienation, at the same time as it prescribed involvement with, and participation in, the world. Oriental religions denied the worth of reality as we know it naturally. The daughter religions of Judaism broke with the mother religion also by denigrating the realm of the material. Judaism sought to sanctify and perfect all of it—men and beasts, matter and energy, time and space.

In that sense alone do I regard Judaism as the only true religion. Truth for me is God's name, His total being. It must address itself to my total being. Much I may never be able to explain, but the explanation exists. It exists in God. And to His will I deliver myself—or at least aspire to deliver myself.

This message is still distinctive. There is not an area of life for which Judaism does not have a distinctive message. But my Judaism provides me with the one integrating approach—I must fathom God's will on every issue. I am, for example, grateful that I have been able to formulate a position for myself regarding anti-poverty programs. I wish I had enough knowledge of the facts to formulate a position on the war in Vietnam and the threat of Red China. All through life I find myself knowing the right at times, but just as often I suffer travail and doubt. That is the human situation with which I must make my peace.

I have no argument with anyone who does not share my religious commitment. I argue only with those whose ideas or deeds are a threat to the messianic vision and the this-worldly olam haba which is the end towards which creation moves. The secular humanist is not my enemy. The Birch Society is. So is the Buddhist who will affirm the meaninglessness of life or history. So is the Christian who will induce inordinate feelings of guilt with regard to the natural. So is the Moslem who glorifies war. But none is my enemy as a person. I must resist such of their views as I find objectionable to my commitment. Yet I welcome their chal-

21

lenge. My Judaism only becomes richer as I encounter challenges from other cultures.

Political and Economic Positions

During the Jews' millennial history, their encounters with various political, economic, or social systems have usually evoked a tendency to seek in their tradition some validation of the particular establishment encountered. Thus, American Jews in the South justified the institution of Negro slavery by resort to biblical texts even as modern Jews find warrant for capitalism and socialism in the same sources. I think it incorrect to identify my heritage with any one viewpoint. My faith institutes rather a certain way of beholding and appraising all institutions in the light of God's will for man. No one system is divinely ordained; the one that was divinely ordained was never implemented and perhaps never could be. Like Plato's Republic, it only furnishes me with ideas and criteria by which to judge. Therefore, racial segregation is unthinkable for me as a Jew. It runs counter to my basic norm—the equality of all men created in the divine image. Similarly, a good Jew cannot be a Fascist. Yet, my Judaism tolerates and even stimulates the most extensive experimentation with sundry economic programs. Vested interests in property play a very minor role, for only God has divinity—not the owners of goods.

Is God Dead?

When I fail to view a situation as I believe God would want it viewed, or when I fail to act as He would want me to act, He is dead for me. In this sense the question which is agitating Christian theologians has validity for me. However, much of their discussion is, I suspect, meant to make Jesus, rather than God, central to the Christian's commitment and behavior. The humanism to which they aspire may be noble. But if Jesus is deified as a son of God, I rebel against the notion that any creature can replace the

22

Creator. And if Jesus is a man beyond whom there is naught, then I cannot let any man be for me the measure of all things. Here I agree with Emil Fackenheim that man as an exclusive source of right and wrong is self-destructive. At the same time, my stature as a man is only enhanced, and my existence ennobled, because God willed both that I live and how I live. Yet it is precisely from the humanism which Judaism encourages that there emerge the greatest challenges to Jewish belief and behavior. As a Jew I must know the world in which I live, for I am God's partner in furthering the process of creation. Man, too, is a part of nature. Thus social and behavioral science as well as natural science must be my concern. And since God is One and all creation is His, I must synthesize all of this with my religious outlook. Can I combine the subjectivity of my faith with methodologies that are objective? Can my mind function with fixed ideas on the one hand, and, on the other, with an openness that makes for an unrelenting relativism? Even when I can achieve this for myself after years of anguish and travail, can I develop the educational techniques to transmit this to the young who I hope will share the same commitment? And when my commitment involves so much autonomy of the soul, can I join with others in the creation of institutional apparatus that by their very nature make for less autonomy? Yet without such institutionalization I cannot conserve and transmit the heritage and hope for fulfillment of the mission.

Perhaps these are also the problems of all freedom-loving peoples. As a Jew, I have them too—only more so.

Chapter Three

THE PRIMACY OF TORAH LAW

It must be apparent that I feel strongly that law is central in my religious commitment—not just law, but God's Law.

Though many Jews choose to ignore this truth, Christians understand it well. In fact, Paul severed Christianity's umbilical cord with Judaism by abrogating the Law for the Gentiles. The Pharisees—guardians and masters of the Oral and Written Law—were caricatured in the New Testament. The adjective "pharisaic" even became a badge of disgrace in Christian literature.

There were times in Jewish history when Jews too rejected the Law. Sometimes they rejected only the Oral Law and remained loyal to the literal text of the Bible. The Sadducees and Karaites did this. They denied the validity of the oral traditions handed down from Moses through the prophets and elders. Others rejected parts of the Law that they could not fully understand. Thus reformers in the eighteenth and nineteenth century regarded only the Law's ethical prescriptions as binding while the more elusive ritualistic commandments were nullified and even ridiculed.

All of these revolts were natural and are easily explained. The Law is a yoke. It has always been regarded as such. And it is always easier not to obey, than to obey. However, the rebels were seldom thus frank. They offered

24

many other forms of self-justification. Alas that the damage they wrought is not easily righted!

Does Legalism Kill The Spirit?

They argued that the excessive legalism of the Pharisees destroyed the spirit of the Law. The reverse was true. The legal analysis of the Pharisees was more often the fulfillment of Judaism's spirit rather than its negation.

The Bible, by way of example, provided for the emancipation of Jewish slaves in the seventh year of their servitude. If the slave was a married man when he was sold into bondage, his wife and children went forth unto freedom with him. This the Bible commanded.

But what was the correct interpretation of the Biblical verse? Did it imply that the slave's wife and children had been subjected to the same indignity as the slave so that they too had to be emancipated in the seventh year? This interpretation was plausible since many primitive legal systems provided for the enslavement of a slave's family with him. Moreover, the rhetoric of the Biblical verse supported this view. The oral tradition, however, was less concerned with rhetoric than with justice. The Bible did not approve of punishment for anyone other than an offender—and slavery was usually punishment for crime. Therefore, if the criminal alone could be punished, how could his wife and children be enslaved! Perforce, the Biblical command which provided for their emancipation must have had a different meaning. And the Rabbis had it. While the slave was in bondage, he could not support his family. Yet, the family could not be permitted to suffer. Consequently the master was required to maintain all of them since he now owned their erstwhile breadwinner. What the Biblical verse provided was that this obligation of the master should terminate with the emancipation of the slave. This was Rabbinic legalism at work—protecting, on the one hand, the innocent victims of another's malfeasance, while, on the other hand,

25

making the ownership of slaves so onerous to masters that slavery itself might disappear.

Even the rule that one could only be sold into slavery for failure to make restitution of a theft was a master stroke of the Oral Law's legalism. The Bible cited only this instance when it discussed the sale of a man as a slave and the Rabbis became strict constructionists. What of an ordinary debtor who could not meet his obligations? What of that historic bane of civilized man—imprisonment or peonage for debt? The legalism of the Oral Law ended this scourge thousands of years ago. It went further. In the case of a man being sold as a slave because he stole and was without the funds necessary to atone, the Rabbis ruled that he could be sold but once—even if the proceeds of his sale were not sufficient to satisfy the claimant's rights. The culprit could not be sold again and again until his obligation was completely discharged. As a matter of fact, it was suggested that he could only be sold if the proceeds of sale were equal to the amount of the obligation due. The Bible said, "And he shall be sold for his theft." *"For his theft"* meant for nothing more and for nothing less. If the bidding at the sale failed to reach the mark, or exceeded it—as the slave's friends could well accomplish for him—he could not be sold into bondage. Here was legalism abolishing slavery. And who can gainsay that it was legalism fulfilling the spirit of the Law, and not defeating it!

The charge that the legalism of the Pharisees destroyed the spirit of the Law was libelous not only with respect to the civil code of Judaism but also with respect to its ritual law.

Legalism in Ritual Observances

The Oral Law, for example, made much of the Biblical command prohibiting the consumption of blood. Undoubtedly, the many observances in this connection induced in Jews their congenital abhorrence of bloodshed. At the same time, however, that Christians ridiculed the minutiae

26

of Jewish dietary practice, they did not hesitate to enforce another command cited in Deuteronomy—immediately after the command enjoining the eating of blood—that a city of idolaters shall be razed to the ground. The Catholic Church applied this command to heretics—particularly Jews—and confiscated their wealth instead of burning it. The Oral Law of Judaism, on the other hand, had virtually nullified this command millennia before, so that it was in fact never applied. Thus by contrast, the much maligned legalism of the Pharisees induced a dread of bloodshed and a respect for religious freedom while antinomian Christians placed both values in jeopardy. And this was legalism at work, with respect to ritual law—and not civil law alone.

Does Legalism Breed Hypocrisy?

Equally libelous was a second justification offered for the rejection of the Law. The Law's critics claimed that it accentuated hypocrisy. The Law, they argued, so emphasized the formal in religion that many Jews regarded fulfillment of the formal prescriptions as a substitute for genuine religious communion with God. Too many Jews mistook conformism for righteousness. They observed dietary laws, Sabbaths and festivals, and even prayed regularly. Their personal and social ethics, however, were hardly praiseworthy.

A modicum of respect for history should have prompted these critics to admit that it was not they who declared war upon hypocrisy. It was rather the devotees of the Law who did this—the prophets and sages who were the Law's dedicated champions. Isaiah rebuked those whose fasting was only a pretext for contentiousness and self-aggrandizement. And the Oral Law tabooed offerings unto God from stolen property. It was the Oral Law that denounced *Mitzvohs*— good deeds—that had their origin in *Averot*—sins. The Talmud cites illustrations without number. However, the conclusion of Israel's prophets and sages was not that the Law should therefore be abolished. On the other hand, they

27

wanted the Law taught more effectively so that man understands how vain it is to observe the letter when one kills its spirit. But to ignore the Law and seek the end by exhortation alone is folly.

Would any sane legislator seek to protect the life and limb of slaves exclusively by exhorting masters to be humane? Thousands of years of exhortation with regard to brotherhood have not yet induced whites even to worship with Negroes in the same churches down south. One good law against discrimination, however, accomplishes beyond measure. A just state does not protect accused men and prisoners by relying on sermons addressed to judges, prosecutors and wardens. On the other hand, it imposes legal curbs on the unbridled vindictiveness of those in power.

This is no less true of the religious life. One can exhort people to pray when they are in the mood, or one can impose upon people the Law's obligation to pray at fixed times every day. Judaism chose the latter method. One can, of course, reject the yoke of the Law. But he who regards the law as binding, prays thrice daily—and though ofttimes his mood may hardly be an inspired one, it is likely that he will be inspired more frequently than one who has no set times whatever for prayer and meditation. Would that Jews were honest with themselves! Those who rejected the Law hardly ever pray—except in times of great distress or on special festivals. Even Rabbis who reject the Law hardly pray except when they are professionally engaged in conducting religious services.

Even in philanthropy—presumably a matter of the heart alone—Judaism took no chances. Minimal standards of giving were imposed by the Law. Sometimes these standards were increased by the Law's exponents—if a crisis existed. Yet, there always remained the area for voluntary action— the area of maximal giving. That was true of every Mitzvoh of the Law. There could be minimal or maximal performance. The minimum, however, was fixed by Law. The maximum was voluntary. It was called "Hidur"—beautifica-

28

tion. One's whole-hearted performance of any obligation constituted beautification.

To argue that the Law should be abrogated because it might be used as camouflage by hypocrites is tantamount to arguing that education should be abolished because totalitarians of the left and right know best how to exploit school systems and other propaganda facilities for their own nefarious purposes. Law has been, and still is, the most effective way human society has for the conservation of its values. And to argue that religion, which gives the ultimate validity to all our values, must deny itself the use of Law is to cripple religion and endanger its effectiveness. True, man shall enjoy religious freedom. But if in his concept of religion the Law is central—and his religious order is a legal order—he can then regard himself as an individual determined to make his religious convictions count.

Are Law And Freedom Antithetical?

In our own age, the hue and cry against the Law is based principally on the universal clamor for personal freedom. Rejection of the Law stems from resistance to curbs on what one may or may not do. Young and old thus rebel. Sometimes rebellion is even difficult and psychiatrists have to help the rebel succeed.

It is difficult to argue with one who no longer loves the Law or finds its prescriptions neither meaningful nor significant. 'Twould be like arguing with a man who no longer loves his wife. One can plead with the troubled husband that if he has a conscience he should remain faithful to his spouse and save the family—for the sake of the children. Similarly one can plead with Jews to conform to the Law for posterity's sake. For more than Israel has preserved the Law, the Law has preserved Israel.

However, even rebels ought be helped to see how much the Law has done to promote that very personal freedom in whose name they reject the Law. One ought ask why it is

29

that Jews, more than most people, have an almost congenital love of freedom? This was brought home to us most effectively when the two principal totalitarian states of modern history—Germany and the Soviet Union—found it necessary to liquidate Jews. Jews could not be regimented easily. They found it almost impossible to accept the adoration and deification of the dictator that a totalitarian state must ultimately project. Jews themselves oft jest about their unregenerate independence of thought and action. They bemoan their own lack of organizational unity because of their inability to squelch differences. From time immemorial they have debated and differed on almost every verse of the Bible and every rule of the Law. What, then, has made possible the preservation of our feelings of oneness as a people despite overwhelming diversity? And what has stimulated the diversity so that few Jews can ever forfeit the autonomy of their own souls?

Paradoxically enough, it was the Law. Law and freedom are presumed to be antinomies. Yet, Jewish law promoted and conserved freedom. It was Jewish law that made the festival of Passover, with its message of freedom, so effective that no Jewish child could escape its impact. It was Jewish education that hammered away—from earliest childhood—at how the Lord loathed slavery. Furthermore, it was Jewish dedication to the God of spirit that ennobled spirit and made the deification of humans impossible.

The Role of Freedom

Moderns resent the law because they have the wrong conception of the role of freedom in human life. Freedom is important not because our natures crave it. Not everything we crave is good for us. Children want many things which we deny them because we are aware of dangers unknown to them. And we jeopardize freedom when we defend it solely on the basis that we want it. Dictators could then easily defend their tactics. Stalin, Hitler and Mussolini simply maintained that they knew better than their constituents

30

what the people ought to want for their own good, and as a result they denied their people freedom. They could and did rely on Hegel's philosophy which justified substitution of the leader's will for the people's will.

Nor can we cherish freedom as a natural right to do as we please. No one can live in society without some limitation on his freedom. No one is free to kill, or steal, or maim.

The freedom we ought cherish is the freedom to do the good. Freedom, therefore, must be fixed to an end. We insist, however, that we shall not be coerced into choosing the good. If we are thus coerced we are no better than animals. An animal can also be harnessed so that it does no evil and only good. Man is superior to the beast and if bound to do the good, he wants to be thus bound not by force but by his own moral nature. He wants to choose the good as a free agent, without compulsion, without fear and without duress. That is why dictators may not impose even the best choice upon us. In order that we may be judged good, we must start with freedom to do either good or evil. And when we choose the good, we want to be adjudged good because we freely chose it.

When we seek political freedom, it is not that we shall do as we please but that we may as moral beings choose the good by ourselves without a dictator forcing us into the choice. When we seek economic freedom we want to be able to choose the good without hunger forcing us to do one thing or the other. When we seek social freedom we want to choose the good without fear of ostracism or discrimination gnawing at our vitals. All the freedoms we seek are, in the final analysis, favorable conditions for the free exercise of our moral natures on the basis of ethical insight and spiritual maturity—and not because compulsion, fear or duress of any kind whatever is exercised upon us.

Law and Freedom Are Means To Same End

Perhaps that is why God gave the Law unto Israel only after they had been liberated from Egypt. To have given the Torah while the Hebrews were still slaves would have defeated God's purpose. For the purpose of the Law is identical with the purpose of freedom. Freedom is designated to help man develop his moral nature as a free agent. And the Law is God's prescription for the same end—to develop man's moral nature and make him worthy of the divine image in which he was created.

That is why rejection of the Law because of a craving for freedom is to abuse freedom and misunderstand the Law. Jews were always great devotees of freedom but no people were ever more dedicated to the Law.

The Law regarded freedom so highly that the only observance for which there could be a "make-up" performance was the festival dedicated to freedom. If a Jew could not observe the Passover at its proper time—the fifteenth of Nisan—he was obliged to observe it a month later. No other festival enjoyed this distinction. Yet, despite this deep concern for the indoctrination of Jews with the love of freedom, moderns regard religion as antithetical to freedom! The irreligious man is now called the freethinker! Judaism, on the other hand, held that only the man committed to the Law was free. By changing the vowels of one Biblical word which indicated that the Law was engraved on stone, our Rabbis caused that word to be read differently so that it meant freedom. The Law and freedom were one and the same thing. How?

Simply because the religious man alone is really free. All of us readily admit that freedom is relative. No one is absolutely free. We are all restrained by physical limitations—we haven't the wings of birds. We are restrained by the deficiency of our talents—we cannot all become brilliant singers or philosophers. We are restrained by economic and social circumstances—our opportunities to climb the ladder of success do vary. Despite our political equality, not all of us have the same chances for leadership and high office. As a matter of fact, almost no choice that we ever make is really a free choice. Our choices are usually determined by a thousand and one factors in our environment. The medievalists assumed that if we had a perfectly free choice, we'd never make a decision. Given two absolutely equal bales of hay, equidistant from the eyes of a donkey who had to choose one to eat, we would probably find the donkey starving to death because of its inability to make a decision. Whenever a decision is made by humans in any situation in which a choice is offered, the decision does not really come from the free soul. It more often comes from social and economic pressures without; it more often comes from habits and prejudices whose slaves we are; it more often emerges from criteria fixed by our heredity or environment. And it is not easy for a human being ever to feel that his choices are truly free. The truly religious man, however, feels that he had a wider measure of freedom than others. When he decides upon a course of conduct the approbation he seeks is God's and not necessarily that of his fellow men.

Only Religious Man Is Free

Many soldiers with whom I served in the armed forces were continent while away from their wives, both in the zone of interior and overseas. Opportunities for infidelity were numerous. The temptations were great and to resist them even meant to incur the gibes and diatribes of the less disciplined majority. Who were the freer persons? Those who yielded to the pressures of the moment, the natural and social drives, or those who were such masters of these drives that they could decline to respond to them? In truth, the continent were freer. Their very resistance to pressures and drives from without, because of higher impulses within, was the badge of their freedom.

While still a student at college, I had this discussion with fellow students who were driven to violations of the dietary laws because it was not always easy to observe them. I deemed myself the freer person because I could rise above the limitations of a given situation. And if my choice was not altogether free either—because of my obedience to the will of my Creator—at least my choice emerged from a

33

freely exercised will which sought identification with a Higher Purpose or Cause.

That the Jew might fathom this Higher Will was also the goal of Jewish education. For the Jew's philosophy of education differed radically from that now prevailing anywhere.

The Philosophy of Jewish Education

The emphasis in Western education is on free expression. Help children to develop their talents as artists, musicians, inventors, producers. The Greeks, in the main, craved education for either the impractical understanding of the world or the successful manipulation of their fellow men. In the Jewish tradition it was the Law that was the principal subject of study that man might know how best to develop his moral nature. Plato concurred with this view in one section of his dialogue on "The Laws." In modern times one great jurist—Petrazhitsky—also revived the lofty pedagogic purpose of the law. Jews, however, consistently regarded the mastery of the Law as the principal purpose of education. By mastery of the Law, it was hoped that the Jew would become the better able to live as a man, finding favor in the eyes of God and fulfilling God's purpose for him.

I was a mere child when first I was subjected to a Talmudic analysis that would be deemed difficult even for mature jurists. It was a passage which in the curricula of most Talmudic schools would be studied much before adolescence. It involved the return of lost property. If lost property could be identified by its owners, then it must needs be returned. If, however, it is property that could not be identified in any way whatever, the finder presumably could keep it.

Yet a moral problem is involved. How can one make use of property which one has acquired neither by gift nor purchase? Is that not tantamount to theft? The answer given by all legal systems is that if the property is non-identifiable then the owner must certainly have despaired of ever recovering it. The property is therefore ownerless and when the finder keeps it, he is acquiring it as one acquires title to wild game. If the Talmudic discussion ended here, neither children nor adults would find it difficult. However, the Talmud then poses an interesting problem. If the finder finds the property before the owner has become aware of his loss, then the property is not yet ownerless. The owner cannot be presumed to have despaired of its recovery before he even knew of its loss. Consequently, the finder has come into possession of an article which still has an owner, and the Biblical command to return the trove devolves upon him. However, he cannot fulfill this obligation. Since the property is not identifiable, the owner can never claim it successfully. Nor can the finder keep it, for when it came into his possession it was charged with a Biblical command to return it. If the finder was certain that the owner was aware of his loss, at least he could presume that the owner despaired of the loss earlier and made the property ownerless. But who can tell when the owner became aware of his loss! Neither the owner nor his state of mind is known to the finder. Alas, the property stands tabooed. To use it would be to use what may belong to another man. The poor finder's dilemma cannot be resolved.

Years after I studied this particular Talmudic discussion (and much of it that I now omit to spare my reader too heavy a dose of legal analysis), I had occasion to teach the same passage to my ten-year-old son. I was then a member of the bar and as a lawyer I was struck by what had escaped me as a child. I realized that the Talmudic discussion was totally academic. There could never be a lawsuit involving the problem that I had so laboriously mastered. Who could ever sue the finder? The property he found was not identifiable. He would, therefore, never be a defendant in a lawsuit. What then was the meaning of all this mental gymnastics? I smiled when I realized that what I had been taught as a child—and what I was now teaching my children—was *how a Jew, as a free moral agent, is to act with respect to found property.* An attitude had been communicated to me, albeit indirectly. A moral attitude with respect to my neighbor's loss was induced. I was to spare no effort to return his property, for *under almost no circumstances could I ever use it as my own without being a thief.* My legal education as a child was the education of my moral nature. This constituted the glory of the Law, its study, and its observance.

Section Two

The Scope of the Law

Introductory Note

There is not an area of life that is not touched by Jewish law. In this section only a sampling of the areas is provided but I hope that the selection is sufficiently wide in scope to reveal how rewarding the quest can be.

The calendar of the Jew is deemed by many his catechism. To say the least, his life is structured by it. That is why Sabbaths and festivals are discussed first. Then we turn to Judaism's unique approach to the gratification of human instincts. Indeed, many Jews know only its gastronomic dimension and this begs for reinterpretation.

Human rights and medical-legal problems are then discussed with a final chapter on the basic value of human equality.

Chapter One

SABBATHS AND FESTIVALS
IN THE MODERN AGE

The Sabbath, Judaism's day of peace, now wages a war for survival. In an advanced technological society, her regulations are considered "dated"; one constantly hears it said, for instance, that a prohibition against riding could not possibly have included the automobile, and laws with respect to fire could not possibly apply to electricity. Furthermore, we are told that the traditional conception of Sabbath rest should be broadened to include newer forms of leisure activity: creative art is urged upon us as a Sabbath goal pretty much equivalent to the older goals of prayer and study. Finally, it is said that even a Jewish state cannot function without flouting the Sabbath: the essential services of modern life must be maintained day and night. How, then, can the Sabbath survive?

The Fundamentalist Approach

Often, indeed, the Sabbath suffers as much from her defenders as from those who would override her demands. Most champions of the traditional Sabbath have a conception of Jewish law which resembles the philosophical position of the "Imperative School" in general jurisprudence. John Austin, the founder of this school, who lectured at the University of London in the first half of the 19th century, regarded the law as a body of general rules laid down by a political superior to a political inferior. To discover the law, one must only discover the commands. The law is. What the law ought to be is irrelevant to the judicial process. It is not the jurist's function to replace the sovereign.

Austin thus abstracted the judicial function from all social and economic desiderata, and made judges neutral with regard to ideal ends. Within the law the great diversity of rules was to be analyzed and classified. If a judge was confronted with a new case—say, trespasses by planes in the air over one's home—he would have to resolve the issue by reference to the existing rules pertaining to the ownership of property. But this decision must be strictly logical and not based on social considerations, such as the development of air transport or its retardation.

Many orthodox teachers of Talmud take a similar view. Torah or Halachah consists of rules handed down by a divine sovereign who will punish disobedience. Man lives to fulfill these rules—for in obedience lies salvation. In dis-

40

covering or applying the rules, there is to be no reference whatever to social and economic conditions unless the rule provides in advance for such considerations. Changes can be made only as the divine sovereign willed them. The judicial process consists in discovering what the law is. Analysis there must be, but the analysis must be strictly legal, arrived at deductively or inductively from existing rules without reference to ideal ends or social facts.

This fundamental approach to Torah has at least one advantage over Austin's jurisprudence: at least the sovereign in Judaism is divine. And it would not be fair to imply that all Jewish fundamentalists are simply uninterested in the problem of Sabbath observance under modern conditions. The ultraconservative, it is true, hesitate to tamper with any divine command and do not even tolerate the suggestion that electricity may not come within the scope of the Biblical prohibition against fire; they do not want to jeopardize their right to eternal bliss by hazarding a decision which may be wrong. Others do venture to make an analysis: perhaps the "fire" mentioned in the Bible involves only that which consumes its objects or yields flame; the Talmud does distinguish between hot coals and hot metals; consequently, one authority in Israel felt that this distinction warranted the conclusion that the extinguishing of hot metals was prohibited only by Rabbinic—not Biblical —law. Electric lights came into this category. A third group of scholars among the fundamentalists simply prefers to delay action. They feel that no Halachic scholar has yet become sufficiently expert in physics to make the analysis as it should be made, and they wait for the day when great Halachic scholars will also excel in theoretical and applied science; the training of such a group of scholars is even projected by one religious party in Israel. But the fundamentalists are united in their reluctance to probe the values implicit in the Halachic texts.

One may ask this: If the Talmud makes distinctions, is the rationale of these distinctions of no consequence? Was

41

there no philosophy of Sabbath ends involved in the dicta of the Rabbis? And shouldn't this play a part in the resolution of new issues?

Hillel recognized that the Biblical law which cancelled all debts in the Sabbatical year was defeating its purpose: the poor simply could not obtain credit. He therefore created the *Pruzbul* which vitiated the impact of the Biblical law by making the court the creditor instead of the individual (Mishna, Sheviith, X, 3).

One of the principal practices of mourning in ancient times was the complete covering of the head—*atifat ha-rosh*. The practice was suggested by a Biblical verse. Yet it was abandoned in the Middle Ages because the practice provoked laughter, and laughter during the mourning period was the very antithesis of the value which the mourning was to conserve (*Tosafot,* Tal. B. Moed Katan, 21a).

The Rabbis were opposed to free and unbridled competition in economic affairs. If one resident of an alley set up a handmill and another resident of the alley wanted to do the same, the former could enjoin the latter and say to him, "You are interfering with my livelihood." Yet a teacher who set up a school was not thus protected; he could not stop a second teacher from coming in. In the propagation of Torah, competition was encouraged, for "the jealousy of scholars increaseth wisdom" (Talmud Babli, Baba Batra, 21b).

Do not these examples—and there are many more—represent something other than slavish commitment by the Rabbis to forms and texts instead of ends?

The Halachah is more than texts. It is life and experience. What made the Babylonian and not the Palestinian Talmud the great guide of Jewish life in the Diaspora was not a decree or a decision, but usage and the preoccupation of scholars with it.

Can a Halachic scholar lose himself in texts exclusively when the texts themselves bid him to see what practice "has become widespread among Jews," what is required socially "because of the precepts of peace," what will "keep the

42

world aright," and many other social criteria? These standards are as much a part of Torah as the texts themselves. A Halachic approach comparable to that of Austin does not conform to the historic Halachic process. In addition, it makes radical creativity altogether dependent upon the existence of a Sanhedrin, which cannot be convoked easily, if at all. As a matter of fact, the proponents of this extreme position in Halachah are generally the most bitter opponents of the Sanhedrin projected for our day. As Austin's jurisprudence ultimately became the basis for reactionary individualism as well as totalitarianism, so this Halachic approach has become the one cherished most by Jewish reactionary theologians who would restrict Halachic creativity to the reconciling of the texts of authorities. This approach has the advantage of offering a simple answer to the question, what is God's will and wherein lies man's salvation; but that is not enough to make it palatable to those who believe there are no easy roads to God and His will. And for the preservation of the Sabbath, it certainly holds no promise.

The Historical Approach

But the approach of the reformers has been equally unsatisfactory. If the fundamentalists in Jewish law approximate the general jurisprudence of Austin, the reformers were in great measure the spiritual heirs of the historical jurists, who viewed the law as a product of the historical process. Rules of law and procedure came into being at certain times and places because of political, economic, social, religious, ethical, or moral phenomena then and there prevailing; the law was simply a reflection of the state of a people's development. The earliest of the historical jurists, Savigny, paid reverential homage to the historical process. The law was like language—the expression of the *Volksgeist;* too much tampering with the law was dangerous, for it is always difficult to ascertain what is in harmony with the internal spirit of a people. Other historical jurists like

43

Kohler felt that "the law that is suitable for one period is not so for another," and thus invited changes suitable to changed conditions.

Liberal Jewish theologians are committed to the latter point of view for Judaism, while conservative Jewish theologians have accepted the former. "Reconstructionists" veer between the two positions—they agree with Savigny, and his Jewish counterpart, Ahad Ha'am, that radical departures from tradition are a threat to the *Volksgeist* and constitute assimilation, but they are finding it increasingly difficult to reconcile their almost humanistic philosophy with resistance to reform. The Jewish layman, without realizing it, most often echoes the historical view, and the vulgar rationalism associated with it. He is likely to claim, for instance, that the prohibition against the making of fire on the Sabbath stems from a time when great effort was required for the purpose, apparently believing that Moses lived in the Stone Age, and that for the Rabbis too it was a major undertaking to light a fire.

One unfortunate effect of the historical approach is that it oversimplifies the process of legal development. First, it tends too readily to accept as historical fact what are mere conjectures. The prohibition against the eating of pig, for example, is vaguely believed to have some connection with the danger of trichinosis, and other Biblical prohibitions with regard to food are then assumed to be similarly "reasonable." Has anyone bothered to find out whether all the other animals, fish, and fowl prohibited in Leviticus (Chap. XI) also carry infection? Similarly with respect to the Sabbath, one must challenge the simple assumption that it was the expending of much effort that was tabooed. How much effort is required to write two tiny letters with a pen? Yet that too the Law prohibits.

Second, though history plays an important part in the development of law, it cannot explain everything. Women may have been subject to certain disabilities in Jewish law because it is alleged the Jews held women in low esteem and accorded them an inferior social status. But even if this was true, can history explain why women need not sit in sukkahs on the Feast of Tabernacles but must eat matzos with the men on Passover?

Third, in Judaism, precisely because it is a historical religion, the past has a unique philosophical and theological role to play beyond the role of shedding light on how that which presently exists came to be. In the authentic Halachic approach, history was always taken into account—reformers were not the discoverers of the role of history in Halachah. The Rabbis, for example, found two contradictory sources with regard to the immunity of a king to criminal or civil prosecution by a court. One source held that a king was sovereign and subject "only to God's punishment." The other held that the king was subject to the rules applicable to all Jews. To reconcile these sources the Rabbis gave a historical explanation. The kings of the Kingdom of Israel —who were idolaters—entertained a pagan conception of kingship and held themselves above the Law. The kings of Judah, however, were more righteous and accepted the Biblical theory that everyone was subject to the jurisdiction of established courts. History accounts for the contradictory sources. (Tal. B., Sanhedrin 19a).

In Halachah, however, history was not resorted to principally to reject a given rule because it arose under given past conditions at a particular time and place, but rather to fulfill a philosophy of history to which Judaism subscribes. Halachah assumed that God was ever revealing Himself in His encounter with man, particularly through the people of Israel. That is why the festival of Hanukah was observed with lights over which a blessing was recited which attributed the performance of the mitzvah to the will of God. The Maccabean victory occurred centuries after the revelation on Mount Sinai. Yet neither conservative nor liberal theologians have changed the blessing to make it appear that anyone other than God willed the ritual of the candles. That was because the Halachic process permitted the expansion of revelation into history.

Furthermore, the authentic Halachic approach recognized that there were rules that were dependent exclusively upon time and place. While men and women were prohibited from wearing each other's clothing, the articles of clothing described in the Talmud as prohibited to each sex were prohibited only so long as they were the distinctive garb of one sex or the other (Maimonides, *Mishneh Torah,* Hilchot Avodah Zarah, Chapter XII, Par. 9). It was even suggested by one great medieval Talmudist that if any Rabbinic rule was established for a reason which the Rabbis who established it could have believed would disappear, then such a rule does not require an equally competent Sanhedrin to nullify it. This Talmudist mentioned only two Rabbinic rules which he felt required formal abrogation: the promulgation of these two rules was predicated on the continuance of Jerusalem as the site of the Temple service, and no Rabbi in establishing these two rules could reasonably have anticipated the Dispersion. Otherwise, most rules were for special situations, and once the situation changed the rule became obsolete (*Hidushei Meiri* on Tal. B., Beiza, Chap. 1, 5a).

Yet while the authentic Halachic approach does take history into account, it cannot altogether substitute *Volksgeist* for Halachah, nor can it substitute human ends for divine ends. The people are only one partner in revelation. To decide what of the past one will retain and what one will reject by criteria which eliminate God's role in the establishment of these criteria is to create the Halachah in man's image, not in God's. Yet the writings of both liberal and conservative theologians abound in both of these conceptions. And if occasionally it is God's criteria that are referred to, then the criteria are most unrefined. That the Sabbath was meant to be a day of rest and relaxation becomes an acceptable postulate. Therefore, what constitutes rest and relaxation for the individual Jew becomes the measure of Sabbath observance—golf for the sportsman, music for the aesthete, dancing for the teen-ager, cigar-smoking for the addict. Is that all these Jewish spiritual heirs of the historical jurists can find in a three-thousand-year tradition of scholarship on the Sabbath? Did they

46

really probe the depths and come up with so tiny a pearl—
that the Sabbath is a day of rest and relaxation? The
answer is that they did not probe. History became an excuse
to make the Halachah suit one's desires and not the means
to fathom God's will.

It is not only reconstructionists or reformers, however,
who abuse the historical method in connection with the Sabbath. Dr. Yeshayahu Lebovitz has suggested in Israel that
Sabbath restrictions be relaxed in the management of state
affairs because such relaxation was permitted in carrying
out the Temple service in ancient Jerusalem. The exemp-
tions which the Temple enjoyed he views as an indication
that the rules of the Sabbath were suspended when the
interest of the collectivity was involved. The state, he
argues, should now have the status of the Temple. But he
has cited a very special instance of Temple service. On the
other hand, it was from the fact that the Temple could not
be built on the Sabbath that we derive all the thirty-nine
prohibited forms of work. Israel's Chief Rabbinate permits
the maintenance of essential services on the Sabbath because they are required for the preservation of life. The
Sabbath's prohibitions yield because the welfare of human
beings is at stake and not because the State, personified a la
Hegel, is superior to the Law.

Many reconstructionists and reformers take a frankly
utilitarian approach to the entire problem. They would
change the Law to fulfill "the consent of the governed." But
the weakness of the utilitarian position in any religious
order is that the utilitarian is concerned with doing what
will make the majority happy. What the Jewish community
legislates occasionally becomes a part of the Halachah. But
the community's wishes alone cannot become the basis for
divine Law. Jewish law would then be no more than the
will of the majority. Would this not be a degradation of the
Halachah! At least the humanist utilitarian does not call
positive law divine.

The Teleological Approach

The only authentic Halachic approach must be that which approximates the philosophy of the teleological jurist. The teleological jurist asks: What are the ends of the law which God or nature ordained and how can we be guided by these ideal ends in developing the Law? He uses the historical method but it is not his only concern.

The Torah, to the devotee of Halachah, is God's revealed will, not only with respect to what man shall do but also with respect to what man shall fulfill. To apprehend these ends, however, requires more than philosophical analysis of some general ideals set forth in the Bible. It is not enough to say that the Sabbath is a day of rest. One must also study the detailed prescriptions with respect to rest so that one may better understand the goals of the Sabbath in the light of the prescriptions, for if one considers the end alone, without regard to the detailed prescriptions, one will be always reading into the Bible what one wants to find there. It is God's ends we are to seek, not our own. The Halachic scholar must probe and probe, and his creativity must itself be a religious experience supported by the conviction that in what he is doing he is fulfilling a divine mandate—a divine responsibility. Thus in seeking to understand the Law he is seeking to understand God, and in developing the Law he is discovering God's will more fully for the instant situation. Needless to say, his results must meet the challenge of revelation in the Bible, the challenge of history in general and Jewish history in particular, and also the challenge of Jewish life in the present.

The teleological approach is to be found at its best in the work of Dr. Joseph B. Soloveitchik of Yeshiva University. For him, the Halachah is "an a priori idea system . . . it postulates a world of its own, an ideal one, which suits its particular needs." To begin with, therefore, any rejection of the revealed character of both the Written and the Oral Law constitutes a negation of the very essence of the Halachah. Jews who thus reject would do better to regard their interest in Halachah as comparable to the antiquarian's interest in antiquity. They may become historians of the Halachah, or borrowers from the Halachah; they cannot regard themselves as actors within the Halachic tradition.

But once one concedes the divine character of the a priori idea-system, one can turn to the second phase of Halachic creativity, in which the Law begins "to realize its order within a concrete framework and tries to equate its pure constructs and formal abstractions with a multi-colored transient mass of sensations." On the level of application and realization, the Halachic scholar has God's revealed method, "a *modus cogitandi*, a logic, a singular approach to reality which the community . . . had to learn, to understand, to convert into an instrument of comprehension of which man, notwithstanding frailties and limitations, could avail himself . . . Man's response to the great Halachic challenge asserts itself not only in blind acceptance of the divine imperative but also in assimilating a transcendental content disclosed to him through an apocalyptic revelation and in fashioning it to his peculiar needs." There is objectivity and stability in the Halachah. "Yet these do not preclude diversity and heterogeneity as to methods and objectives. The same idea might be formulated differently by two scribes . . . Halachah mirrors personalities; it reflects individuated *modi existentiae*."

The observance of the Sabbath is one area in which the teleological approach is of special significance. Simply to assert that God wanted man to rest one day in seven, as the physician prescribes a vacation, is to oversimplify. Even to assert that God wanted the day to be a holy day on which man will come closer to Him is to rush hastily to conclusions on the basis of a few Biblical verses and to ignore a tremendous Halachic tradition which begs for philosophical analysis. Yes, rest and relaxation, as well as consecration, are ends of the Sabbath. But what do the prescriptions with regard to work imply? What is the unity in the thirty-nine types of labor traditionally prohibited? What is the point of the Rabbinic additions? To answer these questions will not only bring us closer to understanding what the Law is; it will also show us how the Law can be creatively developed.

The Law started with the Biblical premise that God wanted man to toil six days every week, thus making himself master of the earth and its fullness. On the seventh day man was to desist from toil. Maimonides correctly asserts that there are two commands with respect to work on the Sabbath (*Mishneh Torah*, Hilchot Shabbat. I. 1). One is negative—no work shall be done. The other is positive—to call a halt to work, to apply the brake to one's productivity and creativity, to desist from the conquest of the earth. Why?

First, man can thereby demonstrate that he is not the slave of greed and envy. When, by self-discipline, man shows that it is in his power to call a halt to the acquisition of things and the exploitation of natural resources, it can be said that his craving for economic power is not altogether his master. Our sages understood this significance of the Sabbath. In a rather elusive passage of the Midrash they made the point. After Cain had killed his brother Abel, he repented and asked God to shield him from attack. The shield God gave him was not his "brand" as a murderer. Most Rabbis did not so understand it. It was rather the badge of the penitent. But what was the badge? It was the Sabbath. The Sabbath was called a "sign" and so was Cain's shield called a "sign." By Cain's observance of the Sabbath, people would identify him as a penitent for his sin of envy. As a matter of fact, say the Rabbis, Adam later met Cain and inquired what God had done to him. "I repented," replied Cain, "and made peace with God." "Is that the power of penitence!" exclaimed Adam, and he forthwith recited "A Psalm, a Song for the Sabbath Day." Adam too wanted to demonstrate his own remorse for his sin of greed by proclaiming the sanctity of the Sabbath.

Thus the Law made the Sabbath a means for the cultivation of personal ethics—the mastery of greed and envy. Jews were first told about the Sabbath when God gave them the manna and tried them by ordering them not to gather

50

it in on the holy day. Many Jews, nonetheless, went forth on the Sabbath to search for more (Exodus, XVI, 27).

Interestingly enough, the thirty-nine forms of work prohibited by the Law deal almost exclusively with the exploitation of nature. Every form of agriculture was prohibited as well as the preparation of agricultural products, including food and cotton. Hunting was prohibited as well as the preparation of meat, wool, and hides. While one was permitted to consume on the Sabbath articles taken from the earth in the six days of toil, the Law forbade the capture, discovery, and conservation of these products on the Sabbath.

Definition of Work

We must remember that many definitions of work were available to the Oral Law. Work might have been interpreted to mean gainful employment of any kind. It might also have been equated with the expenditure of physical energy. It might even have had a physicist's meaning, e.g., Force X Distance. And if the Law regarded the Sabbath as nothing more than a day of rest and relaxation, any one of these definitions would have sufficed. However, it was the taking and creating from nature that was prohibited. That is why the Law derived its concept of work from a surprising source.

The Bible had indicated that the Sabbath was not to be desecrated even for the construction of God's sanctuary. The Oral Law inferred from this that nothing could be done on the seventh day to speed up the rearing of the Temple or the furnishing of its interior. Here, therefore, was a clue to the meaning of the prohibition against work. Work was any activity connected with the construction of the Temple. Upon analysis, thirty-nine categories were discovered. And these thirty-nine, in essence, turned out to be any taking from nature, or any creation from, or improvement upon, matter.

If the prohibition against work were simply a prohibi-

51

tion against physical labor, then the Law should have prohibited the transportation of articles anywhere. From the point of view of physical labor, what difference does it make whether one hauls wood a few yards from a forest or a few yards within one's home? The expenditure of energy is the same in each case. Yet the Law's principal prohibition was against the transportation of things to places where a new use would be made of them. Within one's home the difference in use could hardly vary materially: the articles were already available to the user and their removal from one spot to another could hardly be regarded as an exploitation of nature. But to haul from forests or deserts, or over highways connecting them, was to take something from a place where its manipulation was not easy to a place where its manipulation was more feasible. Or to remove from one's home to a public domain was to expand the usability and availability of the object removed. The Rabbis regarded carrying as a category of work "inferior" to other categories because no actual creation from nature was involved. However, even to expand the use of a thing already created was a remote form of the conquest of nature.

That is why one cannot help but be amused by some of the Law's reformers who, on the premise that the Sabbath is to promote rest and relaxation, conclude that creative art is an excellent form of Sabbath relaxation. To create is certainly permitted—but never to create out of matter. Let the Sabbath observer create ideas, or cultivate sentiments, or even discover God and His Will. But as for things material, only their consumption is permitted on the Sabbath, not their exploitation or manipulation.

Back to Nature

This analysis of the Law had further significance. Often in human history we have had protests against civilization and its compulsions, and Jewish culture, too, has had its impulse to go "back to nature." The festival of Tabernacles is one expression of this impulse. And so was the Sabbath.

"Back to nature" meant a static, as distinguished from a dynamic, existence—living with nature rather than the pushing of nature. That is why the Law prohibited the use on the Sabbath of that which was dynamic in nature—even animals and still growing vegetation. Moreover, just as one may not create instruments, one may not even use instruments, already created, if they have a dynamic character. Dishes for the serving of food were static; they could be used. Millstones, however, were to come to a halt before the Sabbath day. And it is this hostility to the dynamic that is the very antithesis of the mood of our lives in a technological age. That is why the original rules are so desperately needed now. A day to go "back to nature" once a week is more important now for peace of mind and human dignity than it ever was. Living with nature, however, means not living in primitive simplicity. One was only to restrain oneself from creative activity with respect to physical nature and seek instead to live in accord with man's guiding principle: God's will and reason. Man needs at least the one day to ask what are the ends for which he lives.

The automobile, for example, makes the prohibition against riding not obsolete but all the more compelling, for the automobile only increases the dynamism of travel. The deeper significance of spending one day within a limited area is that man shall find meaning to his existence where he is—and not where he can escape to. Similarly, the prohibition against fire was not a prohibition with respect to its use but rather with respect to its creation and its creative power; electrically propelled motors come no less within the scope of the prohibition.

Using the terminology of means and ends, it can be said that the six days of toil are concerned with the means of life and the Sabbath with its ends. The six days of toil represent the temporal and transitory; the Sabbath represents the eternal and the enduring. That is why the Hebrew language has no names for the days of the week. They are all the first day, or the second day, or the third day, "to the Sabbath"—the Sabbath is the goal toward which time itself moves.

A Day for Ends

To make the Sabbath symbolic of perfect and immutable "being," the Law did not permit the use on the Sabbath of anything that did not exist before the Sabbath. For example, an egg laid on a Sabbath or holy day could not be used that day. The Talmudic discussion with regard to the egg evoked many quips from satirists, including the poet Heine. But the egg was only one of countless problems involved in seeing to it that the Sabbath should remain a day dedicated to ends.

The Sabbath was actually a day of transformation. The most bitter existence of peasant or laborer was transformed into something heavenly. From painful preoccupation with means all week, the higher man finally came into his own on the Sabbath.

Is it any wonder then that slaves too were to rest? How could a day dedicated to ends permit the exploitation of human beings as means! Nor were Jews permitted to employ non-Jews on the Sabbath, notwithstanding popular opinion to the contrary. If a Gentile performed the labor for himself, a Jew was permitted the incidental enjoyment thereof, provided that the Gentile expended no extra effort for the Jew's benefit.

God Himself had rested on the seventh day. For six days He caused Himself to be expressed in matter and subjected His omnipotence to the bounds of natural law. But on the seventh day He reverted to His omnipotence, to His infinite freedom and essence as spirit. The fourth commandment, as presented in Exodus, indicated that the Sabbath was to be observed because God was engaged in creation for six days and rested on the seventh. The same commandment, as described in Deuteronomy, indicated that the Sabbath was to be observed so that Jews might remember that they were

54

once slaves God had liberated. But the two explanations are one. Man was nature's slave six days a week. But on the seventh day he was to be free of this commitment, so that he might, in a kind of imitation of God, catch a glimpse of that freedom which is the essence of God's nature.

Rabbinic Additions

The Rabbis of course found it necessary to make many additional rules, to safeguard the Sabbath. In the main, these are the rules against which moderns are most rebellious. As a matter of fact, moderns frequently visualize the Rabbis as misanthropes whose sole purpose is to make our lives as miserable as possible. There have been others in the past who could not understand the Sabbath. Sadducees and Karaites regarded the prohibition against fire as a prohibition against its use, instead of a prohibition against its creation and the use of its potential for still further creation. In darkness they sanctified the Sabbath. Many even outlawed food and sexual intercourse for the day. For them, misery was the keynote of the Sabbath.

The point of view of the Rabbis, however, stands in bold contrast—in fact, as a protest against these tendencies. The Rabbis prescribed the lighting of candles and made the Sabbath lights in the home one of the most significant features of the day. And they made eating and cohabitation on the Sabbath not only permitted functions but virtually mandatory ones. The Sabbath was not to frustrate man, but to help him fulfill himself.

In that large volume of the Talmud which deals with the Sabbath, one whole chapter (Chap. II) is devoted to Sabbath lights and the use of oils that will not only burn well but also without unpleasant odors. The principal passages of this chapter are recited every Sabbath eve by most Jews as an established part of the service. And lest there be Jews who think that eating on the Sabbath is not permitted, the Talmud prescribes not only the minimum number of meals for the day, but also elaborate techniques for keeping the food warm despite the general prohibition against cooking and the making of fire. That husband and wife should have sexual intercourse on the Sabbath became standard; but there is also a full discussion of how women may make themselves most attractive with perfume and jewelry despite the prohibition against the carrying of weights and the preparation of drugs. There was even a relaxation of some of the rules pertaining to the woman's ritualistic immersion after her menstrual period in order that there might be no postponement of cohabitation on holy Sabbath.

Further to prevent the many Sabbath prohibitions from becoming a barrier to the fulfillment of the Law's ideal, the Law emphasized two positive conceptions—*Kibud* and *Oneg*—the honor and joy of the Sabbath. The Sabbath was honored by festive dress and enjoyed with festive meals; it was welcomed with song and candlelight; its departure was toasted with wine and incense. On the other hand, just as concern with the minutiae of Passover observance caused Jews to become more impressed with the love of freedom, so the Sabbath's restrictions made for greater preoccupation with Sabbath goals.

Thus the Rabbis never lost sight of the Sabbath's affirmative aspects, which they expanded in every age. But they also had to expand the Sabbath prohibitions to meet changing conditions. The basic categories of prohibited work were established in times when hunting, fishing, cattle-raising, and farming were the principal occupations of man. In these endeavors there always was a direct taking and creating from nature. True, the Rabbis had to taboo many activities which resembled, or might induce, the basic activity prohibited by the Bible, in order to spread the knowledge of the Law and insure obedience to it. Yet, what of new enterprises—such as trading, which involved only the transfer of ownership with no changes whatever in the nature of the things traded? And what of business planning? And partners' discussions among themselves? And the use of money itself? Relying upon a verse in Isaiah (58-13), the Rabbis expanded the Sabbath's prohibitions to include commerce

56

of any kind, and the prohibition stands despite the fact that many retail storekeepers profess that they are Orthodox Jews. In fact the Rabbis so expanded the prohibitions that they are adequate for an industrial age as well as a commercial one. Thus, without even considering the propriety of using electricity on the Sabbath, the viewing of television was prohibited a few years ago, in a responsum published by Yeshiva University's "Talpioth," because the vulgarity and the commercialism of the programs were not consonant with the mood of the Sabbath. Similarly, one can expect additional new prohibitions; our machine age needs more than ever the reminder that man himself is more than machine.

Our Modern Sabbath Observance

How far does Sabbath observance in modern times fall short of the traditional objectives! For most Jewish families the day has no significance whatever. For others there is occasional participation in a religious service, usually to celebrate a Bar Mitzvah or Bas Mitzvah. Even in homes with elaborate Sabbath meals—with candles and Kiddush and perhaps a few guests—neither parents nor children dedicate their conversation to the ends of life or the spiritual quest of man. Orthodox homes are seldom more inspiring. Their excessive preoccupation with Sabbath prohibitions most often excludes adequate consideration of the positive values to be achieved, and the Sabbath becomes indeed a day of frustration.

To save the glory of the Sabbath, we must perhaps recall Plato's prescription for the state, namely, Jews must become philosophers. That does not mean that non-philosophers can experience no Sabbath joy. But unless our teachers and leaders undertake to expound the philosophical significance of the Sabbath and help everyone to grasp and live its meanings, the Sabbath will become nothing more than a day of leisure for most Jews and a haunted day for those who make the prohibitions ends in themselves. By all means the rules of the Sabbath will change and develop as they have done in the past. But our primary problem is not how to modify the prohibitions, but rather how to follow the path suggested by the prohibitions and give positive content to the day's observance. Only then can we think of modifying the prescriptions for only then will it be possible for our modifications to have any valid meaning. The aim must be not to evade the Sabbath, but to fulfill it. That aim may demand some relaxation of prohibitions; but it may also demand the establishment of new prohibitions.

The Sabbatical Year

What was true of the Sabbath was also true of the Sabbatical year. The Law enjoined that every seventh year shall be a year of rest. Jews were to engage in no agriculture whatever. If the soil did yield fruit, that fruit was deemed ownerless. Anyone could harvest and consume it.

The Bible said, "And the earth shall rest." Perhaps, as many suggest, permitting the earth to remain unplowed and unseeded was a substitute for the rotation of crops. But the Sabbatical year had significance far beyond the soil's conservation. And the Law projected for it ends that were ethical and philosophical.

In Exodus the Law of the Sabbath and the Law of the Sabbatical year were cited together (XXIII, 10-12). Our sages did not regard the association as purely coincidental. While many prohibitions applicable to the Sabbath day did not apply to the Sabbatical year, because one could not afford to be as unproductive for twelve months as one was for a day, nonetheless, the ends of the Sabbatical year must be related to the Sabbath's ends since their statutes are joined together.

During the Sabbatical year Jews were not to cultivate or improve their fields. Thus they had an excellent opportunity to spend considerable time in the study of Torah. It would appear that this study was to culminate at the end of the year in a great mass demonstration of allegiance to God's word. Jews were to congregate in Jerusalem during the festival of Tabernacles immediately following the conclusion of the Sabbatical year and with their king perform the ceremony of "Hakhel," described in Deuteronomy (XXXI, 10-13). Special passages of the Law were read aloud to the vast assembly, which included men, women and children. That this rededication to the Law was to take place after the Sabbatical year suggests that the rest and relaxation of the seventh year were meant for study by the populace as a whole. Interestingly enough, in America today the principal beneficiaries of this goal of the Sabbatical year are America's teachers. Only the academic world has adopted the institution.

The Sabbatical year, however, as prescribed by Torah and understood by our sages, had added significance. By abstaining from the cultivation of the soil, Jews affirmed that the land was not theirs but belonged unto the Lord. This was the meaning of God's proclamation in Leviticus in connection with all the laws pertaining to the Sabbatical and Jubilee years—"Mine is the earth." This thesis is basic in much of Jewish law.

As the Sabbath each week was to constitute a curb on greed and envy, so the Sabbatical year was to deflate man's conception of the nature of his property holdings. Man often exaggerates his claim to what he calls his own. He regards private property as divinely sanctioned and he resists the interference of society and state in his enjoyment of that which he has staked out for himself. He invokes natural law to retain what he has and to accumulate more. In the name of God, nature and constitution, man nurtures his greed. True, the Torah did grant privileges with respect to the enjoyment of worldly goods and their conservation for personal use. However, the Torah would never countenance what became the philosophy of nineteenth century American capitalism as embodied not only in the writings of Herbert Spencer but in the constitutional law decisions of the United States Supreme Court. On the other hand, the Torah with its law of the Sabbatical year wanted to impress Jews with the fact that all land is held subject to God's will. The use

59

of the land was man's. Title, however, remained in God. And even the uses were limited by God. One year in seven the produce belonged to everyone. Any person could harvest the crops and claim it as his own.

One may have noted that for one day every year, in the heart of the world's largest city—at Rockefeller Plaza in New York—pedestrians are denied the right to use the walks and terraces. The owner of the land, Columbia University, thus seeks to inform the public that when they use the walks and terraces they do so only as licensees. However, they are not to deduce therefrom that Columbia has abandoned its title and made a grant of that land to the public. In a similar vein, God willed that Jews exclude themselves one year in seven from doing with their lands as they please. God affirms His own title in that year, and man should spare himself any false inferences from the fact that God permits him to use the land in other years. In the Jubilee year there was to be a complete redistribution of the land but at least one year in seven man was prepared for the ultimate defeasance of what he might erroneously regard as an indefeasible right. One year in seven he was made aware of the limited character of his proprietary interest. The Jubilee year was the occasion not only for a redistribution of property but also for the emancipation of Hebrew slaves, even if they had not completed the prescribed six years of servitude and even if they had theretofore voluntarily prolonged their bondage. Not only the Jew's rights to the land came to an end but also his rights over his fellow-Jew.

During the Sabbatical year, however, property rights suffered another major invasion. All debts were canceled. Landed wealth was not the only form of wealth subjected to God's ultimate title. Personal property too required some weakening lest its holders become too enamored of its sanctity. Tragic it was that the Bible failed in its purpose. Because debts would be canceled in the Sabbatical year, rich Jews refused to extend credit to their less fortunate brethren. The Biblical rule had to be modified to encourage the granting of loans. Yet who can gainsay that the whole pattern of the Law's prescriptions was designed to curb greed and exaggerated claims of ownership and possession.

Judaism, Socialism and Capitalism

One may wonder how the Law could reconcile its virtually socialistic conception of property with many of its property-minded mandates such as an almost absolute rule that lost property may not be enjoyed by its finder, even when the owner's identity can never be ascertained. However, the Law was not self-contradictory. The Law was concerned with the greed of all people—the haves and the have-nots. It directed its prescriptions to rich and poor alike. The rich were not to claim more than the Law permitted; nor were the poor to seize what was not theirs. And the Law veered between two antinomies: it discouraged the propertied interests from exaggerating the value of their holdings and it encouraged the propertyless to respect the holdings of others and not give vent to their greed and envy by seeking to acquire in violation of the Law.

The Oral Law also sought to fulfill the spirit and intent of the Written Law. And it too was concerned with both the haves and have-nots.

With respect to the haves, the Law had one great plan. Though the Law prohibited the cultivation of land in the Sabbatical year, it permitted the use of whatever crops did grow. The crops were deemed ownerless and anyone could help himself to whatever he chose. However, the landowner himself was a member of the general public. He might harvest the yield of his own field. He certainly would have the first advantage in doing so—enjoying as he would proximity to it and knowledge of its readiness for harvesting. If the Law had prohibited owners from enjoying the fruit of their own fields, they might conspire with other owners to exchange crops. The Oral Law, therefore, complemented the Written Law and taught that the crop could only be harvested for use—for immediate consumption. It could not be

61

stored for long, nor could it be traded. As a matter of fact, if stored beyond the permitted period the crop could not be eaten by anyone. Even the proceeds of its sale were tabooed.

Furthermore, the year of rest—presumably for dedication to God and His Law—might become the occasion for work other than plowing and seeding. One might take advantage of the Sabbatical year to make improvements that would affect future crops. All of this was prohibited except such work as was essential for the conservation of the soil and its trees.

Unfortunately, when Jews lost their autonomy, and Roman governors insisted on annual payment of taxes, the institution of the Sabbatical year disappeared. Jewish law yielded to the demands of life. The spirit of the institution, however, and its deflationary effect on the sanctity of private property remained. Private property was subject to the will of God; and the will of Jewish society, as reflected by the will of its duly constituted authorities, was also the will of God. Thus there developed the basic maxim in the Jewish law that a Beth-Din—a Jewish tribunal—has the power to declare property ownerless and thus modify property relationships as it chooses. Jewish law never suffered the constitutional restraints with respect to property that blocked social legislation in the United States for decades. Jewish courts were less powerful in areas other than property. But property in Jewish law never lost its character as means. As means it was ever subject to the public weal. And thus it can be seen how both the Sabbath and the Sabbatical year have implications for man's body and soul—for his personal as well as his social ethic, for his philosophy of life and even his metaphysics.

The Festivals and Israel

It was God alone who sanctified the Sabbath—no human being helped. However, it was God *and* His people who sanctified the festivals. Detached from the history of Israel, the

62

festivals are without meaning. And of this difference the Law was ever aware in establishing how and when they shall be observed. Because the people had a share in the emergence of the festivals, their philosophical significance was also more readily grasped and fulfilled. Together with the Sabbath, they were Judaism's most effective means to help Jews achieve personal fulfillment and ultimate happiness. Indeed, the cycle of the festivals had as its climax the feast of Tabernacles, which was designated the season of their happiness.

Since it was God Himself who fixed the Sabbath day and made it holy, there can be no changes whatever in its incidence. The nations of the earth may decide to change their calendars; they may establish ten-day weeks, as did the French in the late eighteenth century, or six-day weeks, as did the Soviet Union in the third decade of the twentieth century. They may redefine the months or years, and intercalate days which postpone the coming of each new week. For Jews, however, the Sabbath will remain the seventh day computed uninterruptedly from Creation. Calendar changes by the United Nations may cause untold hardship for Jews who may discover that their Sabbath every year will occur on days that differ from those reckoned as Saturdays by the rest of the world—on one day of the week in one year and on another day in the next year. But Jews are helpless to change what God had ordained, no matter how great the inconvenience to them.

Not so is the Law with regard to the festivals. In fixing their incidence the Jewish people were sovereign. The oral tradition was emphatic with regard to the people's power to determine when months and years shall begin and end. Presumably God Himself had abdicated in favor of His people. Talmudic and Midrashic literature make it symbolically clear that when the Lord and His angels want to know when Rosh Hashanah occurs they themselves consult Israel's highest court, the Sanhedrin (Shemot Rabbah, 15:2).

Furthermore, God's abdication was virtually so complete that while technically the court was bound by stellar phenomena—the appearance of new moons to fix the first day of each month and the incidence of the seasons to decide whether any given year shall consist of twelve or thirteen months—the Law permitted the courts to be indifferent to the facts of nature. Human beings had a right to manipulate nature to suit themselves. The Sabbath, on the other hand, was rooted in divine history and no court could change the past or any of its signs and covenants.

What is of interest is that the highest court of ancient Israel did reckon with the people's convenience when fixing new moons and new years. If, for example, the month in which Passover occurred was proclaimed too early, pilgrims might have to wade through mud to get to Jerusalem. If, on the other hand, it was proclaimed too late, then in a year of drought Jews might be discomfited because they might not be permitted to eat of their new crops before a much deferred second day of Passover, when the offering of the Omer released the new crops for general consumption (Bab. T. Sanhedrin, 11b).

Long ago the Rabbis so fixed the calendar that certain festivals could never occur on certain days of the week. Thus, for example, the Day of Atonement can never occur on a Friday or Sunday. Indeed, the calendar which so provides was established more than fifteen hundred years ago. The Rabbis made a very precise calculation for the fixing of the new moons and new years. On this calculation we have relied through almost two millennia of exile. However, this calendar is not the slave of astronomy, or nature, as the Sabbath is bound by divine history. Nature is always a means, and not an end. If anything, history must ultimately vanquish the evil in nature itself. And that is why Jews expect that, even though their calendar as now observed needs no further improvement, they will, nonetheless, ignore it when the Sanhedrin is again reconstituted and the Sanhedrin will once again resort to the ancient manner of declaring new moons—by the examination of witnesses and by judicial decree. In this way they will reaffirm their right to decide when new moons and new years begin. Nature is their instrument and not their master.

Making Time Our Own

The command to fix a calendar was the Law's first mandate to the Hebrew slaves on the eve of their emancipation. It was the first message of freedom, for only he is free who can make his own time. That is the badge of freedom. The Egyptians had used a solar calendar. Jews were told to use a lunar one instead. This was a declaration of independence. Moreover, the month of their liberation would thereafter be deemed the first month of their year. It might be the seventh month of the year as computed from Creation, but of what significance were the earlier months to slaves whose time belonged to their masters! The month of their freedom was really *their* first month and as such it would be regarded forever. Thus did freedom's message become related to the importance of time. And the power to fix the lunar calendar was vested in the people of Israel in perpetuity. They alone would intercalate the months and the years. That is also why they will resume the exercise of this power when the temple is restored. They cherish a monthly reminder of their freedom—their right to make decisions with respect to time, even in defiance of astronomical exactitude.

The rejection of the solar calendar, however, was more than a symbol of the Jewish people's right to compute their own time. The solar calendar was closely associated in Egyptian life with the worship of the sun. And Jews were to reject the worship of the sun together with its calendar. As a matter of fact, Israel's mission to destroy paganism was thus established. Many Americans became famous as trust-busters. Others excelled as gang-busters. But the historic destiny of Israel was to expose and explode the false gods whom men enthroned.

With the rejection of the sun-cult, there came also the rejection of the Egyptian worship of cattle. The law of the

Paschal lamb became symbolic of this rejection. While their erstwhile Egyptian masters looked on, the Jewish slaves were to take the sacred animals of Egypt and slaughter and consume them. The slaves thus learned two additional truths about freedom. First, to be free one must be courageous. Second, a free man must fix his sights upon the true Lord. Otherwise his freedom can become license. Or it might even lead to personal disintegration when detached from an ideal worthy of fulfillment.

One must not forget that even as we crave freedom from fear, one of our greatest fears is the fear of freedom itself. Too many men dread the moral responsibility that freedom entails. They prefer regimentation. They also prefer to transfer to a "leader" the power of moral choice which they ought exercise themselves. The Hebrew slaves were no different. And Moses and the elders had to urge them in advance of their liberation to prepare for freedom courageously. Fearlessly they were to defy the false gods of Egypt and smear the blood of these animals over their doorposts. Only he was worthy of redemption who would make manifest this courage!

He who would be free must also be alert to seize his opportunity the moment it presents itself. People often forfeit their opportunities by tarrying too long. That the modern state of Israel now exists, and enjoys full recognition as a member of the United Nations, is due to the fact that its leaders did not tarry when their historic moment came. And the Law ever impressed this on Jewish minds. It made the *Matzo* the symbol of haste—the symbol of the speed with which the Hebrew slaves were to go forth to freedom from bondage. It was their "instant-bread." The bread that was leisurely baked then became symbolic of all the ills of luxurious civilization, the softening up that comes with comfort, the preoccupation with material values induced by economies of abundance, and the spiritual degeneration that follows self-indulgence. The unleavened bread, on the other hand, was the bread of poverty. Those who were once slaves were to consume it annually as a reminder of their erstwhile misery. Perhaps they would thus become more responsive to the misery of others.

Passover's Social Values

That we shall be sensitive to the plight of our fellow man because we ourselves were once in need of help is the one idea which the Bible did not hesitate to repeat time and time again. We were not to hate even the Egyptian for we had sojourned in his land for many years. The common man of that land of bondage was not to be despised because of the diabolical machinations of its Pharaohs. And the festival of freedom thus nurtured not only a love of freedom but a dedication to every social value which has become a glorious part of our ancestral heritage.

The festival's preoccupation with social values had another important consequence. It was Judaism's first festival and was ordained from the very beginning to be a family celebration, not a private feast. Judaism, in its earliest conception, was a social religion, and not predominantly a means for individual salvation. The Paschal lamb was to be offered by family units, every member of which was to be specifically counted upon for the observance. This became Judaism's unmistakable pattern. Too many religions ask, "What must a man do to make his peace with God that he may enjoy life everlasting?" Judaism is more concerned with what a man shall do in his relations with his fellow man that God's Kingdom may exist on earth as it does in heaven.

That is why the Passover festival should not be called the "Jewish Easter." The philosophies of the two festivals are completely antithetical. Easter is Christianity's holiday to symbolize its preoccupation with the other-worldly salvation of the individual. Passover, on the other hand, is Judaism's festival *par excellence* to symbolize the role of religion in this-worldly social amelioration. It is to evoke a moving regard for human suffering and a burning passion for the liberation of the oppressed. Indeed, our sages exclaimed

(Tal. B., Taanith 7a) that the Torah has little to say to the individual living in solitude. It addresses itself primarily to man as a social animal.

The Law never lost sight of the fact that Passover was meant to be a family celebration. The Bible had suggested the role of children. The colorful observances would prompt them to ask questions and parents were enjoined to reply. Consequently, the traditional Seder service gave prominence to this pedagogic goal.

Indeed, it is impossible to understand the Seder service without taking account of its design for the young. Queer things are done only to initiate their queries. This is the sole significance of the dipping of herbs in salt water. An amusing multiplication of plagues is also offered for their amusement. Since God had promised never to inflict upon Israel the plagues He inflicted on Egypt, the sages tried to multiply the plagues from ten to two hundred fifty, thus to preclude God from even more evil than He had promised to withhold. The humorous reasoning in which they indulged was meant for children. In order that children shall make every effort to stay awake till the conclusion of the feast, charming songs and ditties were reserved until the close of the service. And amid all the action and amusement, there is the telling and retelling of the story of the Exodus.

With no theme of Judaism has there ever been as much concern for its transmission to posterity as with the theme of freedom. God had willed that His people be free that they may fulfill a great purpose for all mankind. They were to be transformed into a society of priests and a holy people. But to fulfill this mission they must themselves sense the joy of God's liberation. The Passover feast was to convey this mood and it was designed to give every Jew an awareness of the reality of his personal redemption.

This feeling of personal participation in the exodus from Egypt was more than homiletics. It meant so much to the anonymous editors of the Haggadah, which is the prayer-book for the Seder service, that the principal selection from the Oral Law which they included in the text was based on a Biblical text involving not Passover, but rather the offering of the first fruits which was due on Pentecost. Why? Simply because the offering of the first fruits was the one ritual which required every Jew unto eternity to make the pilgrimage to Jerusalem and there recite that he himself had shared the misery of Egyptian bondage and the glory of liberation! Only generations that could personally share the experience of bondage would cherish their freedom and preserve it.

Work on the Sabbath and Festivals

Passover and the Sabbath are related to each other. The Sabbath has a message of freedom for the individual. Passover addresses its message of freedom to the group—to the nation. On neither may one work, thereby expressing an independence comparable to that of God.

However, the Sabbath differed from the festivals in that it had prohibitions with respect to work that were stricter than those applicable to the holy days. On the festivals the use of fire was permitted for the preparation of food; cooking and baking were encouraged for lavish feasts; and even the transportation of objects for immediate use was not enjoined. Only the Day of Atonement was in the same category as the Sabbath. Yet, why was it permitted to do some things on the festivals that one might not do on the Sabbath?

Here, too, texts, history and philosophy played their part in molding Jewish law. In connection with the festivals, the Torah used the term "melechet avodah" while in connection with the Sabbath the term "melachah" was used alone. The latter term is more generic and includes even less creative types of work, such as the preparation of food, which involves no substantial taking from nature and only the remaking of things already taken. Since the making of fire on the Sabbath was prohibited, and fire is used principally to refashion matter already apprehended from nature, the Oral Law affirmed that on the Sabbath even cooking and

69

baking would be prohibited, even though the foods cooked and baked were harvested before the Sabbath. However, on the festivals only "melechet avodah" was prohibited and that meant creative work. The use of fire was permitted and so was the transport of articles, since neither is truly creative enterprise. (*Sefer ha-Hinuch,* Chavel, ed. Mosad Rav Kook, Jerusalem, Mitzva 315.)

History too supported the Oral Law. When Moses transmitted to his people the laws of the Passover he specifically permitted the preparation of food. When, however, the manna was given to them, and Moses then and there—even before the promulgation of the Decalogue—ordained the institution of the Sabbath, he ordered that the cooking and baking be done before the Sabbath. Moreover, Moses could not have prohibited the preparation of food on the festivals since the Paschal lamb itself had to be broiled on the night it was eaten.

However, the ends which the festivals were to fulfill were as important as texts or history. The festivals have one command repeated again and again in the Bible. They must be observed in joy. Even more than on the Sabbath, Jews were to be happy on the holidays. And as if to accentuate this theme the Torah seemed to say to man's appetites that on the festivals even the Sabbath's restraints upon them could be relaxed. Therefore, for the festival, one did not have to prepare everything in advance on the eve of the festival and thereby risk inadequate preparation, or spoilage. One could always prepare on the holiday what one required—and in abundance.

But what is happiness? Happiness should not be equated with pleasure, for one can be happy even in pain. Happiness is that which brings us closer to the fulfillment of the ends of our being. Yet the means to the fulfillment of ends can also afford pleasure. On the Sabbath, however we ignore these means for on the Sabbath there is no special command to ponder the meaning of happiness. On festivals we take some cognizance of the means too as a potential for happiness. Thus we have limited license with regard to some work. And what kind of work may we do? Never work that God would do. God performs creative work—and as He desisted from creative work on the Sabbath to express His freedom, so we desist from creative work on Sabbaths and festivals in imitation of Him. However, He never performs the work permitted on festivals. He never refashions things to make them more palatable or delightful for Himself. But having made us as He did, and having ordained that we rejoice on festivals, He permits us to enjoy some means in the midst of whose enjoyment we might the more readily relish the pondering of the ends of life.

The Festival of the Law

Happiness, however, could not be commanded to a free people until it had received the Law, for in God's word lay the ultimate happiness.

Moreover, the transformation of the emancipated people of Israel into a society of priests and a holy people could only come as the consequence of a great covenant between God and His flock into which all parties entered voluntarily. This covenant was consummated at Mount Sinai and is commemorated by Israel's second festival—the festival of Weeks.

Seven weeks after the exodus from Egypt, God gave the Law. Of course, not all of it. But because the Decalogue was then given, Jews have always conveniently regarded the date of Revelation as the date for the giving of all the Law.

Archaeologists and anthropologists remind us that both the Feasts of Passover and Weeks had great agricultural significance. Even some of the observances prescribed in the Bible had their analogues in primitive religion. Does that detract one iota from the genius of Revelation which transformed primitive institutions so radically that the most exalted of modern men can still delight in the new meanings and derive inspiration from them? Brahms was once told that his first symphony was very similar to Beethoven's Ninth. He retorted that any donkey could tell that. He

71

wanted credit for his achievement with respect to familiar themes. Judaism's thoroughly gradualist approach required that it transform the already familiar. Where Judaism could permit no gradualism, as in the case of human sacrifice, it did not hesitate to prohibit without equivocation. Where, however, it could proceed by modification, reinterpretation, or re-evaluation, it preferred the method that, though slower, insured greater effectiveness and more enduring success.

In this way the festival of the first fruits—the perennial occasion of rejoicing—became the festival commemorating the giving of the Law. Interesting it must be, however, that this festival was the only one that ultimately lost every trace of its agricultural antecedents. Even after the destruction of the Temple, and the dispersion of the Jews from the land of their fathers, Passover and Tabernacles retained some evidence of their association with the soil and its seasons. The festival of Weeks, on the other hand, was the only one dedicated exclusively to history. And it is fitting that this should have happened. Until the messianic era, and the restoration of the Temple and its rituals, God's revelation will remain an event whose significance will not be diluted by other considerations. Furthermore, no special observances distinguish the festival. No one Mitzvah enjoys special status by virtue of its association with the most important event in human history. The whole Law was to be pondered and appreciated. To that end, our sages prepared a special manual consisting of selections from the totality of Judaism's sacred literature which Jews might study on the holiday.

The study and appreciation of the Law, however, is to induce its reacceptance. In Jewish tradition, the reacceptance of the Law plays a very important role. On the festival the book of Ruth is read. Ruth—the Moabite—is memorialized for her readiness to take on the yoke of the Law. She thus merited the right to be the great-grandmother of Israel's greatest king, David, the singer of Psalms. Furthermore, the Rabbis visualized that every time the Scroll is read in synagogue services, the purpose is not study alone but a re-enactment of Revelation at Mount Sinai and the reacceptance of its mandate by the people of Israel. Thus, for example, Jews were always wont to stand as the Torah was read even as they stood at the mountain where the Law was given. Even Jews who had already studied on that very day the portion about to be read were to stand at attention during the formal reading. If the purpose were study alone they might have been relieved of that obligation. But there was also the requirement that upon attending any formal reading one should visualize oneself as a participant in historic Revelation assuring the Lord that one will perform as well as listen.

The Festival of Happiness

The festival dedicated to the Law added a new dimension to the conception of happiness. Through the study of the Law one could come closer to the ends of one's being. Physical delights in freedom might make for pleasure. However, intellectual preoccupation with God's word would bring "Simha"—joy in a loftier sense.

Yet, the holiday that was dedicated to the most comprehensive notion of "happiness" was the festival of Tabernacles. That festival seemed to complement all that was omitted in earlier conceptions and gave more depth and meaning to significances already noted. The High Holy Days, which were also joyous festivals—although not discussed herein—made the Jew mindful of the religious values of penitence and purity, and placed the accent on communion with, and commitment to, God. Once all of these values had been introduced into the calendar's round, the Jew could observe the festival which merged all of them into a unit and became the "season of our rejoicing" *par excellence*.

This festival of Tabernacles had the least historical significance; it was the feast of the Ingathering of the Fruits. Until this day it is the most prominent nature festival

Judaism has. Volumes, however, have been written on the spiritual significance of every one of its many agricultural symbols. To summarize this literature would take one far afield from the theme of this chapter. What is more important is to consider what the Law did with the symbols.

The Law fixed the character of the symbols—the dimensions of the temporary dwelling to be occupied, the requirements for its roof and the physical appearance of the four fruits to be taken in hand—including the number of leaves on the myrtle and willow. The minutiae of the Law are such that one has good and sufficient cause to wonder whether an observant Jew may not forfeit all the joy of the festival by becoming preoccupied with all the details of the prescriptions. One must, therefore, ponder the philosophy which the Law's method here suggests.

A harvest festival is always a joyous occasion. However, it usually brings with it a weakening of religious sentiments and a relaxation of moral standards. One's sense of gratitude gives way to feelings of pride and power. "This is my achievement," says man. He is not then as conscious of his dependency upon God as he was at the time of plowing and seeding. Nor is he as apprehensive as he was when the rains were due. The harvest suggests hilarity and with hilarity the sensuous is accentuated. The drive to wine, women and song is also stronger when one's success overwhelms. The discipline of the Law must, therefore, come into play with greater stringency than ever. Joy there shall be but never without awareness of Him Who is the Source.

The ceremonial of Judaism helps in moments of great emotion. "It reduces the expenditure of emotional energy and steadies our heartbeat, preventing us from losing balance alike in hours of extreme happiness or unhappiness." That explains why the most joyous season of the year required especially effective regulation. When man was most apt to boast of his own prowess, the Law subjected him to the sovereignty of the Lord, and even made him leave his secure dwelling to live in the frail Sukkah.

However, it was more than an awareness of God that

74

the symbols brought to the Jew. Precisely at a time when because of the harvest we might become too impressed with ourselves and our good fortune, the symbols were to induce a sense of God's nearness and our dependency upon Him as well as feelings of equality and brotherhood for our fellow-Jews.

The "back to nature" character of the Tabernacles festival, which made it so similar to the Sabbath, beckoned another period of nuptials with God as after the exodus from Egypt. Yet, "back to nature" also implied a break with the inequalities of civilization. Therefore, all Jews were enjoined to leave their homes—no matter how palatial —and spend a week in huts which could be neither too small nor too large, neither too frail nor too sturdy; neither too sheltered nor too exposed. The rich and the poor met on a plane of equality at least from the point of view of their residence. And if this were not enough to make everyone conscious of his creatureliness—his utter dependence upon God and consequently, his inability to boast a superiority over other humans—God ordained that we take the four species, the citron, willow, palm-branch and myrtle, each of which represents a different type of human organ or a different type of human being, and acknowledge the interdependency of all humans upon each other and their several parts.

When the meanings of particular prescriptions were least apparent, thereby calling for more unquestioning obedience to the divine mandate and consequently evoking a more complete resignation to God's will, the imagination of Jews was most exercised to discover the mysteries behind the observances. Everyone recognized the basic point—that in one's greatest joy one must never forget its Source. But many important historical and ethical insights were gleaned from the prescriptions themselves. Through these ethical insights, the festival of joy would not nurture selfcenteredness but rather induce a conviction with regard to the basic brotherhood of men and their responsibility for each other. The Sukkah itself was regarded sometimes as the symbol of the frailty of life, and sometimes as the symbol of Israel's temporary sojourn in the many lands of dispersion. Sometimes it was even deemed the symbol of Israel's earliest history when Israel lived as if in the lap of God, trusting only in the Lord and His bounty. Aye, the symbolism was colorful and fired the imagination in every age. Basic, however, was the authority of the Law disciplining man's rejoicing and making him mindful of the fact that it was not he, man, who achieved the success but rather He to Whom the bounty of the earth must be ascribed.

The many prescriptions, however, did not mitigate from the "happiness" motif of the festival. As on all festivals, Jews were to eat and drink and be merry. Yet, as on no other festival, there was to be intellectual activity and spiritual commitment. As one Rabbi put it, this was the one festival that one could only observe with one's whole body —the entire body had to enter the Sukkah. (*Siah Sarfei Kodesh*, J. K. K. Rokotz; Lodz, 1929; Hebrew; Vol. IV, 29. Quoted in Newman and Spitz, *Hasidic Anthology*, p. 465.) But the Sukkah was also the one Mitzvah that one was commanded to perform with *knowledge* of its historical allusion. The performance of the Mitzvah was incomplete without awareness of its association with the exodus from Egypt. This required intellectual activity. And like the citron, which clings to its tree no matter what the changes in temperature, Jews were to find happiness—in the harvest season itself—in their cleaving to God. This meant spiritual commitment.

It should be no surprise, therefore, that the ultimate fulfillment of the festival came on *Simhat Torah*—the occasion for song and dance with the Scrolls of the Law. This was happiness: when one could truly feel exalted because one really belonged to God, His people and His law.

Perhaps it would have been more appropriate to have such a celebration on the festival of Weeks when the anniversary of Revelation was observed. Why did our sages choose Tabernacles instead and make *Simhat Torah* the climax of the season of joy? The famous preacher of Dubno suggested the answer.

The Jews rejoice on the festival of Weeks because they then received something which on faith they assumed to be of great value. However, that which they first accepted on faith, they learned to appreciate with the passing of time. Six months later when they had already had ample opportunity to study the Torah and glean its insights, they had another celebration. It were as if, said the preacher of Dubno, a man had married a beautiful woman but had never seen her until after the wedding. Months thereafter as he learns to appreciate her beauty and virtue he wants to celebrate another wedding.

It is in this mood that the Festivals are brought to an end. The Jew starts their observance because of his commitment, because of his faith. However, his observance of the Sabbaths and Festivals helps him to achieve the ultimate in happiness.

Conclusion

"Happiness," said Justice Holmes to a class of graduating lawyers, ". . . cannot be won simply by being counsel for great corporations and having an income of fifty thousand dollars. An intellect great enough to win the prize needs other food besides success. The remoter and more general aspects of the law are those which give it universal interest. It is through them that you not only become a great master in your calling, but connect your subject with the universe and catch an echo of the infinite, a glimpse of its unfathomable process, a hint of the universal law." One can hardly offer a better explanation of why Jews have dedicated themselves to the study of Torah. Torah was the revealed will of the Infinite and a reflection of His universal law for the lives of men. The ultimate goal of its study was not only guidance and direction; it was also to help one catch a glimpse of God. That is why Jews who never owned an ox spent many a night and day mastering the intricate rules of torts committed by animals and why Jews who as aliens in the countries of their birth could never acquire land, intoned page after page of Talmud on the manner of taking title to real property. They did this to catch "the echo of the infinite."

It is such an echo that we are to seek on the Sabbath and the Festivals. As the world and its needs change, certainly the problems of the Sabbath and the Festivals become more complicated; no one has the right to turn away from the voices of those Jews who find themselves troubled and disturbed in their holy day observance. It is not enough to say "the Law is the Law." We must understand the Law and its ultimate purposes as best we can, and we must be prepared to interpret and develop the Law as the Rabbis did in the past. It is our privilege and our responsibility to do this. We need the Sabbaths and Festivals perhaps more than ever, and we must save them. However, just as their salvation does not lie in an arid fundamentalism, so their salvation cannot lie in the encouragement of the typical pastimes of American Jews. Jews must live in their tradition. But it would be fatal to forget that the tradition itself must also live.

Chapter Two

HEALTH AND HOLINESS

In Judaism, the proper slaughter of animals is a religious rite, and the slaughterer himself a religious functionary. Circumcision, too, is a rite and its performer must be a devout and observant Jew, not just a competent surgeon. To certify to the "kosher" character of foods remains a significant function of Orthodox rabbis and a frequent stimulus to their polemics. Facilities for ritual immersion continue to clamor for recognition by zoning authorities as religious establishments.

Can all of this be made intelligible to non-Jews and even to Jews who conceive of religion as involving only metaphysical principles and ethical commitments?

It is with regard to these and other of Judaism's countless prescriptions on food, sex, personal attire, and personal appearance that the Law's opponents have been most vociferous. In these areas also has the rejection of the Law been most common. For moderns often assume that hygienic considerations prompted God to ordain many of the commandments found in the Bible. Thus it is argued that the consumption of pork or horseflesh may induce trichinosis, and the eating of dairy and meat products during the same meal may make the fat imbibed excessive. Cohabitation during a woman's menstrual period may increase the likelihood of cancer, while circumcision reduces the incidence of this disease. However, with the progress of science and medicine, when other means are found to avoid the mentioned evils, these religious rules are regarded as obsolescent.

Despite the popularity of this opinion, no one has ever undertaken a truly scientific analysis of the effects of any of the biblical ordinances on personal health. Certainly no one has identified what diseases may result from eating the scores of mammals, fish, and fowl of which the Bible disapproves, while at the same time demonstrating that the animals which one is permitted to eat induce no such infection. At least this much proof is necessary to sustain any hypothesis based on hygiene. Some time ago one well-known chemist, who was also a devout and observant Jew, did propose the establishment of a laboratory for just such a purpose. However, the overwhelming majority of Orthodox Jews did not concur, despite the suggestion of Maimonides and others that the commandments are related to our physical well-being. They did not feel that the results sought were relevant, for they were not prepared to reject or modify the Law because of any such findings. Indeed, there are rules which the Rabbis promulgated specifically as measures to safeguard health, such as the prohibition to drink water that had been exposed.[1] But these are not related to the Levitical commandments which have religious, and not hygienic, significance. Non-observant Jews, on the other hand, are content with their assumption that in an age of sugar-curing and artificial refrigeration one can eat almost anything without fear of infection.

However, a teleological approach to the Law, with due regard for its own methodology, can yield a harvest of insights that enrich Jewish experience. For the Bible itself suggested religious reasons which the Oral Law developed and these reasons have lost none of their original validity, relevance, or urgency. Even if personal health may be the immediate desideratum, it is the spiritual component of health that is the Law's ultimate concern. And if our forebears linked the commandments with our well-being, it was

1. Mishnah *Terumot* 8:4.

80

usually the well-being of our psyches that they had upper-most in mind. Can this be made cogent for moderns?

The Law's major contribution to the spiritual well-being of its adherents was to add to the *dignity* and *sanctity* of human personality through prescriptions involving inges-tion and procreation.

Man is an animal and as such has appetites which must be satisfied. Judaism never regarded the natural instincts as evil. Even sex was not evil. The so-called "Fall of Man" is not an authentic Jewish idea. If God had wanted the com-plete repression of appetites He would have created man differently. What God asks of man is rather that the satis-faction of his natural desires shall be achieved on a higher plane—a reflection of the divine soul which man has. We do not eat as cavemen. The preparation and the serving of food must appeal to our eye as well as to our stomach. Aesthetic considerations play an enormous role—the floral settings, the dishes, the table ornamentation. In sexual intercourse, too, our erotic tastes and deportment are more refined—we hope—than those of beasts. What the Law sought to achieve was to add considerations of holiness to the aesthetic. Satisfy the appetite, but do it in accordance with the divine will. The gratification of the instinct is thus transformed from an animal-like performance to one charged with dignity and sanctity. To the value of the beautiful we add the value of the holy. Eat and sleep and clothe yourself, even shave, and build your home, as God willed that you do so. Be aware of God even as you fulfill your basic needs and requirements. In that way you will transform acts that are presumably without spiritual value into acts that are religious in character—acts that link you with the Infinite. In that way, too, you will avoid the feel-ings of guilt and even disgust with yourself that frequently accompany the satisfaction of appetites.

The Talmud makes this point clear in a beautiful text discussing the purpose of Torah—and the Torah is the Law. The Torah is compared to a drug; not an opiate of the masses, as Karl Marx thought, but quite the contrary, a life-giving drug. 'Twere as if "a man had severely wounded his son and placed a poultice upon the wound, saying, 'My son, so long as this poultice is on your wound, you can eat and drink and bathe as you please, and you need not fear. If you remove it, however, the wound will become ulcerous.' Thus spoke God unto Israel, 'My son, I have created Satan but I have also created Torah. Study and observe the Torah and you will not only be saved from Satan; you will become his master.' " [2]

Apparently, God had handicapped man by endowing man with instincts that could lead to evil. However, God gave us Torah. So long as one lives within the Law one can eat and drink and cohabit—one can satisfy one's basic impulses—but their satisfaction will not be the fulfillment of man's animality as a result of which he may even forfeit his self-esteem, but rather the dignification and sanctification of those self-same drives which would otherwise be regarded as the hallmarks of his depravity.

One may ask *how* divine prescriptions add the dimension of holiness to human performance. The answer is suggested by Judaism's theology. As Martin Buber observed, for Israel to be a holy nation it must imitate God Who at one and the same time is immanent and transcendent—a part of the world and yet beyond it. Holiness, according to Judaism, implies a capacity to be a part of nature, and yet capable of transcending it. Judaism never advocated asceticism or isolation. It is a social religion, and personal happiness—physical as well as spiritual—is to be derived from and with one's fellow man. This God Himself ordained. Yet in every situation the Jew must be capable of God's immanence and transcendence. He must be of this world, and yet able to transcend it. The Jewish people itself is a segment of total humanity, and yet must retain its character as a whole apart from the group. Similarly individual Jews are to enjoy the pleasures of the body, but yet not be their slave. It is in this way that the disciplines of Judaism make for

2. *Kiddushin* 30b.

holiness, and *imitatio dei*. Holiness is thus to be attained in the willful control of one's own immanence and transcendence vis-à-vis Nature.

Perhaps it would have been enough for the Law to impose disciplines to make the Jews a disciplined people. No one will deny the value of self-control, and an observant Jew does in fact learn how to master his natural appetites. Especially for Jews is it essential that there be an elaborate pattern of prohibitions. They had been singled out by God for a special mission—they were to be a blessing unto all the inhabitants of the earth as the standard-bearers of the truths embodied in the Torah. The assignment was not an easy one, as history well demonstrated. So unique and dedicated an army required much regulation to deepen its capacity for self-sacrifice. This the Law might have sought to achieve by prescribing the manner in which Jews satisfied their basic needs and impulses. But self-discipline is not enough, if the discipline is self-centered. The discipline of Judaism had to be God-directed—a responsiveness to His will and an imitation of Him.

It may be difficult to prove that the Law fulfilled this end in fact. Yet, it is a fact that the prohibitions did make Jews aware of their Jewishness and of their separateness from other peoples and their kinship with each other. The prohibitions insulated the Jewish people and prevented their assimilation, even though there was no period of Jewish history when Jews were without frequent and intensive contact with other peoples.

This is no less true today than it was centuries ago. Children reared in homes where the so-called ceremonial laws were observed were far more conscious of their Jewish identity than children whose Jewish indoctrination depended exclusively upon their study of Jewish history, ethics, or theology. Reformers learned this lesson—though late. They are now urging the reintroduction of more and more rituals into the home for the preservation of the Jewish people. For children cannot grasp the abstractions of Judaism. Yet they are impressed by tangible observances—

special foods, candles, palm-branches, citrons. The Law advanced this view millennia ago. Let the child be aware of his group affiliation from the very moment that he can identify the food that he eats.

Yet neither the personal goal of self-control nor the social goal of group solidarity is the principal reason for the prohibitions that circumscribe the natural appetites of the Jew. The philosophical end is the only one which the Bible mentions, and that end is holiness—life in nature but yet transcending it as God had directed.

Occasionally a Rabbi would become so addicted to asceticism that he would advocate fasting and celibacy, with sex serving no purpose other than child-bearing. However, the more authentic rabbinic view was that God must be served by the very fulfillment of natural instincts whose enjoyment was God-ordained. But the Law reared ramparts around the gratification of the impulse so that man may be its master rather than its slave. And this was holiness—to be capable of immanence and transcendence with respect to desire itself.

Dr. Aron Barth also suggests that the Law sought to convert every natural impulse into an act of rational choice. The pause that the Jew must make before he yields to an impulse in order to ask whether that which he is about to do is, or is not, permitted, converts action that is otherwise impulsive into action that is rational—action that involves selection, deliberate choice.[3] This, in and of itself, is an ennobling influence in man's spiritual growth.

In still another way, the Law sought to safeguard the dignity and sanctity of human personality. The Law did this in consonance with its own method which not only prohibits objectionable behavior and punishes those who permit its evils to come to pass, but also takes measures to make the very incidence of the evils impossible. A few illustrations may be helpful. The Written Law, for example, enjoined covetousness. But how does one prevent its incidence? The

3. Aron Barth, *Dorenu Mul She'elot ha-Netzach*, 3rd ed. (Jerusalem: Religious section of the Zionist organization, 1959), pp. 21, 49.

Oral Law induced a fear of the "evil eye" [4] in those who were wont to boast of their possessions and thereby caused others to be jealous. The Law thus inhibited those who might be inclined to ostentation. And as men refrained from boasting and showing off their worldly goods, the incidence of jealous feelings in others was reduced. Similarly, the Law did not simply order husbands not to abandon their wives and punish them when they so sinned. Long before the abandonment—at the very moment when the marriage was consummated—it vested the wife with rights which would deter husbands from abandoning them. Furthermore, the Law often achieved its goal not by preaching or exhortation but by rules which paved the way to the end desired. Thus, the Law did not just urge the sharing of the flesh of one's animal offerings in the temple with the poor. It prohibited the eating of that flesh after a day or two no matter how well preserved, and in that way gave the donor of the animal offering no choice but to share what was his with others less fortunate, for the only other alternative was to let the food go to waste altogether.

Now, there is no greater threat to human personality than homicide and the Law feared that its incidence would increase because of man's carnivorous habits. It appears from a chapter of Genesis that God had hoped that man would be herbivorous. Only after the Flood, in Noah's day, was permission granted unto man to eat the flesh of animals.[5] This, however, might cause man to esteem life lightly. Therefore, the command against murder, and also suicide, was promulgated simultaneously.[6] Sharing the fears of ethical vegetarians, the Bible suggested that the shedding of the blood of an animal even for the purpose of food might make man callous to the shedding of the blood of fellow humans. The Bible, therefore, did more than prohibit murder. It sought to induce an aversion for blood. The Law's maxim was that the blood was life. Consequently, the

4. *B. Metzia* 107a,b.
5. Gen. 9:3.
6. *Ibid.*, 9:5.

drinking of blood was prohibited. Moreover, the horrifying practice of barbarians to cut steaks out of the live animals for food was also enjoined.[7] These were minimal prohibitions incumbent on all humanity. For Israel, however, there were additional prescriptions. Jews were not to eat meat unless the animal was so slaughtered that the death of the animal was immediate and at the same time the maximum amount of blood was removed from the body and tissues. Even after this manner of slaughter, the meat must be soaked and salted, or broiled, so that its blood content was further reduced. Perhaps some nutritive benefits were lost, but no Jew could fail to be impressed by the moral suggestion that though the eating of meat was permitted, Jews must be ultra-careful, even squeamish, about the eating of blood. Thus their almost congenital aversion for war, dueling, and murder was no accident. It was definitely the consequence of the Torah's preoccupation with the prohibition regarding blood. In one instance [8] was the method of slaughter varied so that the blood was not speedily removed and that situation involved the ritual which constituted atonement for murder. This different method of slaughter, so to speak, was a reflection of the murderer's performance.

Yet, even if the manner of removing the blood had ethical significance, what of the act of slaughter itself? What act could induce a greater disrespect for life than the very act of killing the beast! Visitors to slaughterhouses may have beheld how coarse and vulgar are the men who get the grip on the animals, swing the sledge hammers, and then in fun and frolic cut up the cadavers. That we might have meat, alas, some human beings must be made callous. This Jewish law sought to avoid. And in order that no Jew who eats meat shall do so at the cost of a brother's loss of humanity and refinement, the qualifications to become a slaughterer were so numerous and so exalted that the slaughterer became a religious functionary upon whom higher standards of ethical and ritualistic behavior were

7. *Ibid.*, 4, and *Sanhedrin* 59a.
8. Deut. 21:4.

imposed than upon rabbis or cantors! To prevent his degradation, the requirements were exalted to the opposite extreme. He was to be learned in Torah, a man of unimpeachable trust and integrity, capable of great personal sacrifice, and absolutely immune to any kind of pecuniary appeal. Pious Jews were wont to boast that they ate from the *Shehitah* or slaughter of only saints. No greater compliment could be paid a man than to say that a famous rabbi ate the meat of an animal which he did slay. Such was the Torah's method to save from degradation not only him who eats the meat but him who makes it available!

That the Torah through its prescriptions wanted to save the dignity of human personality and protect it against brutalization is made clear from a verse in Leviticus that deals with the covering of the blood after the slaughter of the beast. The Bible provides for an additional prescription regarding the "life substance." After it is shed, it shall be covered with soil or ashes and hidden from view. Yet this additional rite was limited only to the slaughter of fowl and animals, and not to sheep and cattle. The rationale for the limitation is suggested in the verse containing the command.[9] That verse refers to the hunt, from a superficial point of view an irrelevant circumstance. However, fowl and animals, other than domesticated ones, usually had to be captured from nature and the hunt cannot help but involve the captor in more inhumanity than is normally involved in the case of beasts of the farm. That the hunter may act out his added guilt and be restored to feelings of humanity, his shedding of the animal's blood in the process of the slaughter must therefore be followed by a special commandment—the covering of the blood. That is why the commandment is limited to creatures whose usual means of apprehension was the hunt, and in antiquity most fowls that Jews could eat had to be hunted. In several instances the Talmud considers even domesticated fowls as requiring capture.[10] Thus did the Law take special precautions when

9. Lev. 17:13.
10. *Betzah* 25a. V. Tosafot, 9a.

87

greater human degradation might ensue, and the Oral Law expanded the rule to cover even situations not involving the hunt. Any special regard for blood served a moral purpose.

Indeed, the hunter was hardly respected by Judaism. Esau—and not Jacob—was his prototype. Walther Rathenau once exclaimed that he never knew a Jew who enjoyed the hunt. In any event, more than the slaughterer, the hunter had to have an antidote to the meanness of his vocation and both hunter and slaughterer had to be spared the inevitable hurt that their occupations could cause to their spiritual personality. Moreover, those who ate the meat had to be assured that they did not have to wrestle with their consciences because their indulgence was at the sacrifice of a fellow human's dignity.

Jewish philosophers sought to discover meanings that were implicit even in the details of the dietary prohibitions, not alone in their overall pattern. Some detected a divine intent to impress us with the importance of avoiding some of the objectionable habits or characteristics of the animals tabooed. Others saw in the law forbidding the boiling of a kid's flesh in the milk of its mother a reminder to be grateful. The dietary prescription was to inspire a grateful heart, especially since the same biblical verse ends with a command to bring the first fruits of one's harvest unto the Lord as a thanksgiving offering. For still others this, and many additional rules, was designed to exorcise ancient pagan rituals of which we now know very little.

However, the net effect of all the prescriptions was that the selection of the animal, its slaughter and its preparation, and finally its very cooking and eating were subject to the Torah's mandate. Thus hunter, slaughterer, butcher, and cook performed their tasks in accordance with God's command. The Law determined what the Jew may eat, how he shall slaughter that which he wants to eat, how he shall remove its blood, and with what else he might cook or eat it. Curiously enough, the only edibles which are subject to absolutely no control by the Law are fruits and vegetables—except for the worms within them. Were the Jews to become herbivorous again, so many of his dietary laws would become unnecessary. His unremitting reverence for animal life itself would fulfill the demands of a holiness code.

But the Jew, like the Gentile, has been becoming more carnivorous rather than less so. And the Law, through the millennia, has expanded in many ways to make the Jew more conscious than ever that as his physical existence requires food, so his spiritual life requires *kashrut*. One may jest about gastronomic Judaism, or one may seek to deceive for profit as so many hotels and caterers do with their offers of "Kosher style" products. To the devout, however, *kashrut* remains the way to sanctify life.

While man's use of beasts may degrade him, nothing is more detrimental to the cause of human dignity than man's use of his fellow man, living or dead. The sources from which the prohibition against autopsies developed are few but Jewish sentiment and rabbinic understanding compensated for the paucity of the texts.[11] Again two results were to be accomplished. First, respect for human life was to be induced by the respect accorded even the dead. Consequently, there was a general prohibition against rendering their limbs and tissues asunder. Second, if it became necessary to do this in order to save life—which purpose supersedes most commandments—then the person so acting was to be safeguarded against any possible irreverence with respect to life and he was expected to be reverent until such time as he had fulfilled his last duty which was the proper burial of the part dissected. As in the case of the slaughterer of cattle, those who handled the dead among humans were expected to be saints. What a difference between the undertakers of today and the *Chevrot Kadisha* of old! And what a difference between the traditional watching of the dead until burial, accompanied by the uninterrupted recitation of Psalms, and the atmosphere prevailing in some morgues and dissecting rooms of today's luxurious hospitals, with even "rock 'n' roll" music coming in via radio!

11. See I. Jakobovits, "Dissection of the Dead in Jewish Law," *Tradition*, Vol. I, No. I, 77-103.

Indeed, the dead must be handled. They must even be dissected at times. And some men must become callous in the performance of these duties. Yet Jewish law would never let them become so callous that their reverence for life was in any way diminished. Only saints qualified for the task. And saints they must remain. One wonders whether one should not seek some parallel pattern for the training of modern physicians who, instead of being exposed to a program of "hardening" vis-à-vis blood and suffering, ought not to be exposed continuously to religious and moral indoctrination regarding the sanctity of life. Perhaps they would perform needless surgery less often, and not agitate as much for euthanasia. But undertakers and gravediggers already need saving more than doctors. Modern Jews are happy that undertakers have made burials so aesthetic— the family is shielded from everything unpleasant. The death occurs, and all they must ever view with their eyes is a magnificent casket reposing either in a soothing chapel, or in a memorial park, blanketed with greens. That some human beings have to make of death big business, of embalming a licensed profession, of gravedigging the occasion for jesting (presumably to save the gravediggers from an inevitable morbidity), does not disturb anyone. But why should any human being be caused to suffer an irreverent attitude toward life only because we need someone to perform unpleasant tasks? That is why Jewish custom called for the gratuitous handling of the deceased by a man's friends as an act of brotherhood—or by the saints who were members of the *Chevrah Kadisha*. The last shovel of earth was to be thrown by one who loved and respected the deceased so that in no event could ministry to the dead become the occasion for the degradation of another human being to whom the service had become only a vocation or a job.

If Jewish law would suffer no degradation of man in his use of the dead, then *a fortiori* that it would not suffer any degradation of man in his use of the living, especially his use of his own wife. Much of Jewish law pertaining to ritual immersion after the menstrual period had its roots in this goal.

A woman was never to become only an instrument for man's pleasure. Nothing would make for greater mutual hostility between husband and wife than the feeling that one is only an object for the other's gratification. Even the exploiter would ultimately hate the exploited—such is the mechanism of the mind in sexual performance. If spouses were to respect each other forever as persons equally created in the divine image, then the gratification in sexual intercourse was to be mutual. However, mutuality in climax could not be attained until at least the man learned to be disciplined and artful. The ritual immersion itself may or may not have fulfilled some hygienic purpose. But the fact that during the menstrual period there was continence meant first that humans do not cohabit as or when animals do. Second, it meant that for a good part of the month the husband was to cherish his wife, even though he could not enjoy her body. In truth, every month there was reenacted the drama of the wooing and nuptial periods with which the marriage began. It were as if each month husband and wife reenacted the relationship of bride and groom—with a period of restraint comparable to the period of the engagement, followed by a honeymoon comparable to the wedding night. Indeed, a Jewish wife is to come to her husband at least once each month as a bride after a ritual immersion.

Hygienic reasons have been advanced for the Torah's strictures with respect to sexual intercourse during a woman's menstrual period and thereafter for a specified number of days, especially since the Law prohibited cohabitation for a period of time after any vaginal discharge. Yet, it would be the sheerest folly to defend all the rules as health measures. The present state of scientific research would hardly warrant such conclusions. The Law, however, did seek to conserve certain moral values, and no moral value played a more prominent role in Judaism than the value of the woman's consent to marry and cohabit. Her

91

vaginal cleanliness always was—and still is—an important factor in her readiness to consummate love relations with her husband with maximum gratification. No less significant was the possibility that either spouse might find cohabitation distasteful or unaesthetic and consequently nurture an antipathy to the other. The Torah's goal, therefore, was to achieve in marriage a proper balance of so-called Platonic love with passionate love. A wife was to be employed both as a fellow human and as a woman, and in due time, when she reached menopause, she would be both to her husband simultaneously.

The renowned Dr. Kinsey, alas, did not understand this principle of Judaism. Rightfully it may be said that he did not even understand sex. A quantitative study of sex on the basis of "outlets" and "incidence" with no attention whatever to the qualitative aspects of the phenomenon must needs be misleading. Conclusions thus reached must be distorted. Judaism, on the contrary, was more interested in the qualitative aspects of the love relationship than its frequency. And the Law with respect to *Taharat ha-Mishpahah*—family purity—sought to provide periods of complete continence thereby to promote romance and heighten the mutuality of the spouses' ultimate gratification of their desires.

A charming text of the Talmud is illustrative of this intent. The Talmud was very much aware of the desire of males to have sons. Capitalizing on this preference, the Talmud reminded husbands that sons are conceived in their mothers' wombs only when the female reaches climax earlier than the male in the consummation of the love relationship! [12] If the male ego was to be flattered by the bearing of male heirs, it must excel first in the art of love. It does not really matter whether the Talmudic dictum is scientifically correct. It is at least an abiding invitation to men to be preoccupied with the desires of their wives, and

12. *Niddah* 31a.

92

if younger women are, by their very natures, less capable of achieving climax speedily, then men must be the more patient and the more artful to that end.

In the final analysis, however, it was the Law that dignified and sanctified the satisfaction of man's most urgent drive with full regard for the shared character of the experience, and the mutuality of feeling of the spouses, at the same time that the period of continence made not for frustration but rather for shared experience of the spouses on a level other than the physical.

Sexual intercourse, however, involves more than the sanctifying of life as in the case of dietary laws. It involves the very creation of life itself in holiness. Religious persons will never cease to wonder that God made man His partner in creation. It is God and man together who populate the earth. And in the final analysis, that means that man fixes the number of immortal souls with which God must endow His children. That is why it is inconceivable to the devout Jew that the process of conception should be without religious mandates.

Furthermore, the Law accentuates the role of the Jew as a partner in the creation of other Jews through the rites of circumcision. The covenant with Abraham became symbolic of more than one's Jewishness. An uncircumcised male was regarded as incomplete. His circumcision was the final act of his creation—his final fashioning. For females too there was a final act of creation, according to Judaism.[13] The piercing of the hymen was for a woman what circumcision was for a man—only in the former case it was the husband, not the father, who was God's partner in creation. To such an extent were perfectly natural processes woven into the warp and woof of the holy life.

And the code applied to the postnatal period as it did to events preceding. After a birth there was again a period of continence followed by the reenactment of nuptials—with a

13. *Sanhedrin* 22b, and Rashi's comment thereon.

difference, however, between the birth of a male and a female. The periods of both continence and nuptials were doubled in the latter case, perhaps because vain males needed the benign effect of the Law more when their wives bore them what they wanted less.

To many moderns all of this regulation may be unacceptable. Yet moderns should remember that virtually all of it was personal regulation—self-discipline. In a remarkable inference from a biblical verse the Rabbis ruled that Jews were "on their honor"; males and females alike could certify to their own observance of the Law. Needless to say, the word of the suspect was not always acceptable to the cautious devout. But Judaism frowned upon public supervision of the extent to which wives practiced ritual immersion (as some rabbis in America and Israel have instituted it), and Judaism also attached no legal stigma to the issue of parents who did not observe the rules. Indeed, the acid test of one's commitment to God was one's willingness to heed His will in the most private, the most secret, of all human performances.

Self-discipline or God-directed discipline, however, was not the only religious value that the Rabbis gleaned from the code of personal holiness. Even the rules pertaining to the ritualistic preparation of utensils yielded religious insights. Dishes normally had to be cleansed with the same heat that prevailed when they were improperly used. Boiling water or steam might be enough for pots that had been used in non-kosher cooking, since the maximum temperature for cooking is that of boiling, but higher temperatures were required to qualify old stoves for baking by the observant. It was not difficult to conclude from this that in the measure that one sinned, one must atone. Of what value, for example, would be the atonement of an old man—altogether spent— for sins he committed in his youth? Or of what value is the belated verbal apology of an anti-Semite when the millions of dollars he had expended earlier had already resulted in the death of millions of Jews?

To the uninitiated the Law may appear bleak, even unbearable. To those, however, to whom the Law is life itself, observance is not a chore but a daily delight, dignifying existence, ennobling the spirit, and yielding not only a consciousness of God but fresh insights into His will.

Chapter Three

TALMUDIC INSIGHTS ON HUMAN RIGHTS

As never before in human history, the safeguarding of human rights has become a matter of international concern. The Charter of the United Nations acknowledged that their violation was a cause of World War II and that their protection had become vital to peace. Furthermore, in the debates within the Israeli Knesset the principal argument advanced in favor of the adoption of a written constitution was that it would protect human rights. Jews, therefore, might well consider some Talmudic insights with regard to the nature and implementation of those human rights that have become particularly controversial in our day. Perhaps both Israel and humanity at large could profit by these insights.

Judicial Review

In the American political system, judicial review is one of the most important techniques for the protection of human rights. As a result, one may successfully challenge before the courts the constitutionality of a law duly enacted by a legislative body. One may also challenge the constitutionality of an official act performed by a state or federal officer. Many scholars argue that the power which the courts thus exercise really constitutes a usurpation on their part. Nonetheless, they concede that the power has had a benign

96

effect upon civil liberties. That is also why several modern states now provide for judicial review in their own constitutions, while several others have urged a similar system for the United Nations, whereby a special international tribunal would hear cases involving the violation of human rights protected by international covenant.

When Dr. Leo Kohn drafted a constitution for the State of Israel, he too proposed assigning to the Supreme Court of his country the power to declare statutes unconstitutional. The proposal was publicized in the United States as an Israeli borrowing of an American pattern. The doctrine of judicial review is, however, one of the most ancient of Jewish jurisprudence.

In effect, the doctrine makes it possible for an individual to challenge the mandate of a law-making body or law-enforcing officer on the ground that the law violates the highest law of the state, which, in the case of the United States, is a written constitution. Similarly, according to Jewish law an individual may disobey the mandate of a king and defend his disobedience before the Sanhedrin on the ground that the mandate is in violation of the provisions of the Torah. If the court upholds the contention of the accused, he is acquitted.

Joshua was told, "Whosoever would rebel against thy commandment, and will not hearken unto thy words in all that thou commandest him, shall be put to death" (Joshua 1:18). Queries the Talmud: [1] "(Is the punishment to be applied) even if (the disobedience is due) to words of the Torah?" The answer is no. Wherefore Maimonides [2] expounds: "He who disobeys a king's mandate because he is engaged in the performance of one mitzvah or another, even an insignificant one, is relieved of guilt, . . . and *one need not add that if the mandate itself involves the violation of one of God's mandates, it need not be obeyed*" (my emphasis).

In addition, Talmudic sources support the view that the

1. B. Sanh. 49a.
2. Mishneh Torah, Hilchot Melachim, III, 9.

king could not suspend the rules of the Torah even in an emergency. Only the Sanhedrin could do so and the Sanhedrin was a quasi-legislative and judicial body.

Courts in ancient Athens reviewed laws. They tried a law even as they tried a man. Cicero too was wont to appeal to a higher law in the light of which an unjust law might be regarded as a nullity. Jews, however, applied the principle with regard to a written constitution—their Torah—and retained it even after the institution of kingship. This whole outlook goes back to the Bible. The Pentateuch subjected kings to the rule of law, and the prophets ever pressed this point. Here, it seems, we have the closest analogue in antiquity to the modern view that courts may supervise the exercise of political power and make sure that it remains within the framework of the state's written constitution. If an official violates the fundamental charter of government, the aggrieved party has recourse to the courts. Individuals thus have rights which they can assert against the sovereign.

This principle was later extended to apply not only to a Jewish king—subject to the rule of the Torah—but also to a non-Jewish state within which the Jewish community enjoyed a measure of autonomy in the administration of justice. The Jewish courts protected individuals against the unlawful mandates of those who exercised executive power within the community. Above the community, however, there was the state whose law superseded the law of the autonomous community, at least with regard to civil matters. Yet the rabbis held that if the state's action was discriminatory in character and offended against the fundamental rule of equal protection of the laws, Jews were not bound to respect the law of the state. Some modern scholars deem this a form of civil disobedience which constitutes a precedent for similar action in the present.

"The general rule is that if a king promulgates a law applicable to everyone, and not to one person in particular, then property (acquired by the king in consequence thereof) is not regarded as a theft (in his hand)".[3] Otherwise, it is theft, and Jewish courts will not protect subsequent purchasers even though they may have acquired their titles from the sovereign. In the same spirit, the rabbis reasoned that God rewarded the Egyptian midwives who had saved children of the enslaved Hebrews, though in doing so they had violated the command of their monarch; this command was discriminatory, affecting only Jewish males, and therefore was not to be obeyed. By the same token, Jewish courts might very well hold today that, in the light of an international covenant on human rights, an act in violation thereof by any duly constituted legislative or executive body, whether local, federal, or supranational, and whether within or without Israel, was a nullity. Few modern states are prepared to go this far.

The Right To Work

The assertion of rights against the sovereign has been appropriately called "Liberty against Government." [4] There are indeed many ways in which, in democratic countries, government may be restrained from action. More recently, there have emerged rights in the sense of privileges—ways in which one may expect one's government to act positively for one's welfare. One of the most significant of these rights is the right to gainful employment—the right to work—or at least the right to subsistence.

Within the Commission on Human Rights of the United Nations, this matter was the subject of much controversy between East and West. The right itself, however, was proposed as early as 1789 in the French National Assembly, when Deputy Target suggested the inclusion of the following in the Declaration of Rights of Man and Citizen: "The

3. Shulhan Aruch, Hoshen Mishpat, CCCLXIX, 8.
4. See E. S. Corwin's book so entitled (Baton Rouge: Louisiana State University, 1948).

state must guarantee to each man the means of existence by assuring him property, work or aid in general."

There is a situation in which the Talmud recognizes this right and its rationale is most significant. According to Jewish law, a willful homicide might be punished by death. Asylum from the wrath of the next of kin was, however, offered to him who committed an accidental homicide. In most cases, such asylum involved exile from one's residence to a special city. But that meant losing one's means of livelihood. Therefore, the rulers of the city in which asylum was sought were obliged to provide the refugee with subsistence and a place to live.

Rabbi Isaac explained the significance of the verse, "and that fleeing unto one of these cities he might live" (Deut. 4:42). This implies, "provide the means of livelihood." [5] If the refugee was a scholar, he was even to be provided with a college for the continuance of his calling.[6] As a matter of fact only such cities were to be designated for purposes of asylum as could easily afford employment.[7] The rationale is clear. If the refugee was denied a livelihood, he was, in effect, made to suffer a death penalty and the death penalty was reserved only for those who committed willful homicide. The refugee who had committed an accidental homicide was entitled to live, and that meant that he had to be furnished employment or subsistence.

The United States Supreme Court in *Traux* v. *Raich,*[8] by Justice Hughes, virtually expressed the same view. The State of Arizona had enacted a statute which placed certain limitations on the employment of aliens. As a result, Raich lost his job. He sought relief in the courts and the statute was held unconstitutional as an interference with the power of Congress to offer hospitality to aliens. "The authority to control immigration—to admit or exclude aliens—is vested solely in the federal government. The assertion of an

5. B. Makkot 10a.
6. J. Makkot 6.
7. B. Makkot 10a; Rashi's and Meiri's commentaries ad loc.
8. 239 U.S. 33, 36 Sup. Ct. 7 (1915).

authority to deny to aliens the opportunity of earning a livelihood when lawfully admitted to the state would be tantamount to the assertion of the right to deny them entrance and abode, for *in ordinary cases they cannot live where they cannot work"* (my emphasis).

The right to live in a state must inevitably mean the right to work, and what was a special instance in Jewish jurisprudence must become the rule for all inhabitants of the earth. That is why the proposed Israeli constitution set it forth unequivocally for Israeli citizens, as did the Fundamental Principles of Israel's First Knesset.

Immunity Against Self-Incrimination

Particularly acute at the present time is the violation which civil liberties are suffering under the impact of the Cold War. Forced confessions have become the principal basis for convictions behind the Iron Curtain in crimes of a political nature, and to some degree also in the United States in crimes of violence, particularly when members of racial minorities are involved. Moreover, the constitutional immunity with regard to self-incrimination is being weakened at the hands of many agencies of the state.

Traditional Jewish law held any and all confessions—no matter how voluntarily offered—to be without legal effect as far as the state was concerned. Confessions of debts or thefts might obligate one to make payment or restitution to an aggrieved party at the latter's instance. But the confessions were nullities in criminal proceedings. As a matter of fact, the person making the confession could not even be impeached as a witness in a subsequent and different proceeding on the ground that he had confessed to the commission of an immoral act.

Furthermore, even if such a person did confess to a crime he had himself committed and the confession was made while testifying with regard to a crime committed by another, the court would usually strike out the confession unless it was absolutely impossible to separate the confession from the remaining testimony. In such a case, all the testimony would fail. The confession was still without significance. So inviolate was the rule against self-incrimination!

The Talmud [9] establishes this rule against self-incrimination by means of a syllogism. Relatives are incompetent to testify against each other. A man is a relative to himself. Therefore, he is incompetent to testify regarding himself. Nonetheless, one does find that a man may make admissions against his interest which might give rise to suits for money judgments by persons in whose favor the admission was made. Logically, the same syllogism ought to apply. Yet the Talmud indicates that with regard to financial obligations, an admission might create a liability in the maker of the admission and a power to sue in the party for whose benefit the admission was made. It is only the state that is barred from taking this advantage. This is thus another instance of "liberty against government."

What is of special interest, however, is the rationale of the Jewish rule. The confession is a nullity because of the incompetency of the confessor to testify. In the United States, in a federal investigation, a man was forced at one time to incriminate himself with regard to an act which was a crime under state law, but not under federal law. The immunity against self-incrimination guaranteed by the federal constitution applied only to self-incrimination under federal law.[10] This position is now overruled.[10a] The Jewish rule would bar any self-incrimination whatever because of the incompetency of the confessor. In addition, the immunity guaranteed by the federal constitution applies only to crimes, and not to matters which are not punishable by law. Jewish law, on the other hand, would apply to anything.

The truth is that while law-enforcing agencies have been aided by the gradual contraction of the immunity against

9. B. Sanh. 9b.
10. *U.S.* v. *Murdock*, 284 U.S. 141, 52 Sup. Ct. 63 (1931).
10a. *Murphy* v. *Waterfront Comm.* 378 U.S. 52 (1964).

self-incrimination, personal freedom has also suffered. Jewish law, on the other hand, gave legal recognition to admissions against interest when they involved the waiver of one's wealth. One, however, could not waive one's flesh or freedom.

One modern scholar has even essayed to give a psychoanalytic interpretation to the Jewish rule—the immunity prevented one from indulging his impulse for self-destruction.[10b]

The Right to Defense Counsel

Another problem that is becoming of increasing importance to lovers of freedom in America is the difficulty one is presently experiencing in obtaining defense counsel when one is accused of a crime in which public passions are engaged. Yet a way must be found to insure an adequate defense. Otherwise, the trial is in danger of becoming a mockery of justice. Jewish law was deeply concerned about the adequacy of the defense.

Trial procedure according to Jewish law did not call for representation by counsel; the judges were usually counsel for the accused as well as his tribunal. It is therefore significant that no one could be convicted in a criminal case unless there was at least one judge who found grounds for acquittal and was the champion of the accused. A unanimous agreement as to guilt meant the prisoner's release.[11]

Rabbi Kahane said: "If the Sanhedrin is unanimous for conviction, then the prisoner is acquitted. We derive this from the requirement that even if only a majority wants to convict, the verdict must be delayed for a day in the hope that the minority for acquittal will influence the majority. But if there is unanimity for conviction, the delay would be futile. Thus a basic requirement of fair criminal procedure

10b. Norman Lamm, "The Fifth Amendment and Its Equivalent in The Halakhah", *Judaism*, Vol. 5, No. 1-Winter, 1956, pp. 53-59.
11. B. Sanh. 17a.

cannot be effectively fulfilled. And if there cannot be such fulfillment, acquittal follows."

The meaning of this rule is often misunderstood. It does not mean that at the conclusion of the trial and the judges' deliberations there had to be at least one vote for acquittal. That would not protect the accused at all from a court bent on conviction, for obviously one judge could always vote perfunctorily for acquittal and satisfy the legal requirement that there be at least a lone dissenter. The rule called instead for at least one judge to discover grounds for defense, which he could press. And if, in conclusion, the majority of judges were inclined to convict rather than acquit, the case could not be disposed of until the judges had spent at least an additional day in deliberations—so vital was adequate consideration of the defense to meet the requirements of a fair trial.

The Right to Dissent

It would thus appear that Jewish law was very much concerned with those human rights whose protection is sought by the most recent champions of these rights. However, there was also concern for one's freedom to dissent from the established religious authority, even in a system erroneously called "theocratic."

Needless to say, there was no compromise with anything resembling idolatry or its propagation. The law, however, permitted such diversity in thought and practice that it is difficult to imagine that the constituted authority ever sought excessive regimentation. The law of "Zaken Mamreh" indicates that our sages even distinguished between overt acts in defiance of constituted authority, which were punishable, and verbal criticism, which was permitted. The distinction is brought out in connection with an elder who had taught doctrine or decided a case in a manner which the highest court held to be in error. The elder in his official capacity could not apply the rule which his superiors had reversed but he was free to say—and even to teach—that

104

his superiors had erred.[12] "If the elder returns (from the appellate court) to his city and continues to teach as he had originally taught, he is acquitted. He is guilty only if the erroneous teaching was used in a practical decision."

According to one school of thought, the elder could be penalized in only one instance for defiance of the Sanhedrin. That instance was when his official act forthwith caused the person aggrieved to lose his heavenly reward for the performance of a religious duty. If the victim of the error had the opportunity to verify the elder's decision with other elders before relying thereon, the elder bore no guilt for his own defiant negation of the Sanhedrin's will. The Talmud could discover only one such possibility.[13] This view bears interesting resemblance to the "clear and present danger" rule, for only when the elder's defiance of constitutional authority caused immediate danger did it involve the offender in criminal liability.

The Right of Voluntary Giving

Most interesting of all, perhaps, was a Jew's immunity from being compelled to support what might be regarded as his country's established religion. The Biblical system of tithes and its abuse by non-Jews during the Middle Ages have blinded most moderns to the fact that according to the Talmud there were no legal sanctions for their collection. The state did not collect the tithes.[14] "The tithes . . . are fundamental in Torah. Nonetheless, their collection was left to the (free will of the) common people." Nor were the priests and Levites permitted to solicit them. They were not even permitted to assist in the harvesting of crops lest their presence constitute an indirect hint that they should receive their share.[15] Jews were exhorted to pay the tithes, but that was all. As a matter of fact, a man might simply set the

12. B. Sanh. 86b.
13. B. Sanh. 88b.
14. B. Shab. 32a and 32b; and Rashi's commentary on 32b.
15. Mishneh Torah, Hilchot Terumot, XII, 18.

105

tithe aside and do no more. The rest of his crop might be eaten without violating any religious prohibition. And thereafter he might forever withhold delivery of the tithes to the Levites. He was honor-bound to deliver them but no more.

Two objectives were achieved by permitting the system of tithes to operate on a voluntary basis. First, philanthropy would remain within the province of free will. Second, the clergy would receive their due in the measure in which they were beloved by the people. Both objectives would have been defeated had the state enforced collection. And that is why, despite the great laxity that prevailed in the payment of tithes by the peasants, the rabbis never gave these tithes the status of a tax.

The same was generally true of gifts to the priests who took care of the sacrifices in the temple. In most cases, the priests were to receive only a share of voluntary offerings for services rendered in connection therewith.

The rabbis, of course, applied even more stringent rules to themselves. They could be compensated only for time lost from the pursuit of their gainful vocations. In any event, support of the established religion was in the main voluntary.

The Talmud is a veritable mine of materials pertaining to human rights, and he who would probe its folios will be rewarded with the enrichment of his insights as well as the enhancement of his appreciation of historic Judaism. One hopes that Jewish social scientists will apply their talents to these neglected sources.

Chapter Four

MEDICAL–LEGAL PROBLEMS

For many years there has been considerable discussion
in the United States with regard to the liberalization of
many laws pertaining to the practice of medicine and the
rights of patients as well as physicians. It has been argued
that patients should be given the right to know the truth
about their condition. Doctors should be denied the privilege
to withhold information. In the same vein, patients and
their physicians should be accorded unlimited access to
information and means for contraception. Sanctions against
artificial insemination shall be removed and sterilization and
euthanasia shall be made more readily available and even
compulsory in some instances. Resistance to autopsies has
become the subject of much controversy in the United States
and in Israel, and much legislation is offered.

Generally I hold that the liberalization of state laws is
not opposed by the Halachah, although individuals may
choose on ethical or religious grounds not to take advantage
of them. This essay deals principally with this one aspect
of the problem: Shall Jews, especially in the United States,
resist the legislation?

The Patient's Right to Know the Truth

Ethical integrity requires freedom of choice based upon
full knowledge of the facts. For that reason I personally

would always want my doctor to tell me the whole truth. Only then could I act as a moral person in the situation calling for action. However, for that very same reason I cannot accept changes in the law which would deny physicians the very freedom of choice which I crave for myself. For to impose criminal, or even civil, liability upon doctors for not telling their patients the truth is to deny them the prerogative of weighing the many circumstances that they, as moral persons, ought to consider before they arrive at decisions as to what they shall do. I do not see it as a function of the law to relieve doctors of the onus of making decisions, for they are more than the mere observers of symptoms and prescribers of remedies. A statutory requirement that they invariably tell their patients the "truth" would make of each of them an "it" instead of a "thou," and while patients may have the "right" (in an ethical sense) "to know the medical facts" about themselves, such right should not be converted into a "claim" (in the legal or "Hohfeldian" sense) so that a correlative duty devolves upon the physician to reveal everything he knows or suffer the consequences provided by statute.

Such a law would also be unenforceable. For it is in the rare case that doctors conceal their diagnosis. In some cases, as in psychotherapy, everyone concedes that disclosure might adversely affect the cure and aggravate the patient's symptoms and misery. Yet, who knows better than doctors how virtually indistinguishable are psychic from somatic diseases! Therefore, to enact a law which would permit the withholding of facts in the case of the former and deny such permission in the case of the latter is to enact legislation that will become a mockery. A doctor could always certify that he deluded his patient because in addition to the cancer, the patient had one neurosis or another. It is much more expedient to leave the problem where it belongs—in the realm of ethics. Perhaps more and more people want the truth. However, if the doctors will have misjudged the moral caliber of their patients, then, alas, they will have erred and to err is human. A mandatory law might spare them the possibility of error, but it hardly enhances their freedom, and they too are entitled to the freedom required to be moral persons who can make moral choices.

The legal character of the contract between the physician and the patient plays too important a role in the thinking of those who crave a law forcing the doctor to reveal everything. It is not a legal contract that gives rise to the obligation to tell the truth. Let us assume that I am not a physician but I know facts about my friend which are unknown to him. Must I not disclose them if they are of significance to him? Though the Bible prohibits "tale-bearing," in the same verse it orders me to testify when I have information that would, for example, save a prisoner from execution,[1] though I am under no contractual obligation to the accused and though my testimony may incriminate another. Yet, at the same time, Jewish codes[2] regard him as a fool who divulges information to a friend when such information can only cause grief and inconvenience, albeit that the friend might be a masochist and might prefer to suffer distress. Furthermore, the fact that the doctor has a contractual relationship with the patient means no more than that for a breach of the contract he can be sued for damages. Whether or not he will "specifically perform" the contract will always remain a moral question for the doctor to resolve, and it is no different in essence from the moral problem of any human being having knowledge of facts that are material to another.

By the same token, one goes too far when one virtually creates a property right in the patient to the facts which the doctor acquires in the course of the physical examination, and which facts the doctor may "steal" from the patient by failure to disclose them. Even if those facts became the basis of a case history, the patient has no claim to them. The most that one could say about facts means that the patient's right of privacy has been yielded in vain. But no legal system would go so far as to provide sanctions to

1. Leviticus 19:16.
2. Karo and Isserlis, Shulhan Aruch, Yoreh Deah CDII:12.

protect such a right of privacy in the patient-physician relationship, when to do so would inhibit physicians in the course of their examinations lest they exceed the bounds within which they are protected by law. Thus to expand the scope of the law's protection of the rights of privacy would be against public policy.

In Judaism generally the greater emphasis is always on the duty aspect of the "right-duty" correlative. If we place the emphasis today on the physician's duty to do the best for his patient rather than on the patient's right, we will achieve the better result.

Contraception

As in the case of the doctor's telling the truth, so in the matter of contraceptives I favor minimum interference by the law. The most that the law should do is regulate their production and sale in the same manner that it regulates the purity of other drugs and surgical or medical equipment. It is not the law's function to protect one moral code in the community when an antithetical one enjoys as much loyalty from citizens of the state.

Judaism has a considerable literature on the subject and there is no agreement among rabbis as to the morality or immorality of planned parenthood. The rules applicable to continence during, and for a week after, the menstrual period already greatly reduce the incidence of pregnancy. Moreover, abundant authority there is for the use of contraceptives when the welfare of an already born child may be affected by another pregnancy, as in the case of a mother who is breast-feeding her child and another pregnancy would cut off the flow of milk from her mammary glands. Some rabbis see no difference between such a case and planned parenthood for the economic welfare of offspring, particularly since the Talmud regards nursing as an economic rather than biological function of the mother.[3]

3. Babylonian Talmud, Ketubot, 60b.

Thus, for example, if the child is so young that it does not yet recognize its mother, the husband may in many instances be required to engage some other woman to do the nursing, and relieve his wife of that responsibility. One of the most distinguished Talmudic commentators, Rabbenu Tam (12th century), held that there never was a prohibition against birth control by the wife.[4] In some cases, however, he regarded it mandatory. The case of the nursing mother is one such instance. Most authorities insist that only the wife may practice contraception on the theory that hers is not the command to be fruitful.[5] She is even permitted to imbibe drugs to prevent contraception.[6] Her role in procreation is only passive. And since it is the male who must fulfill the mandate of Genesis to multiply, it is urged that he should not be guilty of active evasion of his obligation. Yet a man fulfills his obligation when he has already had a son and a daughter. Moreover, the mandate of Genesis is explicitly for the purpose of "filling the earth."[7] One could reasonably argue that when there already exists a threat of overpopulation the divine command has been fulfilled. In any event, overpopulation has more than economic importance. It is at least as directly related to the health of humanity as the conception of any second child is to the breast-feeding of the first.

With many others I concur that there has been too much sophistry in all religious traditions with regard to the subject and anyone who will grapple with the total Jewish legal tradition will have to concede that sexual intercourse is not exclusively for procreation. By Jewish law, one may cohabit with one's sterile wife.[8] And one may cohabit with one's wife during her pregnancy and after her menopause. If anything may be learned from the story of Onan in

4. Commentaries on Babylonian Talmud, Ketubot, 39a.
5. Maimonides, Mishneh Torah, Hilchot Ishut, XV:2
6. Talmud Bavli, Shabbat, 110b. Maimonides, Mishneh Torah, Hilchot Isurei Biah, XVI:12.
7. Genesis 1:28.
8. Rabbenu Tam, op. cit. supra note 4.

Genesis,[9] it is that contraception by withdrawal is to be discouraged—for good psychical reasons. But the story may not be authority even for such a limited prohibition. As many exegetes say, it is authority for the proposition that he who would fulfill the Levirate law cannot vitiate it by dropping his seed earthward. Onan had married his deceased brother's childless widow and the only justification for such a marriage, in the face of the prohibition against it, was that he would cause her to conceive.

In any event, the law should not be the instrument for the further benighting of the benighted. Ignorance may be bliss but it is immoral to use the law to withhold from the depressed elements of the population information already available to the majority. The least that Jewish law insists upon is that all Jews shall study the Law which includes discussions of the facts and methods of contraception. As I oppose the use of the law to compel the disclosure of facts by doctors, so I oppose its use to prevent the dissemination of information by the same people or equally competent and trained individuals. Whether or not the information will be used by the adherents of different faiths should always remain a matter of moral choice.

Artificial Insemination

I do favor the legislation which the renowned Dr. Joseph Fletcher, author of "Medicine and Morals," seeks with regard to all forms of artificial insemination. The legislation he seeks would correct existing statutes or vitiate unfortunate interpretations already given them. In this connection Jewish law is exceedingly liberal. A woman is not guilty of adultery when she is impregnated artificially with the sperm of a donor and the child is legitimate, whether or not the mother is married.[10] The doctor cannot be regarded as a criminal since the wife or unwed mother has committed no crime and one cannot be an "accomplice" to "no-crime."

9. 38:9.
10. B. Z. Uziel, Mishpete Uziel, Even ha-'Ezer, No. 19.

112

According to Jewish law, however, the donor remains the natural father of the child—so that the child by A.I.D. would not be permitted to marry any other children that the anonymous donor may then or subsequently cause to be conceived. Such a marriage would be incestuous. It is principally for this reason that A.I.D. has not been encouraged by rabbis. Though a few rabbis question the moral character of the donor's act in permitting sperm to be taken from him, the greater objection is that A.I.D. increases the possibility of children marrying their half brothers or sisters, whom they don't know to be such. Yet even this remote fear would hardly convince many in a Jewish state to prohibit the practice, particularly since no stigma ever attaches to donor, mother, or child.[11] The most that the law would do would be to encourage the selection of donors in such a way that incest could never follow (e.g., by using donors of a religious faith other than the mother) or to require registration of donors so that the state's authority charged with the task of solemnizing marriages would be able to ascertain whether incest is involved.

It has been suggested that while A.I.D. is not adultery, nonetheless, when the wife continues to cohabit with her husband while A.I.D. is being performed upon her, one may never know through whom she became pregnant and Judaism does regard the unequivocal identity of one's parents as a goal much to be cherished. For this reason one rabbi even suggested that while A.I.D. is being performed upon the wife, the husband and wife should be divorced from each other for the duration of the pregnancy.[12] While the suggestion may help to make sure that we know who the real father is, it is hardly humane, for it is precisely during that period that husband and wife require all the warmth and

---

11. No stigma whatever attaches to the child if a record is kept of the name of the donor, even though the record is not available to everyone.

12. Rabbi Meyer Karlin of Brooklyn, N.Y., made this suggestion in an unpublished responsum read before the Rabbinic Alumni of Yeshiva University.

understanding of which they are capable. Nonetheless, it seems clear that Jewish criminal and personal status law creates no problems with regard to the alleged adultery of the A.I.D. mother or the legitimacy of the issue.

More difficult to resolve, however, is the civil liability of the father-donor to the offspring. By Jewish law he is the natural father and a natural parent can never rid himself of his tie to his child, nor can the child ever sever his tie with his natural forebears. Yet this rule does not preclude the fostering of a foster-parent relationship in addition to the natural relationship. That is why Jewish law never provided for adoptions, though one could always voluntarily raise another's child. Insofar as the adoption releases the natural parent from all parental obligations it was objectionable. Yet Jewish civil law is flexible enough to permit such amendments as will relieve the father-donor of liability for support of his offspring, and remove his estate from claims of inheritance by children he has never seen. Israel's Chief Rabbi Herzog has already recommended proposals which would modify the traditional Jewish law of inheritance in other respects and make it accord with such sentiments of obligation as prevail in the modern family.[13] Further amendments of Jewish law to protect the father-donor would also appear to be possible and necessary.

That Jewish law is so much more liberal than Christian law is due to the fact that the two legal systems parted ways centuries ago with regard to their conceptions of illegitimacy. According to Judaism, the child of an unwed mother is not illegitimate. A child is illegitimate only when it is *conclusively* established that it was born of an adulterous or incestuous relationship, and since it is virtually impossible ever to prove that any conception is due to adultery or incest—for the husband is always presumed to be the father of his wife's children, even if he proves that he was on another planet for years—illegitimacy is a status that is more a threat than a legal reality. Furthermore, to be guilty

13. "Hazoat Taqonot bi-Yerushot," in Talpiot 36-50 (Yeshiva University 1953).

of either adultery or incest, the male must at least begin to penetrate the vagina or anus. Anything less than that may be immoral but it is not punishable, nor does it ever create any clouds over status. A.I.D. involves no such penetration.

Sterilization

With regard to compulsory sterilization, Jewish law is not so liberal as are already prevailing statutes. Who better than Jews know the consequences of allowing the state too much control over the gift of life! As modernistic in outlook as we essay to be, the memory of Nazi terror is still too fresh for us to permit any tampering with time-honored rules. And it is not the Fascists alone who have created states with no respect for human life and dignity. The whole story of Communist terror must yet be told. Liberals, and I among them, have helped the Communists to conceal their nefarious achievements. We were deluded for a long time by the profession of high ideals and we presumed that a better society was really their goal. I have visited behind the Iron Curtain and I have one firm conviction: states must be kept at bay. And to vest the state with more power over life and death than it already has is dangerous. Judaism is very much "anti-statist." No legal philosophy is more inconsistent with Judaism than Austin's, Kelsen's, and now the Soviet Union's, to wit: that law is the creature of the state. And this "anti-statism" must have inspired Jewish sages millennia ago to deplore even capital punishment.[14] They did not altogether abolish it as many people believe; even in the Middle Ages they resorted to it, particularly in the case of informers. But the trend to shear the state of power over life and death was unmistakable.

Killing in self-defense remained a part of the law. On that basis one can defend the compulsory sterilization of criminals. Though the Bible prohibits sterilization, that prohibition yields, as do all others, to the supreme command to

14. Babylonian Talmud, Makot, 7a.

save life; and the sterilization of criminals may be necessary to save lives. Society may do it in self-defense if no other preventive is absolutely effective. But the procreation of idiots is an evil against which the state can protect itself. Idiots can be institutionalized. True, the cost is great but unless the cost is so great that the survival of the group is threatened by it, compulsory sterilization is the exercise of a police power not for the good of the sterilized—who are incapable of knowing good or evil—but for the convenience of the majority. This is precisely the type of logic by which Hitler justified the cremation of millions of "inferior" peoples.

Dr. Fletcher's plea for the right of children to be born normal is an appealing one. Would we, therefore, kill children born blind? Or crippled? Dr. Fletcher really sheds crocodile tears for the rights of idiots who are unaware of their lot or status. The ultimate rationalization of our defense of their sterilization is that we, the normal ones, want to be spared the burden of their maintenance. And I submit that that burden is a small price to pay for the safeguards we require against the enlargement of the state's power over life and death.

Judaism's general position on sterilization is quite clear. It is prohibited. At least, the rabbis so understood the prohibition of Deuteronomy.[15] And in the light of the anthropological data available to us, which indicate the extent to which sterilization was a rite of pagan religion, one can understand why the Bible sought to exorcise this vestige of paganism. In its unalterable opposition to paganism it outlawed this pagan practice as well.

Yet, while the Bible prohibits him who caused himself to be made sterile from marrying into the Congregation of Israel—this is his punishment—the Talmud did make it clear that the prohibition does not apply to those made sterile by acts of God.[16] For that reason a group of rabbis informed the Veterans Administration that those who be-

15. 23:2.
16. Babylonian Talmud, Yevamot, 75b.

116

came paraplegics as a result of injuries sustained in combat may marry in accordance with Jewish law.

Furthermore, the question was raised as to whether, in the light of the Biblical prohibition against castration, one may permit the removal of one's prostate gland. However, as already indicated, almost all Biblical prohibitions yield to the requirement of self-preservation. If the prohibition against murder must be suspended to save life, it is an *a fortiori* case that the prohibition against sterilization can also be suspended to save life.

With regard to the Sabbath we have a recent unpublished rabbinic ruling that extends the suspension of the Sabbath's operation when life is at stake to such an extent that a state—the State of Israel for example, where the problem is not an academic one—may render through its employees many services on the Sabbath that individuals may not perform. The state may maintain dynamos and generate electricity which an individual for personal reasons may not do. However, for the state, the availability of electric power is essential to operate the round-the-clock activities in diplomatic and military communications centers and in hospitals. To secure the state is tantamount to securing the lives of its citizens and consequently many Sabbath rules are suspended.

Can the same reasoning be applied to the sterilization of incompetents? Should not the Biblical prohibition against sterilization—of far less significance in the hierarchy of Jewish values than the Sabbath—also yield to the need that the state protect itself against such procreation as can only constitute a drain on its resources and energies? I am not prepared to answer affirmatively. True, the state could use the money it will require to maintain the incompetents for the greater good of the competent. But I dread the extension of the state's police power to include control of the procreative faculties of one person for the benefit of another.

117

Even more than in the case of compulsory sterilization, Judaism would be unalterably opposed to any legislation that would make homicide by physicians or by agents of the state mandatory or permissive. Judaism's position may appear paradoxical. On the one hand, he who accelerates the death of a patient may not be tried as a murderer—for he killed one who was afflicted with an incurable malady and is therefore, from the point of view of the homicide, already legally dead.[17] Moreover, no people can boast as many martyrs as Jews do and martyrs are individuals who for the glory of God permit themselves to be slaughtered when they could save their lives by one form of apostasy or another. This means that the tradition did not glorify the continuance of life as an end beyond which there is no end. Yet, at the same time Jewish ethics prohibit suicide—without exception—and also euthanasia—without exception.

However, the seeming paradox makes for the very ethical integrity which is the heart of the moral position described in Dr. Fletcher's book.

For the law to relieve men of all crucial moral decisions is to deny them that spiritual autonomy which is of the essence of their moral and religious experience. Confronted by a suffering fellow man, the doctor must make decisions. Or the members of the family must make them. And they must steer a course between two antinomies: the inviolability of the right to life and the command to mitigate suffering. Whatever the decision, there will be no punishment by human tribunals—according to Judaism. Mercy killing will not be murder. The *freedom to act morally* is, therefore, absolute. One acts only under God and with one's own conscience as one's guide. And one will have to live with that decision forever after. The law, however, plays no part.

The Model Legislation.—Petitions for euthanasia would

17. The victim must be suffering from an incurable disease, not simply an old man who would soon die anyway.

definitely be objectionable from Judaism's point of view. If the patient wants to commit suicide, he will have to make a moral decision comparable to that which the physician makes when he commits a mercy killing. However, the law should not be amended so as to give the state more power over life and death than it already has. The misery of the few who might seek to take advantage of the legislation proposed is naught by comparison with the misery of multitudes whom the Leviathan will destroy when and if we raze the ramparts which religion has reared for millennia around the sanctity of life.

Dr. Fletcher's plea for the afflicted is moving. But alas, as mindful as one wants to be of the welfare of the individual, one must not forget that the law, and ethics, must also be mindful of the general welfare of society. Lawyers often speak of hard cases making bad law. In the refinement and development of justice, one must frequently ignore the hard case and permit the generally just rule to remain inviolate. The proponents of legislation regulating euthanasia are preoccupied with the plight of individuals who, at best, will be few in number. For while many patients may beg for death, few will petition for it. And while doctors technically kill with pain-relieving drugs, the drugs do relieve pain and diminish the likelihood of legal action by patients. For the rare case, therefore, in which legislation would be used, it would be most unfortunate if, in an age which has tolerated as much wholesale slaughter as ours already has, we should take further steps to let the state play God.

Chapter Five

JUDAISM AND EQUALITY

Introduction

Biblical Hebrew has no word for "equality." Nonetheless
in the book of Leviticus the Jews were told, "Ye shall have
one law for the stranger and citizen alike; for I the Lord
am your God" (Lev. 24:22). Equality before the law, according to Judaism, was divinely ordained. By the same
token Hebrew has many equivalents for "differentiate," and
God Himself presumably ordained many of the differences—
not only natural but also legal. Can such antithetical mandates be reconciled so that God's attribute of justice is not
impugned and His role respected as "judge of all the earth"
(Gen. 18:25)? Not easily, but the literature of Jewish law
and theology reflects a continuing tension between the ideal
of human equality and the many inequalities that result
from differences for which the tradition holds the Creator
Himself responsible. In the emerging dialectic, values other
than equality play their part, as do the different functions
assigned to human beings in society as a whole.

The paradox encountered in the Biblical texts is aggravated by the fact that it is more than equality before the
law that God has willed. Indeed, even at creation did He
will human equality as a *fact*. Because of this extraordinary
notion, Judaism's contribution to the idea of equality differs
from that of Stoicism.

In Stoicism it is the possession of reason that marks man off from the external world. Men are deemed equal because the part of them that reasons, their "souls," is the same in all men. Judaism also held that God endows all humans with His image—the *Tselem Elohim*—which Jewish philosophers in the Aristotelian tradition often equated with reason. The dogma was so basic in Judaism that the fundamental rationale for executing a murderer was that he destroyed a divine image. He killed, in a sense, God's likeness. "Whoso sheddeth man's blood, by man shall his blood be shed; for in the image of God made He man" (Gen. 9:6).

Judaism, however, also derives human likeness from the fact that God had created only one man from whom all humanity is descended. No one could ever argue that he was superior in birth because of his genealogy. "Man was created alone. And why so? . . . That families might not quarrel with each other. Now, if at present, though but one was originally created, they quarrel, how much more if two had been created!" (Babylonian Talmud; tractate Sanhedrin, 38a.) That all men have only one progenitor, whereas animals were created by God in the plural number, was held to mean that all human beings are born equal. They enjoy this equality by virtue of the very fact that they were born, even if they never attain to the faculty of reason. This was the only source on which Thomas Paine could rely in his "Rights of Man" to support the dogma of the American Declaration of Independence that all men are created equal. And this dogma was basic in Judaism.

Augustine later modified the Jewish doctrine considerably and as a result Western civilization did not have the full benefit of its implications. Were it not for Augustine's introduction of the need for grace resulting from the Fall of Man and of the elitism of those who are blessed with grace, the merging of Jewish and Stoic conceptions might have accelerated progress toward equality in all human affairs. There would have been no blithe acceptance of inequality as a punishment for sin, for historic Judaism had no dogma of the "Fall of Man"; consequently the Jewish and Stoic views might have complemented each other for a more rapid fulfillment of the ideal of equality.

Nonetheless, even as all men are born equal because they all descend from the one Adam, men do differ. "The creation of the first man *alone* was to show forth the greatness of the Supreme King of Kings, the Holy One, blessed be He. For if a man mints many coins from one mold, they are all alike, but the Holy One, blessed be He, fashioned all men in the mold of the first man, and not one resembles the other" (*ibid.*). Men differ in voice, appearance, and mind; men differ in sex and color; men differ ethnically and nationally. What is more, God Himself willed that they shall differ in language and geographic distribution. Within their national groupings, there are freemen and slaves, kings and subjects, priests, levites, and prophets—and of all these differences the Bible takes note. To some it gives *de facto* recognition; to others even *de jure* recognition. Some differences it prescribes itself and it accords to the differentiated special duties and privileges. How can this be reconciled with the command to have one law for the citizen and the stranger? And how consonant is this proliferation of mankind with the prophetic protest, "Have we not all one Father?"

To this very day the annals of Jewish history, the folios of Jewish law, and the apologetics of Jewish theologians reflect continuing concern with this dichotomy. This essay purports to deal principally with the legal norms and parenthetically with the theology that undergirds them. The facts of Jewish history—a record of successes and failures in attaining the ideal—are beyond its scope. Too often the legal norms were ignored and the prophets inveighed against the oppressors; sometimes rabbis were progressive and at other times conservative and reactionary; communal leaders were often on the side of the status quo and often against it. As among all national and ethnic groups, there were forces other than the law that precipitated or retarded the movement toward maximum social, economic, and political equality. Scriptures and Talmudic materials were quoted by all sides. Yet Jews have adequate cause for boasting that the ideal of equality suggested by the very first chapter of the Bible was fulfilled in their society to a greater extent than among the many peoples with whom they had contact in their millennial history, and today the collectives of the new state of Israel are not only living laboratories of the ideal's fullest fruition but also seats of very impressive philosophical discussion on the meaning of equality. Despite the absolutely equal sharing of goods in these collectives, there is growing concern that some members enjoy more prestige than others by virtue of their positions as decision-makers or of their greater ability to produce, think, or lead. Even this concern, this feeling of guilt, bespeaks an enduring preoccupation with an absolute ideal and the difficulty encountered in fulfilling it in practice.

Male and Female

From the seemingly divergent accounts in Genesis describing how God created Adam and Eve, one derives at least, first, that a man leaves his parents to cleave to his wife—wife in the singular. Thus while polygamy was practiced lawfully by many Jews, as it is in some Oriental countries even today, monogamy appears to be the ideal. Second, women share the divine image; their lives, limbs, and property are to be accorded the same respect accorded those of men. Third, men and women have different functions. Judaism is, therefore, less receptive to the idea of a natural hierarchy but accepts the legitimacy of functional inequalities.

Polygamy and Polyandry

That a man might lawfully wed many women while a woman was bound to one husband at a time was a flouting of the ideal of equality. But Jewish law was committed to another value—the importance of the identity of the father in the case of offspring. Therefore, it could not countenance polyandry, which would result in children's uncertainty as

123

to who their father was. To abolish polygamy was not easy, for most men resisted change. It required a considerable moral and social development that finally, in about the year 1000, culminated for Occidental Jews in the ban of Rabbi Gershom against the practice. The Biblical ideal of man cleaving to one wife gave impetus to this moral and social development. Whenever it did discuss the polygamy of the patriarchs, some special reason for it was given: Abraham impregnated Hagar at Sarah's request; Jacob married two sisters because of his father-in-law's fraud and took two concubines at the request of the sisters. Kings were warned in it, moreover, not to enlarge their harems unduly. Especially noteworthy is the word used in the Bible to describe the relationship between two wives of the same man; it is *Tzarah*, which also means "misfortune" and suggests that two wives of one husband can only bring grief to each other. Yet, as will be demonstrated, the advantage of the male over the female still predominates in the inequitable law of divorce.

Marriage and Divorce

Whereas males and females who had reached their legal majority were absolutely equal in consummating a marriage, they were not so in divorce.

Because the husband performs the formal act creating the marriage, the Law assumed that it is he who must give the order to write and deliver the bill of divorce. He who created the sacred bond must undo it. In Judaism, including the Kabbalah, the male is regarded as the active principle in the universe and the female as the passive principle. Therefore, in marriage and divorce it is he who must perform the legally operative acts.

Yet without the consent of the female, a marriage could not be consummated. But until the year 1000, her consent to the divorce was not required. The need for her consent was slower in coming because the Law assumed that it served no purpose to keep her wedded to a man who did not respect her. The Law sought only to provide for her maintenance after divorce.

Moreover, her right to sue for a divorce is suggested by the Talmud, not the Bible. The Law labored under a presumption that any woman would prefer a bad marriage to no marriage; "It is better to live with any other, than alone." Yet virtual equality is now achieved and today where there is mutual consent, no court approval is required and no grounds for divorce need be offered. If either spouse withholds consent, a court of competent jurisdiction is able to adjudicate and act against the will of either spouse.

Nonetheless an inequality, which begs for correction, persists. Because it is the husband who must give the order to write the bill of divorce, the court is still impotent to terminate the marriage when the husband is not subject to the jurisdiction of the court, when he is missing or insane, and especially in states in which rabbinic tribunals have no authority except such as the parties want to vest in them. Therefore, wives are often helpless in getting the necessary bill of divorce and without it cannot marry other men. In similar circumstances, however, men could remarry. They could, for example, deposit with a rabbinical court a bill of divorce for an insane wife. Because by Biblical law there is no objection to a man's being wedded to more than one woman at one time, a man can marry a second wife while his first is hospitalized. Or if a wife has disappeared, the husband can, again, deposit a bill of divorce with a rabbinical court. This inequity is very much the subject of discussion among modern rabbis who will have to promulgate new rules to solve a problem whose incidence is greater now.*

During Coverture

The extent to which the separate property of wives survived the creation of the marriage relationship was extraor-

___
* See infra, pp. 241 ff.

dinary. What a woman brought into the marriage as dowry became the husband's, but he was obligated, in the event that he predeceased or divorced her, to return the full amount he received. His liability in this connection was that of an insurer. The loss of the dowry because of acts of God or non-negligent management was no defense. What a woman acquired during her marriage by gift from friends or inheritance from relatives remained hers. Her right to separate property was well established. The husband became trustee of that property, taking the income for himself and conserving the corpus for her in the event of a divorce or his predeceasing her.

However, the one significant inequality was that she was not an heiress of her husband whereas he was her sole heir. She acquired from his estate her dowry, all separate property received by her during the marriage, and support until her remarriage. However, if she predeceased her husband, he took all of her estate to the exclusion even of the issue of the marriage.

In rights of inheritance generally males had the advantage. It would appear that the advantage enjoyed by males was due to the central importance, in the wealth of the community, of land, which the men were expected to cultivate and defend. The role of woman was truly domestic; she was to serve spouse and offspring. The rest of the family's economy was the responsibility of the man. Thus differences in function may have contributed to the advantage of males.

But the husband had no special privileges with regard to the life and limb of his wife. He could not kill her even if he apprehended her in the commission of adultery. He was also responsible for torts committed against her person not excluding torts committed in the course of coitus.

The Equality of Offspring

Jewish law limited the right of the father to disinherit his children—or, for that matter, any of the heirs entitled to the succession. In his lifetime the father could dispose of his

126

property as he chose. But even a written document altering the Biblical pattern of inheritance was a nullity. The Oral Law did permit him to alter the disposition among his sons, or among his daughters if he had no sons. He could prefer one to the others. Yet the rabbis frowned on such behavior; their rationale was based on the religious value of penitence. One ought not to disinherit a child in anger or resentment because the child might repent, or the child's offspring might prove worthy of the estate. Saints are often born to parents who are villains.

The rights of issue were so vested that it did not matter whether the children were born in or out of wedlock, or whether they were even legitimate. A child was deemed illegitimate only in the rarest situation when proof was incontrovertible that he was born of an adulterous or incestuous relationship—and to prove this was almost impossible. The child born out of wedlock was legitimate even if there was no subsequent marriage between its parents. And these children were heirs. They were not subjected to the indignity of proving that they were entitled to take a share of their father's estate so long as their paternity was either generally known or admitted by the father in his lifetime. Moreover, if an illegitimate son, and *a fortiori* one born out of wedlock who was not illegitimate, was the first issue of the father, he was entitled to all the rights of primogeniture.

The rights of the first-born were generally proscribed. The Bible had said that they were entitled to a double portion. Did that mean two-thirds of the estate in every case, or two portions of the estate after it was divided by the number of sons plus one? The latter interpretation was upheld. The Biblical verse was strictly construed in this respect, as it was with every other problem that arose.

The first-born took his double portion only of such property that the deceased actually possessed at the time of his death. Claims of the deceased were not to be included. In addition, the first-born had to prove beyond the shadow of a doubt that he was the father's first-born. If a stillborn preceded him, he forfeited his special position. He must also have been born before his father died—he did not acquire special privileges as a fetus, and thus could not take more than his twin brother born moments after him. Moreover, he must have been born naturally from the womb and not by a Caesarean operation. This was strict construction of a verse, proscribing a right which the Oral Law deemed anomalous and inconsistent with the ideal of equality.

Perhaps the institution of primogeniture should have been abolished altogether rather than only radically proscribed. Certainly the narratives in the book of Genesis reveal how much grief resulted from the deeply entrenched preference for the first-born—for example, the rivalry between Ishmael and Isaac, Esau and Jacob, Reuben and Joseph. The Midrash so dwells upon these rivalries that one wonders whether some of Adler's psychoanalytic theories did not derive from it. But the rabbis did not abolish the institution. The Bible had approved of it even if it did curtail its benefits, and the rabbis were not prepared to abolish it altogether as they might well have done. Perhaps they regarded the first-born as the bearer of special social, economic, and educational responsibilities in the family. The first-born had been the family priests until the tribe of Levi replaced them as religious functionaries. As the eldest in the family, they were also expected to provide leadership after the father's death and even during his lifetime. Perhaps as Philo suggested, the first-born was owed a debt of gratitude by the father. After all, he made the father a father. Therefore, some special consideration was accorded him in the distribution of the estate. But to that extent the ideal of equality remains compromised.

If rabbis frown upon a Biblical law but refrain from nullifying it, is their thought to be regarded as deontological and Kantian rather than as teleological and utilitarian? It would be more accurate to say that it was all of these: The Law was theocentric—divine in origin and with creative achievement ever oriented to the fulfillment of God's will. Never to lose sight of this commitment, the Law had its suprarational mandates not readily explicable in terms of human values and interests. Every branch of the Law had them. But the Law was given to people, who alone were responsible for its development. The Bible itself appeals to man to comprehend the justice-content of the Law. It also bids him to live by the Law, not to perish because of it. Thus suprarational norms remain the Law's theocentric roots and prevent it from becoming altogether positive in character. But rabbinic creativity had to be mindful too of ends and utility.

Slavery

Jewish law distinguished between slaves who were Jews and slaves who were non-Jews, usually called Canaanite slaves. Their legal status was not the same, and the inequality derived from religious values that conflicted with the value of equality.*

The abolition of the ownership of one Jew by a fellow Jew was accomplished centuries ago. Those who heard on Mount Sinai that all Jews were God's servants were not to become further indentured to coreligionists who shared with them a common bondage to the same Master! But what is most significant about this result is that it represented the achievement of Jewish jurisprudence—that very legalism of the Pharisees which became the butt of Christian criticism.

No one became a slave for failure to pay a debt. The sale was permitted only for failure to pay for one's theft. Furthermore, a man could be sold only if he failed to pay the principal amount due on the theft. If he could pay the principal but not the double or quadruple or quintuple damages due, he could not be sold into slavery. Nor could he be sold as a punishment for false witness. The Bible said "theft" and theft alone it shall be!

Having become a slave, the person kept a status virtually

* See supra, pp. 25 ff. and infra, pp. 206 ff.

like that of a freeman. He could not be disgraced by a sale at public auction. The work he could do for his master was not to be difficult or degrading. Wherever possible, he was to continue in his former occupation. He was also to enjoy the same food, clothing and shelter as his master.

His life and limb were as protected as the life and limb of any freeman. The master was as liable for homicide or mayhem as if the slave were an equal. The slave's wife and children were not sold with him, as was the custom in most other contemporaneous cultures. As a matter of fact, the master was obliged to support the slave's dependents.

The slave could acquire property and redeem himself to freedom. At most his bondage would last six years and out of any property he acquired he could pay for any part of his unexpired term. According to Maimonides, his wife could engage in gainful employment. None of her earnings belonged to her husband's master, even while the master remained responsible for her and her children's maintenance. If the slave were ill for any part of his term—up to one-half thereof—he did not have to serve any extended period to compensate for the time of his indisposition.

He could sue and be sued. He was also competent as a witness. In one respect only was his legal status different from that of a freeman. The master could compel him to take a Canaanitish slave woman as a wife. The progeny would belong to the master, for the status of the progeny was that of their mother. In an age when polygamy was quite prevalent, this was not a serious invasion of personal rights.

Even in those isolated instances where the master was permitted to cause the Jewish male slave to mate with a non-Jewish female slave—the only instance justifying the contention that the master owned the very body of the slave —the moral standards of a monogamous relationship were applicable. Promiscuous relationships were prohibited. The institution of slavery was never to place in jeopardy the lofty moral ideals of the Law.

To demonstrate the high value set upon freedom, a slave

130

who refused to become free had his ear pierced with an awl. Unlike the Hammurabi code, which prescribed this penalty for a runaway slave, Jewish law prescribed it for the slave who did not avail himself of an opportunity to become free.

When the slave's term expired, the master was to give him a gift—severance pay. Talmudic jurists fixed the amount instead of relying upon the master's generosity. Moreover, they exempted the gift from execution by the slave's creditors to insure the slave of the wherewithal for a new start in life.

With this kind of legal development, it was to be expected that one would hardly ever want to become a master of a Jewish slave. And thus by a rigid legalism slavery was abolished—a result sermons and homilies could hardly achieve.

A Jewish girl could become a slave only if her father sold her into bondage prior to her reaching puberty. The sale, however, was less a sale than a betrothal, for she was automatically emancipated upon reaching puberty unless her master or her master's son wed her. If the master or his son did wed her, she had the status of a wife with all the privileges thereunto appertaining. Moreover, her consent to the betrothal was required.

In all other respects her legal status was that of the male Hebrew slave. And neither the male nor the female could be resold by the master to another.

The Oral Law did not permit even a non-Jew to be enslaved without giving him sufficient status as a Jew to insure the protection of his life and limb and his partial participation in the religious life of the family and community. As such, he had a higher status than even a free Gentile. If the non-Jew was bought with the express proviso that he should not be converted to Judaism, then he had to acquiesce at least in the observance of the seven Noahide laws.

It would appear, however, that non-Jewish slaves preferred Jewish owners. As a consequence of their becoming members of a Jewish household, pursuant to the performance of the appropriate rituals, they could not be killed with impunity. There was no difference whatever in the law of homicide, whether willful or accidental, as to whether the victim was a Jewish freeman or a non-Jewish slave. Torts committed against the non-Jewish slave by persons other than the master were actionable. Though the recovery was the master's, the injuring of slaves was deterred by the very fact that a tort against him was actionable. And the master himself did not escape with impunity for his own torts against his non-Jewish slave. Emancipation of the slave might be the consequence of the master's tort. Under certain circumstances the master would even pay the death penalty for having killed his slave, although the Law also sought to protect his disciplinary authority. If a master refused to feed his non-Jewish slave (presumably as a disciplinary measure), the community performed this obligation for the slave as it performed it for the poor generally. The rabbis even penalized a Jewish master for selling his slave to a non-Jew who would not respect the non-Jewish slave's right to observe Sabbaths and festivals. The master was compelled to repurchase the slave though the cost of the repurchase might be ten times the amount of the original sale. Moreover, the master could not sell a non-Jewish slave even to a Jew residing outside the territorial limits of the land of Israel. Such a sale automatically emancipated the slave.

True, the Law frowned upon the emancipation of the non-Jewish slave. Such emancipation would give the non-Jewish slave the status of a full-fledged Jew, and the Law did not encourage this way of increasing the Jewish population. The Law abhorred the less stringent sexual code prevailing among non-Jews. Many authorities even observed that the non-Jewish slave would prefer slavery, with its license for promiscuity, to freedom as a Jew with its stern limitations on sexual relationships. Not having been reared in a milieu stressing the high moral standards the Law imposed, the non-Jewish slave was not to be catapulted into a free society that would make him unhappy or that he would feel constrained to corrupt. Nonetheless, the rabbis ruled that if by emancipation a moral purpose was achieved, or a *Mitzva* (a religious goal) was fulfilled, one might violate the injunction against freeing the non-Jewish slave. If, for example, a non-Jewish female slave had been promiscuous with the people at large, the Law urged her master to free her in the hope that she might marry and establish a monogamous relationship with a husband, infidelity to whom would be less probable because of the threat of the death penalty.

Society and State

In the liberal tradition equality is stressed as a means to freedom and inequalities are often justified when they promote freedom. In the Jewish tradition equality is not principally a means but rather a fulfillment of all men's "creatureliness" under God, the only Master. Despite inescapable functional inequalities, equality was achieved within the family and household. It had to be achieved also within society and state. Indeed, equality must be achieved for the sake of order as well.

According to Maimonides, society requires a ruler "who gauges the actions of the individuals, perfecting that which is deficient and reducing that which is excessive and who prescribes actions and moral habits for all of them to practice always in the same way, until the natural diversity is hidden by the many points of conventional accord, and so the society becomes well-ordered."

Yet, shall the goals of equality and order negate the possibility of differences, in intellectual and moral excellence or in economic productivity, which freedom makes possible? Freedom is also a means to serve God better and improve His earth and its inhabitants. The Law certainly cherished the value of freedom, but equality was to be safeguarded by many principles.

Equality before the Law

Judaism was committed to the general principle that all are equal in the eyes of the Law. This applied to kings as it did to commoners.

With respect to racial differentiation, Judaism always was, and still is, color blind. Males and females, except as previously indicated, were equal in all matters civil and criminal. Women could not be judges or witnesses because this was inconsistent with their primary household roles. This did not mean that their credibility was impugned. With respect to all matters in which strictly formal testimony was not required, they could impart information to religious functionaries and would be believed. It was in a trial that might lead to capital or corporal punishment, or in the creation of a new personal status such as marriage or divorce, or in an action in tort or contract, that they suffered exclusion. Indeed, there were matters in which they might be the only or most readily available witnesses and the Law had to make exceptions and admit their testimony. A classic example is a tort action for an assault committed in the women's section of a synagogue where no men could possibly be present. Moreover, they could act as judges in a civil action if the parties consented. Thus their exclusion from participation in the judicial function was not a reflection on their inferiority—although many rabbis were unchivalrous enough so to hold—but rather on the need for keeping women unseen that men might be more chaste.

Paradoxically, the one great exception to the principle were persons who had achieved greater intellectual and moral excellence. They were held accountable to stricter standards in tort and contract. "A distinguished person is different." More is expected of him, says the Talmud.

Equal Right to Positions of Leadership

In their earliest history Jews maintained the idea that leadership was the responsibility of merit rather than the prerogative of a class or family. In the religious sphere one tribe did ultimately become responsible for the performance of specified rituals, and in the political sphere one family acquired an indefeasible right to kingship. However, this situation did not long endure and all of the most important opportunities for leadership in temporal and spiritual matters became available to all equally. Even Moses divided the temporal and spiritual authority between Joshua, of the tribe of Ephraim, and Aaron, his brother, of the tribe of Levi. The "Judges" were recruited from all ranks to deliver the people from oppressive invaders, and they founded no dynasties. The prophets especially championed the ideal of equality, denouncing as they did the exploitation of the poor by the rich and disregard of the Law, which sought to achieve economic equality by such institutions as the Jubilee with its redistribution of the land every fifty years. The prophets also gave the world the messianic vision of an age when there would be universal peace and justice and nature itself would become perfect. The rabbis, who succeeded the prophets as the "Law's doctors," were also recruited from all ranks and even from among converts to Judaism. The requirement that they take no remuneration for their services made their labor one of love with the result that as a group they wielded more authority over the people than did priests or kings whose limited authority was hereditary. Thus the Jewish community ever enjoyed the circulation of the intellectual and moral elite and there never was a bar to the emergence of new leadership.

The most effective safeguard against the evils of any kind of monopoly on spiritual or temporal authority was the fact that Judaism was an exoteric rather than an esoteric religion; the law was promulgated, taught, and interpreted by all. "Would that every man in the camp of Israel were a prophet!" exclaimed Moses.

In this instance, equality advanced the cause of freedom.

Despite the unequivocal establishment by the Bible of a hereditary priesthood, the virtual obliteration of the difference between clergy and laity was achieved almost two thousand years ago. This was a giant step in the direction of social equality.

The priests and levites of whom the Bible speaks were the only persons in the Jewish community who had special status by virtue of their birth. Even long before the destruction of the central shrine in Jerusalem, their claim to hegemony over the spiritual lives of the people was successfully challenged by prophets and rabbis who came from all classes of society. In the year 70 they lost their special roles and rabbis became the guardians and exponents of the Law. And a rabbi never had any special sacerdotal power. He is nothing more than a layman who has more knowledge of Judaism than most people and can, therefore, offer them religious guidance. He does not even conduct religious services except as a layman might.

How the Bible created the anomaly of a hereditary priesthood in the face of so much concern for equality is itself a revelation of its commitment to the ideal that men shall not crave power over their fellows. Students of political theory are well aware of the discussions from Plato to the present about citizens' avoidance of civic responsibility. The best people often choose not to hold political office. Particularly with regard to the performance of sacred tasks in God's shrine, one may expect that the truly pious and devout will shy away, deeming themselves unworthy in thought and deed of any special role in the public service of God. Failure to decline is itself proof of the lack of the humility necessary for the purpose. Therefore, one must be drafted and only one who is drafted can qualify. Thus one never chooses to be a priest or levite. One has the obligation thrust upon him, and this is the only way it could possibly be unless the

136

temple was to be staffed by people driven by ambition to rise above their brethren.

The tradition regards Moses himself as a drafted leader. When Aaron, his brother, was asked to be the High Priest, he too hesitated. Moses had to order him to serve. Moses also had to seize the levites forcibly and ordain them keepers of the shrine. And because they were drafted, it did not mean that they were rewarded. On the other hand, they were told of the greater hazards that would be theirs because of their service of the Lord. They would have to fulfill prescriptions meticulously and risk punishment for sins of omission or commission. Furthermore, they were given no share of the Promised Land. Fear, perhaps, of the extensive landholdings of the Egyptian priesthood—whom even Joseph could not expropriate—may have been behind the Law's denial to the priests and levites of any territory in Canaan. The Law even hedged their statutory gifts and taxes with so many conditions and restrictions that their delivery was in effect voluntary. A Jew was required to set the tithe gifts aside, thus learning the discipline of self-denial, but if he chose to let them rot, there was no one to stop him.

The rabbis' role in classical Judaism was determined primarily by a long-felt need to prevent the surrogates of God from exploiting their position for personal aggrandizement. All the safeguards proved inadequate to stop the priests and levites from abusing their election to serve God. The prophets had to denounce them for aligning themselves with the rich against the poor and the Pharisees had to denounce them for their usurpation of political power as well. The rabbis ruled that no one might derive a profit by his pursuit of Torah. Rabbis were to be volunteers. If they did perform services for another, they could lawfully be compensated only for time lost from their non-rabbinic vocations (no fewer than one hundred named in the Talmud were artisans). Indeed the rabbis were not clergymen. The measure of their authority was based principally on the confidence of the community of believers.

Equality of Converts

The Law assured equality of status to all non-Jews who embraced the creed and practice of Judaism. Although there were some minor restrictions, one can generalize that all converts enjoyed the same privileges and were subject to the same duties as Jews. Yet, whereas their legal status was one of equality, socially they were often subjected to discrimination and suspicion. By the same token many rabbis held them in higher esteem than those who were born Jewish, but not always did these rabbis prevail against popular prejudice. Notwithstanding the prejudice, several important rulings reveal that the kinship of Jews with each other is not the kinship of blood but the kinship of a common faith. This is shown by the fact that in prayer the convert, no differently from the priest who can trace his male lineage to Aaron the High Priest, addresses God as "the God of our fathers." The patriarchs Abraham, Isaac, and Jacob are his progenitors too. Moreover, the convert speaks of the land of Israel as the land given to his forebears in a special rite connected with the Pentecost festival.

Social and Political Equality

Jewish society was like all other societies in that social inequality did exist, even though the Law regarded all persons as equal. Yet generally the tradition was no respecter of wealth and the only aristocracy recognized was that based on piety and scholarship. And those so recognized rarely received special privilege or power unless a majority in the community—and this was true especially in the Middle Ages—elected them to comprise the "Seven Good Men of the City" who handled the affairs of the public.

A considerable amount of self-government prevailed in the medieval Jewish communities and by the twelfth century their form of government was democratic.

"The Seven Good Men of the City" were presumed to have been elected by a majority of male constituents and exercised authority because Jewish law recognized that a majority could properly create authority. Yet their powers were circumscribed. On many matters they had to conduct referenda, referring decisions to majority vote of all the male inhabitants of the city. On the other matters they had to obtain unanimous approval. On matters involving taxation and property it was often held that only a majority of taxpayers or property-holders could make decisions. Interestingly enough, if women were among the taxpayers or property-holders, they too were entitled to vote.

If only taxpayers and property-holders were to vote on matters pertaining to taxation or to the use and distribution of property, then the achievement of economic equality under such a system would appear to have been an impossibility. The expropriated would have no political means for improving their status. Paradoxically enough, it was precisely through a non-democratic institution that they achieved amelioration of their lot. The Beth-Din—constituted of the duly recognized doctors of the law—had virtually unlimited power to legislate as well as adjudicate matters affecting property. They could impose taxes and coerce the rich to support the poor as well as all public agencies and institutions. They also adjudicated occasional claims that the "Seven Good Men of the City" had exceeded their authority.

Thus whereas there was no clear distinction between legislative and judicial functions, there was a diffusion of power and a mixed form of government created by the people. Their choice of members of the Beth-Din was limited because the persons chosen had to qualify as scholars. However, once chosen, they had broad power and in patriarchal fashion could protect rich and poor and balance equities. The "Seven Good Men of the City" had more limited power, but anyone could qualify for that position.

The democratic experience of Jews in their own self-governing communities from the Middle Ages virtually up to World War II in Eastern and Central Europe predetermined their total acceptance of universal suffrage in the modern state of Israel. Its legislature has the broadest governmental power comparable only to that of a king, who was anointed by the prophets. The king, however, was subject to the Law and the sovereignty of God. According to Judaism, all the people, not just a majority, are denied the right to violate the basic norms of God's revealed will. Modern Israel's legislature is not now so limited. Yet it does represent the full blossoming of the seed of political equality —"one person, one vote"—contained in the medieval sources.

Economic Equality

It is doubtful whether the Levitical law of the Jubilee, which provided for a major redistribution of the promised land every fifty years, was ever implemented. However, the elimination of poverty was a Biblical injunction. It appears that a poor person even had a legal right to demand support from the community. But before modern times there were no significant experiments with total economic equality such as prevail in Israel's collectives. The Law itself is very respectful of the institution of private ownership of property. Limited the right to such ownership was—much more so than in modern capitalist states. Yet no measures were ever taken to limit incomes or restrict acquisitions. Consequently Jewish communities always had their very rich and very poor. They differed from other communities only insofar as they cultivated and maintained a high degree of responsibility for all their constituents. Jewish historians even maintain that one cause for the failure of Christendom to win more converts among Jews, aside from the suffering and humiliation inflicted on them, is that Jews within their own communities felt more secure than they might have felt outside ghetto walls that their basic needs would be fulfilled. Jews remembered that their exile was predicted by the prophets as a consequence of the exploitation of the poor by the rich; for social and economic inequalities, which were the root of all evil, were to be eradicated in the Messianic era. Augustine regarded inequality as punishment for sin. Judaism, by contrast, regarded the continuance of inequality as sin and the cause for God's anger and national disaster.

Economic equality was the goal. Economic freedom was great. But it was weighted heavily with responsibility.

Giving and Taking Interest

The Bible denies Jews the right to give interest to, or to take it from, Jews. To gentiles Jews were permitted to pay interest and consequently they could also take it. Plato, in his "Laws," suggested the same dichotomy for Athenians and "barbarians." Apparently, within the family, so to speak, free loans were to be the rule. Or it may be that a particular type of economy was to be promoted for the in-group while the out-group could engage in other economic activities, usually more peripheral ones.

During the Middle Ages the inequality became virtually academic because legal fictions were developed and Jews paid interest to fellow Jews as readily as they did to non-Jews and vice versa. Contemporary Israel has as yet done nothing to revive the Biblical prohibition, and modern capitalism is as entrenched there as in most of the Christian world.

Taxation

The greatest tension between the ideal of equality and an imperative need for inequality is in the area of taxation. To justify the imposition of higher rates on the rich than on the poor, moderns have invented the notion of the equality of burden.

Jewish law also exacted more from those more able to pay. But in one instance the system of taxation so sustained the ideal of equality that few, if any, other rules of law gave the ideal comparable popularity and esteem. For the support of the temple, all Jews—rich or poor—gave the same half-shekel. This poll tax became one of the most cherished of all practices of Judaism. Vis-à-vis the central shrine, all were equal.

Theodor Herzl, founder of the Zionist movement at the turn of the century, evoked popular support for his cause by reviving the institution. Commitment to the belief that the solution of the Jewish problem was the establishment of a Jewish state was evidenced by the purchase of a "shekel"— cheap enough for all Jews, no matter how depressed their lot. Fulfillment of his objective required substantial gifts from affluent persons and an unequal burden on donors. Yet membership in the movement was based on a nominal gift, equal for all. The new state in the imagination of many Jews replaced the central shrine of yesteryear and the revival of a time-honored practice gave impetus to the ideal of equality set forth in the Bible's first chapter.

Pagans and Gentiles

In no area of Jewish law is the tension between antithetical ideas comparable to that which exists between Judaism's theological notion that all men are possessed of the divine image and its strict, sometimes seemingly inhumane, attitude towards pagans and gentiles. The literature on the subject is so confusing and the views of the authorities so disparate that only a few guidelines can be indicated.

The Idea of the Chosen People

First, the "chosenness" of the Jewish people—no matter how understood or expounded by prophets and philosophers —never furnished a foundation for a legal norm. The basic norm of the legal order was simply that pagans were "outlaws," for they had not accepted the seven Noahide laws regarded as essential for a society with a minimal morality. They would constitute no threat to Jewish settlements or communities unless they resided among Jews, and, therefore, when Jews conquered and occupied the promised land,

142

they had to get rid of these pagans or compel them to submit to the seven Noahide laws whereupon their status was changed to that of resident aliens with considerable protection by Jewish law. Pagan nations or tribes that created no problem for the Jewish people were not to be attacked, exterminated, or even coerced to change their way of life. Indeed, the prophets had stressed the equality of all nations, and one prophet was even forced to go to the Assyrians to deliver God's message to them. God may have chosen the Jewish people (for whatever reason or mission one can glean from the sources), but He is the Father not only of all creatures as individuals but also of all nations and ethnic groups, and He judges all of them continuously, especially in the Messianic age.

Even pagans who were outlaws could bring offerings to God in the central shrine in Jerusalem. Their divine image was the warrant for this privilege and gifts that they made to the building itself in perpetuity were never to be altered. In this respect they enjoyed an even greater assurance of the perpetuity of their donations than did Jews. Moreover, Jews were obligated to deport themselves so honorably vis-à-vis even pagans that pagans might exclaim, "Blessed is the Lord of Israel."

Yet Jewish law often "recognized" the rules of law prevailing among pagans. For example, their rights of inheritance were respected as were their claims to property personal and real. Jewish law even established special forms for their acquisition of title. In the law of tort there was even the notion of reciprocity—whatever wrongful acts non-Jewish courts regarded as actionable when committed by non-Jews against Jews, Jewish courts regarded as actionable when committed by Jews against non-Jews. This is a far cry from justice but it makes for some degree of equality.

Persons or peoples, however, who had accepted the seven Noahide laws were deemed civilized and it is to them that the Bible refers when it orders Jews to love the stranger.

But Jewish law itself—the written and oral law—was

given by God to the Jewish people for the governance of Jews. This made the law "personal" rather than "territorial." And it applied to Jews no matter where they lived. It was to receive and obey this law that they were chosen whether for the purpose of being a light or a blessing unto the nations, or bearing testimony to the perpetuity of their personal relationship with God, or helping to establish His Kingdom on earth. As a law for a Jewish society, it had only peripheral concern with those whose "personal" law was different. It did provide for rules of warfare when such war was forced on Jews or sought by them. In no instance was the massacre of the enemy justified if the enemy chose to live in peace and accept the seven laws of Noah.

Perhaps the mood of Jewish law can best be understood in the light of the dilemma of modern liberals in the United States who are torn between a respect for human life—even the lives of Chinese communists—and their anxiety that the free world has to reckon with leaders who have little respect for the rule of law within or without their borders. In such a situation one must be ambivalent. To respect life may require inaction. But to insure the survival of cherished values may require wholesale slaughter. This was the dilemma of Jewish law vis-à-vis those who would not abide by the seven laws of Noah, and the law did not move as rapidly or as dramatically in the direction of the equality of pagans with Jews as it did in the direction of the equality of resident aliens.

The Righteous of all Nations

So committed is the Jewish tradition to the equality of the non-Jew who leads a righteous life that it accords to him the coveted title of "Chasid" and assures him salvation just as it is vouchsafed to righteous Jews themselves. Maimonides distinguishes between a righteous non-Jew who pursues righteousness because it is the will of God and a righteous non-Jew whose pursuit of eternal values and moral deportment is derived from reason and natural law. The latter he

144

calls a "Hacham," a wise man; the title "Hasid" is reserved for those who are also God-fearing. But whatever the title, the conclusion is that Jews did not feel impelled to convert non-Jews to Judaism. Commitment to Judaism was not the condition prerequisite for salvation for anyone but Jews. Non-Jews could achieve it by righteous living alone. And Judaism today is still fully committed to this view.

Freedom of belief thus emerged from the recognition of universal equality. The freedom of Jews, however, was more limited. Whereas they enjoyed a considerable measure of latitude in connection with dogma and doctrine, they were held strictly to the fulfillment of the Law. By observance of the commandments they were to play a special role in God's vision of human history.

Conclusion

Since God created all men equal, their natural inequality can only be justified with reference to His service, which means the fulfillment of the very equality God had willed. Freedom does not serve primarily the purpose of man's self-fulfillment, as in the writings of John Stuart Mill, but rather God's purpose—that justice and righteousness shall reign on earth. In Judaic thought, therefore, freedom is more the means and equality more the end.

SECTION THREE

GOD AND MAN

Introductory Note

Judaism places the highest value on man and his potential. But Jewish humanism is not antithetical to the belief in a personal God. On the other hand, it derives from the fact that God created each of us in His image. The supreme worth of man is vouched for in every phase of Jewish law and thought. In the opening essay of this section I affirm the inter-dependence of Jewish humanism with commitment to the Will of God. Naturalism, humanism, and theism all dominate my outlook and find expression in the following essays.

Chapter One

A GOD-CENTERED HUMANISM

I

Moses our teacher himself congratulated the people of Israel for refusing to validate God's appearance on Mount Sinai merely by the accompanying thunder and lightning.

> For these nations that thou art to dispossess hearken unto soothsayers and unto diviners; but as for thee, the Lord thy God hath not suffered thee to do so. A prophet will the Lord thy God raise up unto thee, from the midst of thee, of thy brethren, like

unto me; unto him ye shall hearken; according to all that thou didst desire of the Lord thy God in Horeb in the day of the assembly, saying: Let me not hear again the voice of the Lord my God, neither let me see this great fire any more, that I not die. And the Lord said unto me: I will raise them up a prophet from among their brethren. . . . . I will put My words in his mouth, and he shall speak unto them all that I shall command him. And it shall come to pass that whosoever will not hearken unto My words, which he shall speak in My name, I will require it of him. But the prophet that shall speak a word presumptuously in My name, which I have not commanded him to speak, or that shall speak in the name of other gods, that same prophet shall die.

And if thou say in thy heart, How shall we know the word which the Lord hath not spoken? *When a prophet speaketh in the name of the Lord, if the thing follow not, nor come to pass, that is the thing which the Lord hath not spoken:* the prophet hath spoken it presumptuously; thou shalt not be afraid of him.

Deuteronomy XVIII, 14-22

Thus did Moses admonish his followers to test all future claims to new truths by their intrinsic merit and coherence with fact. Moderns may justly regard it as an invitation to try new truths in the light of mankind's collective experience. This places upon man the onus of verification. And that is why the first problem of religious philosophers, who would cope with a generation of agnostics, is to restore faith in knowledge—even before the attempt is made to restore faith in God.

Without meaning at all to be sacrilegious, one is tempted to say that God's fortunes rise and fall with man's faith in man. The ebb and flow of man's confidence in himself determine man's faith in God. Too often religious thinkers try, on the contrary, to predicate religious faith upon man's incompetence, his unworthiness, his utter dependence on some higher force. Such insistence has its pith and point; but no less important to any philosophy of religion is the emphasis on man's capacity for trustworthy knowledge, and on man's dependability as a medium for apprehending truth.

The Jewish tradition has been equally forceful with regard to both trends.

This tradition must now be revitalized.

To such an extent indeed have Jews held faith in man's capacity for knowledge that Saadiah Gaon, the great light of the tenth century, felt that even without Revelation man would have ultimately apprehended the existence and nature of God. He would have done so by reason alone. Revelation but hastened the process and acted as a guide during the quest. The peerless Maimonides, in the twelfth century, expressed the same thought. He said that the first two commandments of the Decalogue—those proclaiming God's existence and the vanity of idolatry—did not require the intervention of the prophet Moses for all Israel to know them. All men, Maimonides held, are capable of arriving at these precise truths without supernatural aid.

Hence, even Orthodox Jews cannot, with intellectual honesty, allow themselves to be authoritarian. There must be confidence in reason. There must be resort to naturalism.

II

If we would revitalize faith in man's capacity for truth (without which even Revelation can have no validity), we shall find that modern naturalism is not a foe but rather an ally.

Philosophies of naturalism can be used to good advantage for religious faith. True, naturalistic philosophies gave birth to materialism and determinism. But these offspring suffer a fatal weakness. They are not thoroughly naturalistic; they are only partly so. As Professors Randall and Buchler once wrote: "The philosophy of materialism depends for much of its plausibility upon a process which

151

only time has brought fully into the open—over-simplification. Half truths are magnified into truths because of a failure to make one or two important distinctions. The emphasis on the physical as the basis of all phenomena does not warrant the conclusion that all phenomena are physical. . . . The error of materialism is that it confuses the *dependence* of biological, social and psychological phenomena with the unreality of such phenomena. To say that they cannot exist unless physical conditions exist and that yet the latter may exist independently, does not mean that they are 'nothing but' physical. There cannot be thought without a brain, but from this truth the identity of the two does not follow. The physical may be a basis of all else, but it does not exhaust all." [1]

One interesting illustration of the materialist's incomplete naturalism is relevant to our theme. The English philosopher Joad once wrote: "Mathematics is a product of the mind's *a priori* reasoning in accordance with self-evident principles from self-evident premises; it owes little or nothing to experience. Yet when we come to experience the world, we find that it obeys the very laws which our reasoning has derived from the study of abstract principles. Now this is a very surprising fact." [2]

The materialist would explain this remarkable coincidence by pointing out "that the brain is a part of a living organism" and admitting "that living organisms have evolved in an environment which has imposed its characteristics upon them, as a mould will stamp its impress upon the fluid material submitted to it. Our brains, on this hypothesis, function in a manner which reflects the operations of the physical world, and the mental counterpart of this cerebral functioning is our apprehension of the laws of logic and mathematics." But, to be consistent, the materialist should apply the same reasoning to man's *a priori* moral laws as well. Just as he posits a mathematical universe which impresses its characteristics upon the living organism

1. *Philosophy: An Introduction*, pages 196, 198.
2. *Guide to Philosophy*, pages 147-148.

called man, so too he must posit a moral universe which impresses its characteristics upon man. Yet the materialist does not do this. He finds nothing in objective reality that underlies man's moral nature.

A thoroughgoing naturalism, on the other hand, would start with the major premise that *any conception of nature which does not take account of the whole man is incomplete.* And what is most significant for a philosophy of religion is the fact that *when the whole man is taken into account—* and man is surely a part of nature—*then all that is human is natural: all that man is, in fine, is a part of nature.* If man eats, he also thinks. If he breathes, he also perceives.

There is no more reason to deem man's categories of thought or his intuitions as unnatural, or beyond nature, than there is reason to deem his digestive processes as unnatural. Every valid philosophy of religion would thus do well to start with the fact that man is *within nature*—and not an alien *from without.*

This is the essential approach for a philosophy of religion which recognizes the existence of immutable principles of moral law. An agnostic may deny the validity of knowledge. But if he accepts the gift of life at all, he must be prepared to face all the implications of living; and that means he must regard his thinking as *natural.* To be sure, an agnostic has the alternative—which is also a part of nature—to destroy himself physically. So, too, he can retire from contact with other men and frustrate the basic urge for human fellowship. He can deny worth or validity to categories of thought which are natural in man. But if he finds the desire for life sufficiently impelling to restrain him from suicide, he has to take account of all that living implies; and thus he must reckon with the fact that nature, of which his life is a part and within which he moves and acts, endows him not only with the instinct for self-preservation but with all that constitutes his physical, intellectual, emotional, and spiritual life.

It is true that this all-inclusiveness of nature allows for error, evil, and all things that make life depressing and bewildering. But natural too are canons of criticism, standards of evaluation, frames of reference. To make choices is natural; to conceive of purposefulness is natural; to idealize as well as to objectify is natural.

So in any philosophy of religion worthy of the name we must start with man. This is not to say that we are bound to have faith in the competence of human intelligence. One need only say that we must have faith in the fact that we are alive; with this recognition of the fact our very living furnishes us with the data we must explore; and these data are within nature and not exterior to it.

If a naturalistic philosophy underlies our approach, then the difference between the agnostic and the religious man pertains fundamentally to acceptance or rejection of life as a reality. The agnostic, though he professes not even to know he is alive, nonetheless lives. The religious man accepts life in nature and all its consequences. Living means not only eating and breathing, but also thinking and feeling, and evaluating and objectifying. And it even involves the objectification of the source of our religious and moral experience, which leads to faith in God and His ethic.

This conclusion we must now further explore.

III

Some modern men with great faith in the data of human experience have lost their religious faith. But if, on a thoroughgoing naturalism, we hold that man's thinking processes are no less natural than his emotional and intuitive life, our philosophy must encompass the total experience of mankind. A conception of the universe which fails to explain much that constitutes human experience is inadequate; it is in fact myopic; and cannot satisfy our quest for the fullest understanding. Scientific method yields only limited conceptions.

Scientific method is indeed worthy of both our admiration and our loyalty. It has given us a greater mastery over our environment, and has opened up to us new vistas that

154

enrich our religious, ethical and esthetic insights. But the limitations of scientific method are serious. To reject out of hand, as superstitious or illusory, what cannot be interpreted by scientific method because, forsooth, scientific method cannot cope with it, is to place enormous areas of human experience beyond our ken—and this is most unscientific. For is it not of the essence of empiricism to take account of everything that man experiences—even those experiences which laboratory or statistical techniques cannot interpret? And to reject so much of what constitutes our intellectual and emotional life because a highly successful method in physics or chemistry and biology is not relevant to it—isn't that to commit a most serious fallacy?

For our task is to interpret *all* experience. Science helps us to interpret *some* experiences. But it should not presume to say that what it cannot interpret is not experience at all. That would be substituting a method for the material to which the method is applicable. An illustration will perhaps help to clarify this. We can measure some merchandise by the yard; but we would hardly say that because wine cannot be measured in yards it is not salable. Similarly of human experience. We can interpret much of it by scientific method; but because some of it cannot be thus interpreted, it doesn't follow that what cannot be thus interpreted must forever be unintelligible.

Philosophers of science have perceived this. More often it is the layman who equates truth with scientific theories. In his admiration for the remarkable achievements of science, the layman exaggerates the claims of the experts. Enamored of the rapid technological advances, he deifies science, making it omniscient and omnipotent. The extreme caution philosophers urge is not heeded; popular conversation on religion and science betrays almost universal misunderstanding.

But even philosophers are often none too fastidious. There are certain types of experience involving values—religious, moral and esthetic—which they are willing to consider only in part. Modern pragmatists, to be sure, insist on including within the scope of their inquiries all of human experience. But for them an idea is true only if "it has, *through action*, worked out the state of things which it contemplated or intended." [3] To be deemed true, an idea must be capable of consequences. The consequences may be observed in the laboratory, in the social scene, in the political state, in artistic expression. But since truth is "success in inquiry," the idea must lend itself to further verification in a tangible fashion.

This concept of "truth" is valuable from the point of view of communicability. If one can verify a statement by reference to its implied and foreseen consequences, one can communicate the "truth" to another convincingly. But what about values, or ideal ends? With regard to these Dewey says that their reality is vouched for by their "undeniable power in action." This is undoubtedly part of the picture, but it is not the whole picture. *If one takes account of the fullness of human experience, one must admit that the reality of ideal ends is vouched for by intuitive experiences which make them powerful in action.* And it is these intuitive experiences which a comprehensive philosophy must undertake to fit into its overall conception of the universe. Man has experiences which are self-verifying: that is to say, man has experiences which carry with them their own assurances of certitude—experiences which are so strong that they exclude impugning by reference to other data. These are experiences that carry incontrovertible conviction: they are as self-validating as our experience of the sun.

It is this oversight of the pragmatist that impels him, in some instances, to deny truth to the claim that God exists, in spite of the abundance of mystical experiences fully described and authoritatively reported. The pragmatist, like other men, is overwhelmed by the evidence; nor does he impeach the credibility of the witnesses. But the pragmatist makes a distinction between "religious" and "religion." The

3. John Dewey, *Essays in Experimental Logic*, pages 239-240.

156

religious experience he regards as real, for it has verifiable consequences; but the object of that experience—God—is not regarded as real. Thus John Dewey writes:

> The actual religious quality in the experience described is the *effect* produced, the better adjustment in life and its conditions, not the manner and cause of its production.
>
> . . . there are also changes in ourselves in relation to the world in which we live that are much more inclusive and deepseated. They relate not to this and that want in relation to this and that condition of our surroundings, but pertain to our being in its entirety. Because of their scope, this modification of ourselves is enduring. It lasts through any amount of vicissitude of circumstances, internal and external. There is a composing and harmonizing of the various elements of our being, such that, in spite of changes in the special conditions that surround us, these conditions are also arranged, settled, in relation to us. This attitude includes a note of submission. But it is voluntary, not externally imposed; and as voluntary, it is something more than a mere Stoical resolution to endure unperturbed throughout the buffetings of fortune. It is more outgoing, ready and glad, than the latter attitude, and it is more active than the former. And in calling it voluntary, it is not meant that it depends upon a particular resolve or volition. It is a change *of* will conceived as the organic plentitude of our being, rather than any special change *in* will.[4]

This is the result of the *religious* experience which Dewey deems significant and valid. But *religion itself*, "the doctrinal or intellectual apparatus and the institutional accretions that grow up are, in a strict sense, adventitious to the intrinsic quality of such experiences." The idea of

4. *Common Faith*, pages 14, 16-17.

God, of a Being with priority reality, Dewey rejects altogether.

But here the philosopher is again overlooking an important part of the experience he would interpret and validate. From the pragmatic point of view, as we have seen, the experience is deemed valid because its consequences are verifiable in action. But the experience itself almost invariably involves a preexisting Unity, which unifies the person's self. Even if the religious experience could come without such a preexisting Unity, the fact that the experience does most often involve it should prompt us at least to consider that element of the experience. And, certainly, that is the normal situation, not the accidental one. It is the Being of God that is always the unique feature of the religious experience.

Professor Albert C. Knudson has pointed out—in his *Validity of Religious Experience*—that Dewey errs in denying validity to the belief in God simply because that doctrine is *interpretive* of the *religious* experience. Belief in God is, first, the "distinctive element in religious experience." Second, no experience is possible without interpretation. Knudson writes that "all experience is the result of a creative activity on the part of the mind, that no object enters the mind either physically or metaphysically, that the mind builds up its own objects on the occasion of external stimuli and in accordance with principles immanent within itself, and that among these principles is an innate capacity to experience and think the infinite." And just as we attribute reality to the objects of sense experience, and that reality is validated by our natural capacity to interpret sense experience, so we must attribute reality to the object of religious experience. For this reality also is validated by our natural capacity to interpret religious experience.

In any event, it would seem the pragmatist ignores that part of the religious experience which is intuitive and self-verifying—the belief in the existence of God. This is not in accord with a thoroughgoing naturalism that requires us to

158

interpret *all* of our experience, including the object of the experience which is God.

If we should go along with the pragmatist and define truth in terms of consequences, ignoring all self-verifying experiences, might we not be led to some such pass as this: it is impossible to aver that one loves his young wife without waiting for the later vicissitudes of the marital state to prove it. Would not the pragmatist be impelled to say one thing or the other: *either* that future developments will prove the truth of your present experience of love; *or* that the assertion of your love is inconsequential to anyone else but yourself—its truth or lack of truth need not stir general attention. But neither of these alternatives is satisfactory. For neither gives one an understanding of a very basic experience whose meaning is vital to the lover *now*.

Nor can we say it is "true" that you love if you deport yourself as a lover, and we can verify that you love by observing your behavior. That could mean ignoring your subjective state altogether. And your subjective state is as much a part of nature as the flowers you give your beloved.

In short, to define "truth" in such a way that one cannot say, "It is true that I love," while one can say, "It is true that the sun now shines," is to bifurcate nature: it is to hold that truth is applicable to the senses but not to our intuitive life. Yet surely a lover knows that his experience of love is as real, as moving, as convincing, as the sight of the sun. The mechanist may give us some insight into antecedents; the pragmatist may give us some insight into consequences. But both ignore the basic ineffable experience, and both would deprive it of the very value or quality of truth—the *vrai vérité*.

Nor, again, do we solve the problem of interpreting the religious experience by substituting either nature or humanity as the object of that experience, instead of God. The totality of natural phenomena, the totality of humanity, are also objects whose reality is apprehended, not from sense experience, but rather from a self-validating experience

159

which is akin to the religious experience, and is the unifying factor of faith in God. To sense nature as a unity, or to sense its infinity, is—let us admit it—impossible. To sense human society as a whole is equally impossible. One can only apprehend them as one intuitively apprehends God's existence—God as the object of our religious experiences.

It is true, as Dewey points out, that religious men experience different kinds of gods. But this is far from proving that there is no preexisting Reality which is the object experienced—only preconceived doctrines of institutional religion whose very validity is in question. What is proved from the fact that religious experiences are of different varieties is only that they cannot be accepted at face value, any more than sense experience can always be accepted at face value. In the words of Professor Knudson again, the religious experience "must be purged by criticism before its true significance can be brought out." When they are carefully examined it is found that there is something universal in all such experiences—something that unifies the self of the experiencer, giving his life, and even his despair a single direction.

Nor, once more, does it help skeptics to try to explain the religious experience in terms of factors that contribute to its rise. Here again they overlook one phase of the experience not contained in any of the elements which may have partially contributed to its existence. No one feels that an interpretation of color in terms of wavelengths is adequate to explain all that color is to the esthete. Similarly, no philosopher can interpret religious experience exclusively in terms either of its antecedents or its consequences. Fear, wishful thinking, drugs, any number of factors, may contribute to the development of the religious state. Unified personality, moral direction, contentment may be its consequences. But that is not the whole story. Something there is in the experience itself that is not of the nature of any of the contributing factors. Naturalists will interpret the experience faultily if they ignore this added something. Men experience God, they experience new strength, they acquire

160

a new altruism: these experiences are not contained in the causes, no matter how conducive the causes may be to the coming of the experiences.

Harold Höffding expresses the same thought in another connection:

> Consciousness and personality can as little be explained as the products of previously given elements as organic life can be explained as the product of unorganic elements. On the other hand, consciousness and personality, just like organic life, come into being through a perpetual synthesis of elements not originally begotten by themselves. It is this antinomy which makes the genesis of life and of personality so great a riddle.[5]

Just so, the religious experience cannot be explained in terms of only some of its elements. John Dewey errs in ignoring that Object which gives the experience its truly religious character—the reality of God.

IV

That many philosophers glibly ignore the essential cause, or basis, of the religious experience is even more apparent from their writings on the moral experience. If our desire for life, liberty, and the pursuit of happiness accounts for the emergence of certain social laws, a man's moral experience often involves a denial of those laws as appertaining to himself. A man accepts martyrdom, prison, poverty, because of his moral experience. That experience is something more than any contributing cause.

There are, then, experiences which are self-validating, whose emergence can be explained only in part by observable factors. In overlooking them the pragmatist overlooks the palmary fact that men have spiritual experiences which

5. *Problems of Philosophy* (translation by G. M. Fisher), page 19.

impel them to reject ideas whose consequences "scientific method" may find desirable. And these spiritual experiences are as much a part of countless human beings as our experiences of sky or sun, or eating or dancing. Yet the pragmatist cannot call such experiences "real"!

It is not enough to say with Dewey that the reality of ideal ends as ideals is vouched for by their "undeniable power in action." That is putting the cart before the horse. The reality of the ends is vouched for by something which makes them powerful in action; and what makes the ends real is an intuitive experience which is self-validating. It does have consequences, very tangible ones; but the fact that the idea has redounded to the greater happiness of men is not the basis for deeming it true. For even when it detracts from the happiness of men, men will not cast it aside, nor deem the experience unreal or untrustworthy.

Bertrand Russell, for example, holds the "Rights of Man" to be philosophically indefensible. Stating the conception from a point of view a pragmatist would accept, he writes: "The general happiness is increased if a certain sphere is defined within which each individual is to be free to act as he chooses, without the interference of any external authority." [6]

Yet Russell admits a repugnance to certain suggestions which might be deemed necessary for the maintenance and increase of that general happiness. "I am informed by many people," he writes, "that the preservation of democracy . . . can only be secured by gassing immense numbers of children and doing a number of other horrible things . . . I think I should refuse to use such means even if I were persuaded that they would secure the end and that no others would." Here he yields to the proposition that children have inviolable rights which, though indefensible philosophically, he cannot impugn. Therefore, it cannot be said that the idea of the sanctity of human life derives its validity from the assumption that it works well in human society. On the

6. *Power*, page 115.

other hand, because we have that idea we achieve certain consequences and avoid others. Because we have that idea we cherish democracy; but nonetheless we would not preserve democracy at the cost of gassing our children.

Bertrand Russell himself must concede he has this spiritual experience with regard to the sanctity of human life. Yet, in another connection, he fails to see that. He conjectures how civilization developed filial piety in place of parricide. This development, he says, was "a device, however instinctive and unconscious, for prolonging parental power beyond the early years when children are helpless." [7] Here Russell fails to recognize that the idea of the sanctity of human life may have determined the growth of filial piety, precisely as his own conviction regarding the life of children determined his attitude toward their extermination by gas. In his own attitude toward children, Russell cannot make a rationalization comparable to the one he uses for children's attitude toward parents; therefore, it is a spiritual state or feeling or experience that becomes the sole arbiter of conduct. The idea is there; it is real; but its reality is not derived from its consequences. It even obstructs the application of means that *pragmatically* would advance social ends.

Even were the spiritual state verifiable in terms of its consequences for social action, the pragmatist's test of truth would still not be valid. For it loses sight of the fact that Bertrand Russell feels the way he does about children irrespective of the consequences. His experience of affection, or respect for their lives, is final, ultimate. It is valid to him without regard to consequences. That is the way he experiences his affection. And to hold a theory of truth which ignores this type of experience is either to shun or to deny its reality, and the plain fact that it calls for interpretation.

Humanists, on the other hand, acknowledge the reality of the moral experience and also the reality of the religious experience; but as the object of these experiences they

7. *Power*, pages 245-246.

would substitute humanity for God. They recognize man's experience of the sacred; but they would divorce it from any association with God, as a supernatural or metaphysical entity, and attach it to human society.

But the very idea of human society—of a oneness among men—is valid only because our moral experience makes it so.

It is in our moral experience that we conceive of the totality of human souls; in our moral experience we posit its reality. Humanists accept the self-validating moral experience of "human society" as a whole—a "human society" which exists only as the object of moral experience. Yet humanists insist on rejecting a Oneness in the Universe, which is the object in the religious experience.

To sum up. *First:* any adequate interpretation of the universe should explain *all* that we experience; an interpretation which does not take account of self-verifying experiences is incomplete. *Second:* religious and moral experiences involve *a priori* truths with regard to God and the sanctity of human life. *Third:* there is an illogical reluctance on the part of pragmatists and humanists to accept self-verifying religious experiences, and the existence of God thereby established, while at the same time they do regard moral experiences as self-verifying, thus establishing the reality of the oneness of humanity.

V

If the study, analysis, and synthesis of immediate self-verifying experiences are "musts" for the theologian, they are no less so for the political philosopher who would uphold the democratic faith. The extent to which the ideas and institutions of religion have impeded or advanced the development of democratic government is not the issue. The more fundamental problem is whether it is possible to validate the doctrines that are both explicit and implicit in our conception of democracy without relying upon our self-verifying experiences which prompt us to believe in God and the reality of a moral order in the Universe.

The fact is that every great thinker and writer on democracy has made assumptions which are based upon the reality of a moral order in the Universe. Yet many of them would resent the imputation that their thought is theological. Nonetheless, their ultimate rationale involves the validity of self-verifying experiences which underlie so much of modern theology; and it is intellectually dishonest to assume the existence of certain moral and esthetic values on the ground of self-verifying experiences while, at the same time, rejecting religious values which are validated by the same capacity of the human soul.

Bertrand Russell's admiration for democracy, for example, is based on his reverence for the life of the individual and its fulfillment. The highest value is placed thereon. He deems the totalitarian state most objectionable because it makes the welfare of the state, not the welfare of the individual, the end to be sought.

> This is the essential difference between the Liberal outlook and that of the totalitarian State, that the former regards the welfare of the State as residing ultimately in the welfare of the individual, while the latter regards the State as the end and individuals merely as indispensable ingredients, whose welfare must be subordinated to a mystical totality which is a cloak for the interest of the rulers. . . . Liberalism, in valuing the individual, is carrying on the Christian tradition; its opponents are reviving certain pre-Christian doctrines. (*Power*, pages 302-303.)

Mr. Russell acknowledges that the religious tradition has heightened, accentuated the value placed upon the individual human being. But on what basis shall this value become a conviction? Mr. Russell graciously applauds the saints and sages of the religious tradition. Yet he fails to see that they were able to achieve the idealism he cherishes because they felt it to be part of a divine order of things.

Nor can a utilitarian philosophy preserve that idealism when all values become only functions of the general happiness. From the point of view of most men's happiness, a state that guarantees the majority food and shelter and some amusement, and relieves them of the burden of intelligent participation in government is by far more desirable— even if some minorities and some freedoms are sacrificed upon its altars—than a state which imposes governmental responsibilities upon every citizen, and makes all citizens co-partners in the onerous task of self-government. Every fiber of Mr. Russell's free being would rebel against the former. Yet, according to the doctrines of utilitarianism, the craving for security and the necessities of life that prepossesses the vast majority is the criterion of good.

Should Mr. Russell argue further that, while the majority may prefer security now, in the future more men will come to resemble him and entertain his wishes, and therefore we should promote the cause of democracy in behalf of the future, then one can only ask why men should sacrifice their essential desires now for a hypothetical general happiness of unborn generations.

And, while we struggle to preserve democratic institutions, it would be the sheerest folly to believe that our adversaries have no "general happiness" which *they* want to conserve. The enemies of democracy derive very certain pleasure from the magnification of their states. That is the thing they seek. They cherish the thought of dying for their fatherland on the field of battle. To be sure, their success and happiness would not contribute to the happiness of other peoples over the globe: far from it! There would not be universal happiness. But if they are firm in their faith that for a thousand years they can dominate the world, what makes their point of view wrong and ours right? If victory were theirs, their own happiness might have been unparalleled. If sixty million Germans could live on the slave labor

166

of six hundred millions, what a paradise they would have wrought for themselves!

The truth is that the basis for our faith in democracy is not that its achievement will make us happy. It is rather a self-verifying moral experience with regard to the sanctity of human life. We would rather lose our lives than violate the mandate of this moral experience. By our own intuition we sense the rightness or wrongness of a viewpoint regarding rights that inhere in man; and so strong do our convictions become that, for them, we do not hesitate to call upon our sons to make the supreme sacrifice.

It is interesting that Tom Paine, in his classic *Rights of Man*, uses Biblical texts to predicate his most unscientific assumption that all men are equal. You cannot establish human equality by sense perception. No visual or auditory tests will help you. From the point of view of the chemist, an obese man has greater chemical content than a thin man. From the point of view of the economist, men with different talents have different economic worth. Even our legal system recognizes that. Kill a pauper by automobile accidentally, and his next of kin will recover a mere pittance compared to what the next of kin of a banker would receive. So Tom Paine must needs resort to Biblical authority for his assumption.

Today we reach the same conclusion through man's self-verifying moral and religious experience. But to posit man's equality merely as a useful assumption does not do justice to human experience. For we regard man's equality as a real fact, even if that equality leads us to a course of conduct which may not be immediately advantageous to us. We prefer the democratic form of government, even when inefficient, to the most efficient and benevolent tyranny. To say that we exercise such preference because we have the future in mind—the mortality of the despot and the possibility that he may be succeeded by one less benevolent—is to evade the fact that we abhor the paternalism of even the benevolent dictator, because it comes from one who would ignore his basic equality with all other men.

Professor E. M. Sait, in his book *Democracy* (New York, 1929), discusses many of the criticisms that have been leveled in recent years against the democratic state. His concluding defense of "government by the many" is a theological one, though very similar to Bertrand Russell's in tone. For he too finds the ultimate reason for preferring democracy in "the dignity of human personality."

What, then, makes this item called "human personality" so important that we attribute to it dignity and sanctity? If our faith in democracy, and its *raison d'être*, must derive validity from a conception of man as a sacred being, are we not relying upon a self-verifying moral experience no different in essence from the religious experience? The moral experience vests man with an ineffable sacred character, while the religious experience vests all the earth therewith.

Now to deem moral and religious experiences real because they are "powerful in action," and yet not to deem the objects of these experiences as real, is to deny reality to a basic element in all of such experiences. Be the object God, or the Oneness of the Universe, or the Oneness of Humanity, these objects are real—as real as the experience itself. And if one regards the objects of sense experience as real—the sun, the moon, a chair and a table—because the predication of reality to these things is a natural process of thought, so too must one predicate reality to the objects of our moral and religious experience—God, the soul, humanity, and the totality of the Universe.

Professor A. C. Knudson writes:

> . . . there is a psychological "immediacy" in objective experience that carries conviction with it. This immediacy cannot be explained away as illusory in the case of religious experience and accepted as valid in the case of sense experience. If it has epistemological value in the latter case, there is no necessary reason why it should not have it in the former. Suggestion and expectation, it is true, play a larger

168

part in religious than in sense experience; but they do not create the objective reference of religious experience. At the most they determine to some extent the particular psychological forms that the experience takes. The objective reference is as original and immediate in religious as in sense experience. And the assurance that the apparent immediacy of the religious object carries with it has the right to be treated in the same way as the corresponding assurance in sense experience. (*The Validity of Religious Experience,* pages 99-100.)

This type of naturalism in religion, it may be added, does away with the ancient dichotomies of naturalism and supernaturalism, relativism and absolutism.

In moral and religious experiences, supernatural objects and absolutes are the things experienced. But, insofar as they are a part of man's natural experiences, they too are natural. If man believes in the reality of the world he experiences, and its intelligibility to his natural self, then he must accept the reality of those absolutes of which he catches but a glimpse. And man's capacity for moral and religious experience is part of the permanent texture of nature, not an illusory or transitory phase of his existence. With this capacity he comes to know God and the moral law. With it he grasps the Infinite and eternal values.

Furthermore, such an approach makes not only for the reality of good in our conception of the Universe but also for the reality of its purpose, because our capacity for religious and moral experience involves the use of certain categories of thought. In sense experience the categories are space and time. In religious and moral experience the categories are value and purpose. They are just as real as the spatio-temporal categories by which we behold and interpret the objects of sense experience.

These spatio-temporal categories have received the attention of many philosophers in recent years. But what requires more reiteration is the preeminence of the *a priori* in both religious and moral experience. As Dr. Jacob B. Agus puts it, "There is indeed vouchsafed to man, albeit admittedly at rare moments only, an intuition of the eternal validity and of the extra-human source of ethical values." The values, however, are not ethical alone. They involve a perspective with regard to all that constitutes the realm of nature.

Thus one arrives at certain ideas that are fundamental in Judaism's philosophy of religion.

The first conviction is that the idea of God does not grow of itself in the human mind, "owing nothing to God's self-disclosing action." God is real and reveals Himself in the religious experience. Israel's teachers have differed in their interpretation of the account of revelation in the Bible. But all are agreed that there is direct communication between God and man.

Second, the coincidence of moral and religious experiences has always been the rule in Jewish tradition, rather than the exception. The prophets enjoyed self-verifying experiences not only of God but also of His will. His commands and exhortations of justice, peace and human brotherhood were as certain as His reality. Not all Christian philosophers would deem morality and religion inseparable; but Rudolph Otto, in his book *The Idea of the Holy*, asserts an *a priori* relation between the two. That is unequivocally the Jewish point of view.

Third, the conviction that God exists and constantly reveals Himself to man in religious experiences, which are almost invariably moral experiences also, makes Judaism a religious tradition with very few dogmas and with a primarily this-worldly emphasis. Since man's capacity for religious experience and his interpretation thereof vary constantly, Judaism makes no attempt to formulate for all times its basic beliefs. Nor does it attempt to visualize the world beyond, a world beyond physical experience, while it does seek to alter the present world through our moral experience.

Orthodox, Conservative and Reform Judaism all subscribe to these premises.

And it is by our insistence upon the validity of man's experience of God, and the simultaneity of religious and moral experiences, that we establish the validity of those aims and ideals which prompt us to preserve our democratic institutions.

Chapter Two

ISRAEL AND GOD:
REFLECTIONS ON THEIR ENCOUNTER

That God and Man communicate with each other is basic
in Judaism. The dialogue is not limited to Jews. The Bible
itself reveals that Bilaam, a non-Jew, was endowed with the
gift of prophecy. Nor did Judaism assume that God communicates no law to Gentiles. Even before a solitary
Hebrew lived God had commanded Noah and his descendants, as He subsequently commanded Avimelech, Laban and
others. Moreover, the encounter between God and Israel is
a continuous one, and its form and content are subsumed in
the concept of Torah, the totality of the Written and Oral
traditions. Jews experience the Divine principally through
His word, and God still communicates in every newly discovered insight of both the Halachah and the Aggadah. God
also communicates by His participation in Jewish history
and, as an integral part of that history, in the judicial
process of Israel's duly appointed doctors of the law. Yet,
remember one must that the ongoing dialogue between God
and Israel involves both God and man.

Despite their differences, some of the most articulate
Jewish theologians of our day concur in this conclusion.
Heschel, Fackenheim, Petuchowski, Soloveitchik, and a host
of their disciples in the Orthodox, Reform and Conservative
camps, accept the challenge of this encounter. Their controversialists, on the other hand, also to be found in all camps,
are Orthodox rabbis who denigrate the role of man in the

172

unfolding of Torah, and Reconstructionists—Conservative and Reform—who denigrate the role of God. The former shun virtually any Halachic development, except perhaps to provide more stringent safeguards about the law. The latter see no reason for Jews to be deterred from doing anything that furthers their humanistic aspirations. Most Jews, alas, are on the side of the controversialists. They prefer rabbis who play it safe with God, or rabbis who assure them that God is harmless. Only a minority regard Torah as an encounter between God and Israel, in which there is a continuous dialogue between finite man and his Infinite Creator. Yet only this minority can help to prevent Judaism from becoming either the faith of a small group, withdrawn from the intellectual currents of our time, or the folk-pattern of a larger group whose Jewishness will only be a function of their social and psychological situation rather than a commitment to God, whom they can address as "Thou."

The minority cannot transmit its conviction by argument. In the final analysis faith is never induced by reason. However, the minority must—like the prophets of old—speak what they hold to be the truth. They may never be at the helm of Jewish states, communities, or even future Sanhedrins, but they do offer much to those who look to Judaism for something more than merely the culture of a people or the inflexible imperative of a code.

I

As man is God's partner in continuous creation, so the Jew is God's partner in the process called Torah. In that process the Jew is more than God's obedient servant. He participates in the discovery of God's Word for every situation and, therefore, his own needs must enter into the dialogue. It thus appears, for example, that in those areas of life in which the greatest change is likely—man's economic and social life—pure logic and authorities were never, and are not now, the only factors in Halachic exegesis. By way of contrast, an analysis of the Talmudic folios dealing with the duties of the priests in connection with animal offerings reveals almost exclusive reliance upon Biblical texts, oral tradition, and extensive deductive reasoning with respect to the texts and traditions. Logic is the life of this branch of Jewish law. One of the greatest Talmudic experts of our day was wont to say that he loves to study this branch of Jewish law not only because he believes in the immanence of the Messianic era and the restoration of the Temple and its rituals, as a result of which Jews will again have need of this learning, but also because this branch of the law is so "Seicheldik"—so charged with pure reason. In another branch of the law, that dealing with festivals, one discovers more preoccupation with the lives and needs of Jews. In family law and civil law the demands of life are as important as the logical implications of the texts.

This is as it must be. If in the Halachic process there is a Divine encounter, then, as in prayer, the process cannot be oblivious of life. What is more, as in prayer the same texts are discovered to be meaningful throughout the millennia and amid the diversity of human situations in every age, so the same legal texts address themselves to many new legal problems and permit extensive discovery. The Talmud, and several medieval philosophers, visualize the revealed will of God as the blacksmith's anvil which causes a multitude of sparks to fly. In the case of the blacksmith the sparks do not endure. The sparks of God's Word do endure, and in time kindle a fire as the encounter between God and Israel continues. The Jew constantly discovers these sparks which at one time may even have appeared to be ambiguous, contradictory, and multi-directional. Study them night and day, and they speak to one of everything, for every situation, past, present and future.

In the case of the *lex talionis* we have ambiguity in the Bible.[1] Does an "eye for an eye" require exact retribution

1. See next chapter.

174

as in the case of "a life for a life" when applied to a homicide? Or does it require monetary compensation as in the case of "a life for a life" when used in Leviticus in connection with the killing of another's animal? In connection with the phylacteries we have contradiction between the Biblical text and the Oral tradition. The word "Yad" in the Bible means "hand," not "arm." Yet tefilin are placed on the arm. Are the ambiguities and contradictions errors, or are they means of involving Jews in the flowering of the law so that they cannot find security in certainty but must always traverse God's path with awe and trembling and ascertain His Will?

The source materials necessitate the intellectual and emotional participation of the Jew for their exposition, classification, and application. One great medieval scholar points to the fact that even a problem resolved in one generation may be reconsidered and resolved differently in another generation. Maimonides differed. Maimonides held that once a majority of the Sanhedrin had arrived at a conclusion as to what the law was, no succeeding Sanhedrin could overrule it unless its personnel was greater in quality. If it is superior, a succeeding Sanhedrin which agreed with the minority in the earier tribunal could subsequently, by majority vote, make the earlier minority view the authentic one. Somehow, the very fact that the earlier Sanhedrin was closer to the earliest encounter of God with Israel makes it prima facie the superior authority.

Rabbi Abraham ben David yielded to no such presumption. In the ongoing encounter, the later tribunal may adopt what was theretofore only a minority view. The later tribunal may even be inferior to its predecessor in quality but that does not gainsay that the view of the minority in the earlier tribunal may have been the truth which only became apparent to a succeeding generation. Maimonides, the rationalist for whom a dialogue with God was less thinkable than for the sage of Posquieres, made man's continuous participation in the Divine encounter less productive of Halachic change than did his controversialist. Maimonides made of both God and His word ultimates far beyond the grasp of ordinary men. Rabbi Abraham ben David placed both within our reach.

Perhaps this, too, is the essence of the difference between the two men in theology. Maimonides allegorically interpreted all references in the Bible to the corporeality of God and regarded as pagan any conception of God which was anthropomorphic. Rabbi Abraham ben David seems to say to him: "Don't pontificate. One should not pronounce absolutes even in theology. Binding the generations to one view and anathematizing dissenters is a dangerous course."

Because the view of yesterday's minority may become the view of tomorrow's majority, the Talmud devotes almost as much space to minority as to majority views, as students of Talmud well know. Students of Talmud are frequently exasperated by the seeming futility of trying to fathom positions which did not prevail. Yet in an ongoing encounter between God and Israel, and the progressive Revelation which the encounter entails, minority views are important. Who can understand this better than students of American constitutional law wherein the erstwhile dissents of Holmes, Brandeis, Stone, Black, and Douglas, finally become the law of the land!

Thus one should not only master the views of dissenters but encourage them. In one's practice of the Law one should not be a sect unto one's self. This was the heresy of the Karaites and the basic reason for their virtual oblivion. However, Jews as individuals are expected to engage in the encounter and contend with God and the tradition. It is thus that the study of Torah can rank with prayer as a means of confronting God. It is thus also that a theocentric law is always found viable. Humility in the encounter there must be, but not blind obedience exclusively.

The Halachah supports this position. The Zaken Mamreh,[2] the dissenter who defies the Sanhedrin, is punishable only for acts in defiance of a superior authority which, by

2. See supra, pp. 104-5.

majority vote, arrives at a rule of law. However, he is not punished for persisting in his view that the Sanhedrin erred nor for arguing his position publicly.

If Orthodox rabbis continue to denigrate the role of man in Halachic creativity then they shall bear the guilt for failing to reach many of our contemporaries who want to "return" but resent an uncompromising authoritarianism. They must be helped to see that man plays a role in the development of Halachah.

However, God does also.

II

With regard to God's role in the encounter there is even more controversy than with regard to man's. Many theologians, even among those who are committed to the belief in a historical Revelation at Sinai, maintain that it happened once and will never happen again. Those who deny an original Revelation are certainly reluctant to believe in the progressive unfolding of that which never existed. But many Orthodox Jews regard the Law as having been given once, and what Jews have done with it thereafter—within the limits and according to the exegesis originally prescribed—is *their* doing, and their authority is set forth in Deuteronomy, where Jews are ordered to hearken to all that their future judges would teach.

The view that God no longer shares in Torah is supported by texts which deny the validity of supernatural voices (Bat-Kol) and of omens in the resolution of Halachic questions. It is also supported by Judaism's resistance to Christian and Muslim revelations. Maimonides made of the finality of Torah a cardinal dogma of the faith. However, texts as well as experience support the view that, while there shall never be another Torah, sages relied on Divine help and even apocalyptic prophecy to discover God's will in countless Halachic situations. Indeed, it could not be otherwise, for then no religious experience whatever would be involved in the resolution of new Halachic problems.

177

Certainly the saintliness of the scholar would be inconsequential, since what he opines must stand the test of reason alone. Yet in Halachic development it was the scholar who was also saintly and whose views prevailed over those more learned but less devout. Piety was at least as much the hallmark of authority as genius, and unless religious experience is involved in Halachic exegesis this requisite makes no sense.

Heschel has fully documented the thesis that prophecy played an important role in Halachic decisions during the Middle Ages. Certainly it was through the immediacy of their experience of God that Hasidic teachers suspended many binding rules of the law. Moreover, even the most avid of Jewish rationalists know only by mystical illumination when a particular discourse in Talmud is the truth and when it is only intellectual acrobatics.

Yet, the greater threat to the Halachah comes not from those who regard God's role as ended but from those who regard the Law as without a transcendent source. They may not adversely affect the status of the Jewish people or the Jewish State in our day as does the American Council of Judaism. However, theologically speaking, their heresy is of the same caliber. One group denies the role of people in the encounter; the other denies the role of God. That is why Reconstructionists can so readily extend the invitation to secularists to join hands in a common humanistic endeavor for Jews.

But those for whom God is the ultimate source of all law and law-making—and the cause of all mutations in our ethical and religious insights—the ongoing encounter between Him and man is the cornerstone of all their commitment.

Nelson Glueck claims that archaeology sustains his faith in a transcendent Being. Excavating in the area traversed by Abraham four millennia ago, he discovers a remarkable homogeneity in cultural patterns everywhere. The emergence of a new faith in the midst of all this sameness is a mutation that could either be accidental or the result of a

178

Divine encounter. He chooses the latter alternative as the basis for his religious commitment.

Henri Bergson derives it rather from the prophets. He cannot concur in the view that justice is exclusively the product of social need. He poses the famous question:

"What should we do if we heard that for the common good, for the very existence of mankind, there was somewhere a man condemned to suffer eternal torment? Well, we should perhaps agree to it on the understanding that some magic philter is going to make us forget it, that we shall never hear anything more about it, but if we are bound to know it, to think of it, to realize that this man's hideous torture was the price of our existence, that it was even the fundamental condition of existence in general, no. A thousand times no! Better to accept that nothing should exist at all! Better let our planet be blown to pieces.

"Now what has happened? How does a sense of justice which may have emerged originally from social need suddenly soar above it, categorical and transcendent, so that in its name we defy the social need? Let us recall the tone and accents of the Prophets of Israel. It is their voice we hear when a great injustice has been done and condoned. From the depths of the centuries they raise their protest. They imparted to justice the violently imperative character which it has kept, which it has since stamped on a substance grown infinitely more extensive. Could it have been brought about by mere philosophy? There is nothing more instructive than to see how the philosophers have skirted round it, touched it, and yet missed it."

For traditionalist Jews it is in the Pentateuch, even more than in the Prophets, that not only the record of Israel's encounter is to be found but also the warrant for the authenticity of its transcendent source. The twenty-fifth chapter of Leviticus, which in modern times inspired a Henry George, is an eloquent illustration.

A people—every one of whom expected to share in the distribution of the land after its conquest—is unequivocally told that the land will not be theirs. It will always belong to God (verse 23). And because it is God's it will not be exploited every seventh year. Nothing will be gained by this other than a demonstration as to who is truly the owner. Yet, if law is to be defined as the expression of universal self-interest, how can one explain this law which denies the self-interest of everyone in the legal order! Furthermore, if law is to be defined as an expression of the self-interest of the dominant economic group, how can one explain that verse in the same chapter which lets the masters of slaves know that God alone is a Master! It was He Who took His people out of bondage in Egypt to serve Him (verse 55). Any servitude to humans is, therefore, always subject to His will and limited by it.

Nor is law the will of the king, the human sovereign, to aggrandize his authority. For it is obedience to God's law, not obedience to the king, that will insure the peace and permit one to live securely on the land (verse 18). The king has his duties and his rights, but domestic tranquillity is God's gift, not his. What human sovereign would ever promulgate such a preamble to his constitution! Nor is law for the greatest good of the greatest number. The minority of non-Jews is also not to be put at a disadvantage. Their proprietary rights shall be safeguarded (verse 48). And even human nature is not the source of the law. To the contrary, one of the law's principal functions is to alter human nature. The bully in man is to be shrunk (verse 46).

How other than from a transcendent will could such a code emerge! The sages of the Talmud so thought. In a very incisive comment they made their point. They observed that in the opening verse of Chapter 25 of Leviticus reference is made to the fact that the laws therein contained were given on Mount Sinai. According to the tradition the entire law of Moses was given at Sinai. Why, then, the special mention of the mountain in introducing this particular chapter? The answer is obvious. Only from Sinai—only from God—could such a chapter come. Who could believe otherwise! Therefore, let all know that as this chapter can only emanate from Him, so all the Law is from Him.

Moses did not transmit the Law as if from God to strengthen *his* authority and the authority of his successors. That kings in the ancient world were wont to do this gives one no right to assume that Moses must have followed suit. It is the uniqueness of his presentation that bears the certification of its origin in God. For it was only His authority that was being established. Most of the Law was irrelevant to Moses' times. Most of it was to be obeyed only after his death—when Jews would have conquered the Promised Land. And Moses could not have tried to insure the security of his successors. His children did not succeed him. His own authority he diffused among priests, judges, elders, and kings. Nor would any of them ever have ultimate authority. Authority would forever reside in the One, transcendent and omnipotent.

Buber noted one interesting exception in the phraseology of most of the commandments that were given for fulfillment in the land of Canaan. Most of them would be binding after entry into the land. Two would be binding only after entry, conquest, and division among the tribes of Israel. These two laws pertained to the coronation of a king and the annual ceremony to bring Bikurim—the first fruit—to the shrine in the city where the king would reign. That the performance of these two commandments was to await the conquest of the land and its division among the conquerors was God's way of preventing feudalism with its system of land tenure as derived from the sovereign. Jews were not to have a king before they acquired their land. Then they would know that from God they received it and not from a human majesty. Moreover, if after the coronation of a king the king might be inclined to forget this, he was to be annually reminded of his error, when all Jews

181

would appear in the very city in which he held his court with their first fruits which they presented to the priests with a declaration of gratitude to God from Whom they received the gift of the land. And if feudalism might emerge later, as the king and others accumulated land unto themselves, the Law had its antidote in the form of a redistribution of the land every fifty years. Alienation of the land in perpetuity was well-nigh impossible. It takes more credulity to believe that Moses by himself was the visionary social engineer of his day than to believe that he had an encounter with God and transmitted God's will!

III

But God and Abraham also had an encounter. For an understanding of Israel's role among the nations this encounter is even more important than the one at Sinai. And what emerged from Abraham's encounter was equally exceptional and warrants belief in a transcendent source. Kierkegaard made the story of the sacrifice of Isaac the cornerstone of his theology. However, as Milton Steinberg conclusively demonstrated, Judaism does not subscribe to any suspension of the ethical. In Judaism God and the good are as related as a circle to roundness. But that Abraham was commanded to withdraw from his world is a mandate too revolutionary not to be regarded as a mutation of major importance in universal history. He was ordered to leave his country, the city of his birth, even his forebears, so that in his aloneness he might ultimately bring benefit to all the families of the earth—an altruistic goal five times articulated in Genesis to the patriarchs. And Abraham's withdrawal and other-directedness became the hallmark of Israel's existential situation.

Even the rationale for God's choice of Israel differs radically, as Theodore Reik pointed out, from similar conceptions among other tribes and peoples. The Hebrews were not "chosen" because of their quality. Indeed, the Bible indicates that their number least merited God's recognition.

182

Moses was frequently even more insulting. But it was Abraham who merited being chosen, and to his seed fell the lot of fulfilling the promise that through him all humanity would be blessed. This was God's will for Israel and all humanity. And a dialogue which altered the life and career of Abraham became an "I-Thou" relationship for the benefit of third parties.

This component of Judaism is the object of Toynbee's unrelenting criticism. He cannot fathom Israel's separateness, which to him is only a vestigial ethnicism. But the ambivalence involved in a withdrawal for the purpose of ultimate service to those from whom one withdraws is the essence of Abraham's encounter with God and its continuance with his seed. A later confluence of Hebraic and Hellenic ideas in Stoicism yielded the same ambivalence. The Stoic, too—as inspired by Zeno, Epictetus and Aurelius—would have man withdraw unto himself in virtual obliviousness of external facts and circumstances at the same time that he makes empathy and philanthropy for others the basis of his activity as a man. Perhaps the ambivalence involves what are contradictories by logic, but the logic of life and experience transcends the limitations of pure reason. In Stoicism, individualism and universalism are the antitheses; in Judaism they are particular peoplehood and universalism.

Failure to fathom the unique significance of Abraham's, and then Israel's, encounter with God has also led to an exaggeration of the significance of the Hellenic tradition for the values of humanism and the denigration of the Hebraic tradition. John Bowle, for example, in his "Western Political Thought," regards as "typically Jewish" Paul's "blinding vision of God's omnipotence, of the abject condition of man, the overwhelming sense of sin, the passion for 'salvation.'" Daniel Bell also subscribes to the idea that Jewish Orthodoxy induced such resignation on the Jew's part to his fate that he did not resist Hitler's decrees.

If any tradition made man the captive of the gods it was Hellenism and not Hebraism. Indeed, the optimism of an

Aristotle—or to a lesser degree of a Plato—with regard to man's capacity to mold life and institutions to his will was the exception rather than the rule. Hebraism, on the other hand, because of Abraham's encounter with God, catapulted man to such an exalted position that in dialogue with his Creator he could insure the peace and plenty of the earth. Righteousness, which is man's raison d'etre and wholly within his reach, even binds God to fulfill His covenanted obligations. God is the obligee of man!

Furthermore, it was because all men are created in His image that the equality of man is a Hebraic doctrine, while in Hellenism the emphasis is on man's inequality.[3] And since justice was to Abraham God's most pronounced attribute, preoccupation with justice was the hallmark of Judaism throughout the millennia. Notions of equity and equality were, therefore, more Hebraic than Hellenic, and again via Stoicism Hebraic ideas humanized Roman law for the greater happiness of man in the Western world. Subsequently, through Christianity, Biblical Judaism gave to the world the very weapon by which the tyranny of the state—including Rome—could be mitigated and human freedom expanded. This weapon was the faith that there was a right that transcended imperial power—a right derived from God. The individual in opposition to the State, in the name of God, was a conflict unthinkable to an Athenian; but it was the very heart of prophecy in the Bible. This is one of many ways in which it was Hebraism rather than Hellenism that advanced the cause of humanism. And it was Abraham who first held even God to be bound to do the right! The Sovereign of all the earth was also bound by a higher law—albeit His own.

IV

What the West will now do in its controversy with the East may well lead to the end of human life and civilization

3. See Chapter 5, Section 2, supra.

as we know it. However, if the West should capitulate—to prevent the holocaust—then there can be no hope for freedom at any time in the next millennium unless more people individually, because of their personal encounter with God, are prepared to resist the spread of tyranny. Perhaps prudence will dictate that collectively free nations withdraw, suffer shame, and forfeit influence. The responsibility will then fall to solitary humans, in martyrdom to keep alive the hope that some day the right will prevail.

Chapter Three

TRUTH AND WISDOM

I

Notwithstanding popular opinion to the contrary, Judaism does not give its adherents unequivocal answers to the basic questions of life. Nor does it even prescribe for every situation in which the Jew may find himself. While it does have religious, philosophical and ethical imperatives, these are often antithetical in character and man is rarely spared the onus of deliberate choice and decision. It is important to point this out for the benefit of those who are already committed to the Law as well as for those who are about to embrace it.

Judaism affords no escape from the awareness of reality or the exercise of reason. Indeed, the divinely revealed must be true—in the absolute sense—and what is absolutely true can be an anchor for emotional and intellectual security. But the divinely revealed is limited in word and scope. Life, on the other hand, is complicated, nuanced, and calls for cautious application of divinely revealed norms to an endless diversity of situations. To make this application the Jew must constantly muster all of the resources of heart and mind available. And for this he has his Oral Law and the sea of the Talmud. Most appropriately has it been said that while truth is to be found in the Decalogue, the Talmud has wisdom. The former is absolute; the latter is qualified, antithetical, even unsure of itself.

As simple an imperative as "Thou shalt not steal" cannot be treated as an absolute. Is man's right to the ownership of things divinely protected? When can his neighbors, or his fellow citizens, invade the right and subject ownership to the requirements of the public weal? What is the nature of the higher good, or how many its beneficiaries, that in its name the public—a state or a community—may expropriate an individual? The Talmud suggests that the prohibition against the theft of things may not even be part of the Decalogue—the theft of things is too unimportant an evil to be given equal status with prohibitions against murder, incest and adultery. The Oral Law, therefore, regards the commandment as directed against kidnapping. As murder and incest and adultery are crimes involving personality, not property, so must the prohibition against stealing involve humans, not things.

Is the prohibition against murder, however, any more absolute than the one against theft? Apparently, judicial punishment, even when capital, is not murder. Is killing in self-defense murder? And what of the killing of one's enemies in war, or after their conquest? As murder must be defined, so must adultery and incest. Even the mandate to tell the truth may have exceptions, and certainly envy—though generally reprehensible—is often encouraged when it stimulates rivalry in righteous and scholarly living.

Thus, even the revealed truth of the Decalogue becomes qualified and nuanced in life and the simplest revelation provides none of the absolutism that so many moderns associate with Orthodoxy. Man retains a creative role in the very process of applying revelation itself. He cannot altogether abdicate the autonomy of his reason. Nor can he, in Judaism, altogether delegate this responsibility to others. Even his choice of an authority is ultimately an act that calls for deliberation and decision.

However, if with regard to the commands of the Decalogue there remains an area for interpretation, then *a fortiori* with regard to the remainder of the Law, one can anticipate an uncertainty or ambiguity. Many texts of the Pentateuch—in the narratives and in the codes—invite a multiplicity of exegeses. Saadia Gaon argued that the lack of clarity is deliberate, for thereby God stimulated understanding by man on many different levels—literal, mystical, allusive. This diversity in interpretation could also help to make diverse the application of Torah to many different situations. Revelation's importance is then due as much to the process it initiated and continues to mold as to its fixity. Indeed, its poles are many, even antithetical, and the Jew must learn to live by the light of these many suns. Simple and stark truth he may never achieve, but at least wisdom is within his reach. This wisdom is contained in the Oral Law, which helps us cope with the ambiguity and lacunae of revelation. And Moses, who taught the Law to all Israel, could not evade his own part in the process. That is why tradition must regard him as the lawgiver of both that which is written and that which is oral.

II

One of the most elementary functions of reason when applied to revealed materials is classification. In revelation itself there is no classification—there are only particulars upon which an inductive operation must be predicated. Without classification, an evolving body of law becomes incapable of transmission to succeeding generations. Moreover, in the very process of classifying the rules, new insights are born and the creative role of man is seen again. An isolated, revealed truth, becomes part of an organized body of wisdom.

Thus, for example, the Oral Law, as based on revelation, could not subscribe to the distinction which most modern states make between civil and criminal law. According to Torah, all conduct is either proper or improper, righteous or sinful. Consequently Halachic analysis was not troubled, as modern legal philosophy is, with the problem of defining a crime, as differentiated from a tort. The Jew either did or did not do what God had sanctioned. If he did what God sanctioned, he could not be summoned before the court. If he did what God had not sanctioned, or failed to do what God had ordained, then how could one regard his act of omission or commission as culpable only from a civil point of view and not from a criminal one? Judaism's classification therefore, was exclusively functional. It focused attention on the remedy which the court could grant. And the classification of cases was predicated on whether the court could grant a monetary award or a corporal punishment: flogging, imprisonment or execution. The nature of the court's judgment determined the qualifications and number of judges, the nature of the proof required, and the immunities of the persons against whom claims were asserted. That which was intended to be done to the defendant was definitive. If only his assets were to be reached, then the Law was less concerned about the possibility of error. Greater caution had to be exercised when it was his limb or his life that was in jeopardy. The state, however, played no more and no less of a role in the one case than in the other.

Thus, a court of three sat in a suit which involved the payment of money, and a court of at least twenty-three when his life was at stake. In the latter type of case the judges invariably had to be duly ordained masters of the Law; in the former type, the requirement was not so rigid. Decisions were arrived at by a majority vote, but for an execution more than a simple majority was necessary.

In cases involving only money, self-admissions were countenanced to a limited extent; in cases involving corporal punishment, confessions were utterly disregarded—they were absolute nullities. Furthermore, proof normally required two competent eye-witnesses; some circumstantial evidence was valid in cases involving money. In cases involving corporal punishment no circumstantial evidence whatever was considered. Even the thoroughness with which the court interrogated the witnesses differed in both types of cases, for the interrogation of witnesses was by the court, not by attorneys. Some judges in capital cases played their role as cross-examiners so devastatingly that they virtually abolished capital punishment altogether—for this the Halachah became famous. The judicial procedure of Judaism clearly manifests how much higher was the evaluation placed on life and limb than that placed on property.

With regard to the competency of witnesses there were also different standards. Some persons might be competent to testify in a lawsuit involving only money but not for a trial involving corporal punishment. Moreover, in the latter type of case it was necessary that the testimony be of such a character that the witnesses might not only be impeached generally but also be subject to the special form of impeachment as a result of which they could become liable because of their perjury to the same punishment that they sought to mete out to the accused.

It was because the classification of the Oral Law concentrated on the difference between property and life that the eighth commandment of the Decalogue was interpreted as involving kidnapping. The Rabbis understood that all of the last five commandments of the Decalogue involved a hierarchy of values pertaining to human personality—the integrity of one's life (the prohibition against murder) ; the integrity of one's family (the prohibition against adultery) ; the integrity of one's freedom (the prohibition against kidnapping) ; the integrity of reputation (the prohibition against bearing false witness) ; and immunity from being begrudged in what one has (the prohibition against coveting). The prohibition against stealing property is found in Leviticus and it involved no corporal punishment—at most, the return of the theft with double or quadruple or quintuple damages (which excess was a fine).

The preoccupation of the Law with the nature of the court's judgment resulted in many an anomaly. Thus, for example, a tort which was substantial enough to warrant a judgment in the amount of one cent or more was tried by less rigorous rules than a tort which was so inconsequential that it involved damages of less than a cent. Because in the latter case the court could award no money but could order the flogging of the defendant, the more stringent rules applicable to cases involving corporal punishment had to be followed.

On no issue, however, is the contrast so great as with respect to the measure of responsibility. When a money judgment is involved the defendant is usually held accountable without regard to his fault, for no legal system was ever committed more extensively to the theory of strict liability than the Halachah. The only situations in which the defendants might not be liable for the immediate consequences of their acts were either when they were minors or incompetents, or when the acts were not theirs—when their bodies were used by others. Otherwise, they would be liable for torts committed even in their sleep. If the defendant, however, was to suffer corporal punishment, then his act must not only have been willful but he must also have been forewarned in advance by two competent witnesses that if he proceeded with the act, he would suffer the punishment that is involved, and he must nonetheless have defiantly committed the act. Ignorance of the Law in such cases is not only regarded as a defense but the witnesses who bring the crime to the attention of the court bear the burden of proof that they themselves apprised the defendant of the law involved. Needless to say, this was the way in which all corporal punishment was abolished—for who but an insane person would commit an unlawful act in the presence of two competent witnesses who were forewarning him and preparing to testify against him! Furthermore, how could any of the laws against adultery and incest be enforced when the very act of coitus that constituted the offense had to be performed in the presence of two warning witnesses. It was thus that most of the laws which called for corporal punishment became exclusively hortatory. They constituted moral norms for social and educational purposes. Undoubtedly, the leniency of the Law increased the incidence of behavior that was frowned upon by the Law. The Talmud records this argument. When the incidence was too high, emergency measures had to taken. One such instance is recorded with regard to the practice of witchcraft and necromancy which the Pentateuch had forbidden. Moreover, a court of twenty-three, it would appear, had a reserved power to get rid of evil-doers, and if someone offended too brazenly, they could resort to a ruthless form of punishment with torture, to accomplish the result. However, there is no recorded case where this was done. The power remained a reserved power of the judiciary.

Moreover, the greater concern of the Law for human personality, rather than property, prompted the rabbis to develop the law of stealing; what was uppermost in their minds was the reform of the thief and not the return of the theft. Owners who sought to reclaim their property were frowned upon for thereby they deterred thieves from confessing their sin and doing penitence. Those owners, on the other hand, who waived their rights, helped to rehabilitate anti-social beings into honest men. How different the situation today when the criminal law and the threat of prosecution become the principal means whereby stolen goods are recovered, and in exchange for restitution, the offender is released!

It can hardly be claimed that any modern state, including Israel, could base its criminal law on the Halachah. Indeed, few if any rabbis in almost two thousand years have thought that the Halachic system could be restored in its entirety in any period other than the messianic era. Nonetheless, Jews studied the rules as part of Torah and hoped thereby to learn more about God, Who is the Source of their Law, and some of their ethical insights might very well receive more attention in all legal systems of today.

III

The second major function of reason in the Oral Law is to resolve ambiguities in the revealed truths. No ambiguity in the Pentateuch, for example, has attracted more attention in Christian and Jewish history than the *lex talionis*—"an eye for an eye and a tooth for a tooth." Christian scholarship has generally assumed that the Pentateuch required the physical removal of the limb of the person who thus offended against another. The Talmudic rule—that the tort be compensated for with money—was considered a later development. Modern scholarship has exposed the error of this assumption. Some scholars have even demonstrated that the payment of money for the tort antedates the *lex talionis* in the development of some legal systems. Others maintain that the two rules are to be found in force at the same time. Perhaps either the offender or his victim had a choice of remedy. Certainly, Talmudic sources indicate that both remedies were known among Jews and were regarded as normative by one group or another. And the least that could be said about the revealed rule is that it was ambiguous. It remained for the Oral Law to resolve the ambiguity by reason, as well as tradition.

"An eye for an eye" might mean that an eye is to be removed for an eye even as the phrase "a life for a life" means precisely that when it is used in connection with the crime of murder. There the phrase is understood as requiring a life to be taken to atone for a homicide. However, "an eye for an eye" might also mean that a monetary equivalent shall be paid, as the phrase "a life for a life" used in Leviticus in connection with the killing of another's cattle, whereupon it is unequivocal that the tortfeasor pays the value of what has been destroyed, and does not forfeit his own life or the life of his cattle. Furthermore, in Exodus, only a few verses before the so-called *lex talionis*, there is a rule calling for the payment of medical expenses and loss of earnings in the event of bodily harm imposed upon another, which contradicts the phrase "a bruise for a bruise" a few verses thereafter. In Numbers it appears that the punishment for murder cannot be compounded with money but other torts may be thus compounded.

The ambiguity prompted the rabbis of the Talmudic era

and a preponderance of medieval commentators to articulate what is in essence the difference between the simple, stark truth of revelation and the qualified, nuanced wisdom of its application. He who takes another's eye merits the loss of his own. Measure for measure is the principle of divine, absolute justice. But no human tribunal can administer measure for measure. What executioner can remove the eye of an offender with absolute assurance that he will not kill and thus do more damage than he was authorized to do! Or how can one achieve exact equivalence when eyes are not all of the same size or vigor! God may articulate in revelation what is absolutely just but only He could administer it. Judges on earth can only permit themselves a limited retribution—full payment for every manner of loss sustained—in ultimate earning capacity, in pain, embarrassment and healing costs, and also loss resulting from one's unemployment during recovery from the tort inflicted.

The *lex talionis*, however, is not the only instance in which punishments are revealed vindictively only to indicate the extreme displeasure of God with the persons offending while, in fact, human tribunals are incompetent to administer the penalties prescribed, and can only mete out less severe ones. The simple stark truths of revelation are absolute norms in God's justice but mortal man must be content to leave it to God to bring the full measure of His wrath to bear upon the sinner. A human court shall only punish mildly. In this category are to be found scores of commandments with regard to whose violation Scripture says either "He shall die" or "That soul shall be cut off from his people," and the rabbis said that only God will decide how and when. The most that they would do in such cases is to decree lashes against the offender, provided that all the technical prerequisites for any form of corporal punishment had been fulfilled. This applied to many of the prohibitions against incest—particularly those involving collateral consanguinity rather than forebears or descendants—and most of the commandments pertaining to ritual observance.

The dialectic of the Oral Law involved two sets of antithetical norms. On the one hand there were God's exacting standards of justice and the unquestioning obedience He was entitled to receive from the people whom He had taken out of Egypt that they might be His people and receive His Law. On the other hand there were God's compassion and love and His mandate that man be equally merciful. Where the revealed command appeared harsh or vindictive—primarily because the Jews were less likely to obey unless the Torah used fervent exhortation or vituperation—the Oral Law veered in the direction of mitigation. Thus, the provisions for the complete extermination of all the seven nations of Canaan, as well as Amalek, were understood as binding only if these pagans refused to make peace with Jews and fulfill the Noahide code, without which they could hardly be deemed safe to live with. Similarly, the almost inhuman commands of Deuteronomy with regard to the wayward son and the idolatrous city were so understood by the Oral Law that they were virtually nothing but exhortations, with at least one rabbi contending that the laws were never actually applied and another rabbi claiming to have had hearsay knowledge of the application of the Law. To such an extent had the laws become purely academic that no one is reported ever to have beheld an actual trial!

On the other hand, a provocateur for paganism—who thereby endangers Israel's covenant with God—was not regarded by the Oral Law as adequately condemned by the revealed word. His crime is so heinous that he is not entitled to the privileges and immunities of other offenders in capital cases. Moreover, if the Torah did not adequately punish the usurer, the Oral Law added to his grief, and according to one rabbi, he forfeits the principal of, as well as the interest on, his loan. Again, revealed laws are qualified and nuanced in the dialectic of the Oral Law.

In no instance does the ambiguity of the revealed word beg for resolution more than in connection with the problem of individual versus collective responsibility. Repeatedly the Torah ascribes guilt to the group for the sins of the few at the same time that it ordains that "a man shall die for his own sin." The prophets wrestled with the problem and no less so did the Oral Law. For the prophets the problem was theological—for the rabbis, legal. And since theologians do not have to arrive at conclusions while jurists must pronounce verdicts, we find both groups accentuating antithetical views. In Jewish philosophy and ethics it was the principle of collective responsibility that was of paramount importance. The righteous suffer for the sins of their generation and all Jews are mutually responsible for each other. In Jewish jurisprudence, on the other hand, the principle of individual responsibility was carried to such an extreme that an accessory before the fact was not liable to punishment. Only he who does the actual killing or stealing bears the brunt of the law. In his commission of the crime, he has no partners and he cannot look forward to even that modicum of comfort that others who cooperated with him— before or after—will share his plight before the bar of justice.

In life it is a fact that the good suffer because of the bad, and the innocent are placed in jeopardy because of the guilty. The Torah recognizes this truth. It is, however, also given to individual men to choose between good and evil. This is a fact of the moral life and the Torah states it unequivocally. That because of those who choose evil, the righteous are denied their reward, remains a problem of theodicy for philosophers and theologians. However, man cannot claim a right to do evil and rely upon the argument that God Himself breaches His own covenant when He denies them their due. Human justice can only reckon with individual responsibility and act accordingly. On the level of absolute truth there is dilemma, contradiction, paradox. On the level of life and experience, there must be decision.

IV

The third major function of reason in the Oral Law is to fill the lacunae in the revealed word. In Numbers, for example, the Jewish law of inheritance is set forth. A decedent's estate, it is said, passes to his children, and if he has no children, to his brothers. The Oral Law ordains, however, that the father has a prior right to that of the brothers. The revealed word is silent with regard to the father. It is reasonable that the father's right should be antecedent to that of the brothers since the latter inherit only by the virtue of the common ancestor whose claim ought therefore be superior to theirs. Yet why the omission in the revealed word? Because, it is argued, for a father to inherit his child is a tragedy and the Torah preferred in such a case to leave a lacuna and let reason fill the gap.

Many phrases and words of Scripture are also allusions to practices or things whose character is known only through the Oral Law, such as the manner of slaughtering cattle, the nature of the fair fruit used on the Sukkoth festival, the composition of phylacteries. However, there were significant sections of the Law with regard to which there were only the most meager references in the Biblical texts, while it must have been anticipated that there would be a high incidence of litigation involving them. Of these none is more exciting than the field of contracts—the enforceability of a promise made by one person to another. Here, too, the Oral Law compensated for the lacuna, deriving from a few verses a multitude of insights that reveals the tradition's unrelenting concern for equity, the dignity of human speech, the need of the economically disenfranchised, and other values which are of paramount importance in a system of jurisprudence that is theocentric and not rooted only in history, economics, and power.

The Bible did ordain that a man should fulfill "what comes forth from his lips." At least one entire tractate of the Talmud deals with vows and, as one medieval commentator suggested, the goal of its study should be the dignification and sanctification of speech. It is of interest that the sages associated this goal with marital harmony, so important was guarded speech to the cultivation of a proper relationship between husband and wife. But apart from the moral and social implications of all kinds of intemperate talk and broken promises, did persons aggrieved have any basis on which to sue? Since "talk is cheap," when may persons have reason to believe that a legally binding promise was made in their behalf so that they may enforce its fulfillment?

It would be too much for any legal order to insist upon the performance of every promise. Friends may agree to take a walk or play a game of golf and disappoint each other with impunity. Men also make exaggerated statements as to what they intend to do for others. They offend against ethics but it would be too much to set legal machinery in motion to enforce every foolish utterance of mortals. Needless to say, if there has been reliance upon a promise earnestly made, and injury follows a breach of the promise, the promisor should make good the loss. Jewish law concurs. But what of a promise to make a gift which few legal systems ever enforce? Should not such promises be a matter of "honor," with only social, not legal, sanctions to protect them?

Students of jurisprudence know how all legal systems wrestled with this problem. The Romans and Continentals came forth with a doctrine of *causa*, and the Anglo-Americans with a doctrine of *consideration*, two symbols to indicate that the parties to a contract intended to consummate an agreement of which the law should take cognizance. At least two interesting problems emerged in England and America. Pledges to charity were not enforceable since these were gratuitous gifts. Moreover, persons who did not themselves participate in the agreement could not complain that the promises were not performed since they were not principals.

The Oral Law of Judaism generally assumes that only deeds, not words, could create legal rights in others, and thus "nude" promises were a nullity. A formal act accompanied by words, such as a transfer of title to property with a formal possessory act, would be effective. Nonetheless, with words alone one could obligate one's self to give charity. With regard to the poor, and with regard to the

198

Temple, one could not pretend that one was merely jesting. The maxim was, "A verbal declaration in God's behalf was the equivalent of delivery," and the beneficiaries of the promises could themselves recover the gifts even though the words may have been uttered to another. Curiously enough, another type of promise enjoyed the same privileged status —promises of dowry. A marriage was too significant an event to permit of any kind of idle speech.

Another interesting exception was the unexecuted commitment of a person in acute illness. In most legal systems the trend is to impose additional formalities in such cases, as in the case of wills, in order to make certain that there is no undue advantage taken of the plight of the donor or testator. The fears of the Oral Law were quite to the contrary. Unless the patient could really be assured that his desires were being effectuated, he might die sooner as a result of the distress of frustration. In his condition, greater laxity prevailed and the value of saving human life yielded to the value of certainty in legal transactions. Again, the simple truth of revelation evoked in life a pattern of regulation that was complex and nuanced.

And what is true of revelation is true of all profound religious experience. The mystic's awareness of God induces certainty, perhaps salvation. But continuing to live with a constant awareness of God does not necessarily involve certainty. Nor does it relieve one of all perplexity and doubt. The religious experience is only the beginning of wisdom. Its maturation and fulfillment require the Law, which in Judaism is endless—as endless as the sea. Indeed, the Talmud is a sea. It may have shores but it has no termini.

SECTION FOUR

THE LAW'S METHODOLOGY

Having already set forth the thesis that in Jewish law one constantly encounters an antinomy between divine, universal truth, beyond the accidents of time and the exigencies of circumstance, and the need for modulated application to the stubborn uniqueness of life's actualities, I undertake in this section to further illustrate the methodology of the law, and at least some instances of creativity within its frame.

Chapter One

THE DIALECTIC OF THE HALACHAH

Philosophers of Judaism find it impossible to interpret their subject without considering its many antinomies. In Judaism, God is immanent as well as transcendent. The prophets articulate lofty ideals of universalism at the same time that they emphasize the particularistic character of the chosen people. Law is of primary importance while the message of freedom is grafted on almost every precept. Other-worldliness and this-worldliness commingle in virtually all the concepts. And the most visionary of hopes coexist with an unmistakable pragmatism, even with a hardened realism.

Judaism's antinomies are important for an understanding of not only its theology and ethics, but also its Halachah. Indeed, the data of Jewish theology and ethics are usually derived from the Law which fixes the essential character of all of Judaism. Unfortunately, however, many who are presently called upon to resolve questions of Jewish law are often oblivious to the antinomies which are implicit in their subject. Altogether too frequently they seize upon one or another of two or more possible antithetical values or interests between which the Halachah veers, and they assume that there must be an exclusive commitment to that single norm. The dialectic of the Talmud, however, reveals quite the contrary. Implicit in almost every discussion is a balancing of the conflicting values and interests which the Law seeks to advance. And if the Halachah is to be viable and at the same time conserve its method and its spirit, we must reckon with the opposing values where such antinomies exist. An equilibrium among them must be achieved by us as objective halachic experts rather than as extremists propounding only one of the antithetic values.

The very process of halachic development involves the quest for such equilibrium. On the one hand, there are the authorities: revealed texts, revealed norms, and the dicta of sages whose prescriptions are almost as sacred as the revealed data (because what the sages of each generation ordain becomes part of the tradition which the revealed texts enjoin us to obey). On the other hand, the Law's doctors are themselves partners in the development of the Law. Indeed God abdicated in their favor when He bequeathed the Law to them. He thereby restrained Himself from any further revelations. The Talmud tells us that Rabbis are not to rely upon heavenly voices or miracles. They are to act as sovereigns in the sphere of halachic creativity allocated to them. Can one conceive a more difficult equilibrium than this—subservience to mountains of authority coupled with a well-nigh arrogant usurpation of legislative and judicial power over the divine legacy? Yet both poles play their necessary roles in Halachic development.

If not for Halachah's theocentric character, it would be no different from other legal systems that are rooted only in history and economics. Because its students are committed to the divine origin of the Law, their creative achievement in the Law is ever oriented to the fulfillment of God's Will. In order that we never lose sight of this commitment, the Law includes mandates that are also suprarational—inexplicable in terms of human values and interests. Thus Dr. Samuel Belkin, president of Yeshiva University, maintains that even the suprarational commandments of the Torah have a purpose although we may not fathom their reason.[1] These mandates are to be obeyed solely because God decreed them. Such mandates are to be found in every branch of the Law. Obedience to them is of the essence of one's religious experience—one obeys not because one understands but rather because one believes. As children sometimes obey parents not because they comprehend but because they trust, so are we to obey God. It was to conserve this attitude that our Sages hesitated to make too explicit their own analysis of the Law in terms of human values and interests. Such analyses might prompt students to embrace a completely humanistic approach to the Law which would thus lose its theocentric character altogether. In a general way they did explore the rationale of most of the *mitzvot,* but in the articulation of specific rules they did not presume that they completely fathomed the teleology of all the revealed texts.

Yet God gave the Law to the Jewish people who alone were responsible for its development. As humans they crave to understand what they are commanded to perform. Moreover, their needs are not the same in every age or clime. The Torah itself takes note of these factors. It appeals to man to comprehend the justice-content of the law. It also bids him to live by the Law, and not perish because of it. Moses' successors were vested with authority not only to interpret the Law but to constitute themselves as authorities in every generation. The Rabbis often undertook not only to ration-

1. S. Belkin, *The Philosophy of Purpose* (New York: Yeshiva University, 1958).

alize the presumptively suprarational, but also to suspend, even overrule, the revealed words of God.

The late Justice Benjamin Cardozo once essayed to describe what it is that a judge does when he engages in the judicial process creatively. The conclusion is inescapable that one can acquire the art only after years of preoccupation with the law, its history, its ideals, its methodology, its philosophy. So is it with Torah—until one has studied long and much from earlier masters, one does not learn how to balance one's commitment to authority with one's obligation to be the master instead of the obedient servant. Both imitation and originality play their part in the process. Modesty coupled with respect for forebears commingles with self-reliance.

The need to achieve equilibrium among values is even more apparent when one is dealing with the rules of law themselves. Particularly in the area of personal status do we find the dialectic of the Talmud balancing opposing interests and veering between antithetical values. In this chapter we shall attempt to demonstrate that the Jewish law of personal status represents, in part, the achievement of an equilibrium between conflicting interests.

True, many of the norms remain suprarational. Without such theocentric roots, the Law would become altogether positive in character. But there are many areas for rabbinic creativity and in these areas rabbis must be mindful of ends.

The Law of Slavery

Without reference to the existence of conflicting values in the Jewish law of personal status, one might accuse the Halachah of discrimination against the non-Jew in general and the non-Jewish slave in particular. The provisions applicable to Jewish slaves were in fact more liberal than those applicable to non-Jewish slaves. However, an analysis of the different interests which the Law sought to conserve will more than justify the less favored status accorded non-Jewish slaves. For the Rabbis sought to balance their love of freedom with their firm insistence on high moral standards for the Jewish people. In the case of Jewish slaves, the love of freedom was the dominant interest; in the case of non-Jewish slaves that value yielded to the concern for sexual morality. Much of the following discussion is repetitious of sections contained earlier in this book. However, the better to illustrate the point of this chapter, the repetition is warranted instead of resort to cross-references.

Jewish Slaves

It is incontrovertible that the elimination of Jewish slavery was a goal of the Halachah. Those who heard on Mount Sinai that all Jews were God's servants were not to become indentured to co-religionists who shared with them a common bondage to the same Master. Therefore, the circumstances under which the Written and Oral Law tolerated Jewish slavery were very limited. A Jew could be sold by the court only if he had stolen and was so destitute that he could not atone for his crime by the payment of money.[2] However, to punish such a sinner with slavery meant that the plight of his family would be even further aggravated. For that reason the master was required to support the slave's entire family.[3] The Halachah was, nonetheless, concerned that wife and children have the benefit of a free head of the household. It therefore ordained that the slave be permitted to redeem himself from his bondage whenever he acquired funds for that purpose. His wife was allowed to engage in gainful employment in order that he might accumulate such funds. None of her earnings belonged to her husband's master, even though the master remained responsible for her and her children's maintenance.[4] The amount the slave was to pay the master for his freedom was proportionate to the still unexpired portion of his six-year

2. *Kiddushin* 18a.
3. *Ibid.* 22a.
4. Maimonides, *Hil. Avadim* 3:2. Nachmanides disagrees; see comment of *Mishneh le'Melech, ad loc.*

term of slavery. If the slave had no wife and children of his own prior to his enslavement, the master was not permitted to give him a non-Jewish slave as a mate, lest he become so attached to her that he choose to remain a slave and never wed and raise a family of Jewish freemen.[5] The Law sought not only to advance the ideal of freedom but also to conserve the many values of Jewish family life. Even in those isolated instances where the master was permitted to cause the Jewish male slave to mate with a non-Jewish female slave—the only instance justifying the contention that the master owned the very body of the slave—the moral standards of a monogamous relationship were applicable and promiscuous relationships were prohibited.[6] The institution of slavery was never to place in jeopardy the lofty moral ideals of the Law. That is also why no compromise whatever was permitted in connection with the Jewish female slave. She was automatically emancipated at puberty unless she had theretofore wed her master or his son.

Non-Jewish Slaves

In the case of Jewish slaves, the ideals of freedom and family morality are seldom in conflict. However, the Law pertaining to non-Jewish slaves can only be understood in the light of the conflict that prevailed between these values. The Halachah rarely permitted even a non-Jew to be enslaved without giving him sufficient status as a Jew to insure the protection of his life and limb and his partial participation in the religious life of family and community. As such, he had a higher status than even a free Gentile. If the non-Jew did not want to be subject to the Law, his master was required to sell him to a non-Jew.[7] If he were bought originally from a non-Jew with the express proviso that he not be converted to Judaism, then he had to acquiesce at least to the observance of the seven Noahide

5. *Kiddushin* 20a.
6. Maimonides, *Hil. Avadim* 3:5.
7. *Yevamot* 48b.

laws.[8] It seems, however, that non-Jewish slaves preferred Jewish owners. As a consequence of their becoming members of a Jewish household, pursuant to the performance of the appropriate rituals, they could not be harmed with impunity. There was no difference whatever in the law of homicide, whether willful or accidental, between one who killed a Jewish freeman and one who killed a non-Jewish slave.[9] Torts committed against the non-Jewish slave were actionable. Though the recovery was the master's, the injuring of slaves was deterred by the very fact that the tort was actionable. The master himself did not escape with impunity for his own torts against his non-Jewish slave. Emancipation of the slave might be the consequence of the master's tort. Under certain circumstances the master would even pay the death penalty for killing his slave,[10] though the Law also sought to protect his disciplinary authority. If a master refused to feed his non-Jewish slave (presumably as a disciplinary measure), the community performed this obligation for the slave as it performed it for the poor generally. The Rabbis even penalized a Jewish master who sold his slave to a non-Jew who would not respect the non-Jewish slave's right to observe Sabbaths and festivals.[11] The master was compelled to repurchase the slave, though the cost of the repurchase might be ten times the amount of the original sale. Moreover, the master could not sell a non-Jewish slave even to a Jew who resided outside the Holy Land.

Nonetheless, the Law frowned upon the emancipation of the non-Jewish slave. Such emancipation would give the non-Jewish slave the status of a full-fledged Jew and the Law did not encourage this way of increasing the Jewish population. The Law abhorred the less stringent sexual code prevailing among non-Jews. Many authorities even observed that the non-Jewish slave might prefer slavery, with its

8. Maimonides, *Hil. Milah* 1:6.
9. *Makkot* 8b.
10. Exodus 21:20.
11. *Gittin* 43b.

209

license for promiscuity, to freedom as a Jew with its stern limitations on sexual relationships.[12] Not having been reared in a milieu which stressed the high moral standards of the Law, the non-Jewish slave was not to be catapulted into a free society which would make him unhappy or which he would corrupt. Nonetheless, the Sages ruled that if by emancipation a moral purpose was achieved or a *mitzvah* fulfilled, one may violate the injunction against freeing a non-Jewish slave. For example, the Law urges that a promiscuous non-Jewish female slave be freed in the hope that she marry and establish a monogamous relationship with a husband, infidelity to whom would be less probable because of the threat of the death penalty.[13]

Rules applicable to non-Jewish slaves thus involve a delicate balancing of the values of freedom and family purity. In the case of Jewish slaves the two values usually yield the same result, or at least are seldom in conflict with each other.

Employer-Employee Relationships

While an analysis of the master-slave relationship may be altogether academic, the relationship of employer and employee has contemporary significance. Jewish law was always aware of the danger that the wage earner might sink to the low status of a slave. It does not matter that he freely contracted to work—a man might also freely contract to be a slave! Therefore, the values which the Law seeks to conserve in the rules governing the employer-employee relationship are essentially those of master-slave relationship— freedom and morality. However, an added value was considered—the sanctity of the pledged word. Jewish labor law developed as a delicate balancing of all these values.

If a man sold himself as a slave for a fixed term, the Law might tolerate the voluntary forfeiture of his freedom.

12. *Ibid.* 13a.
13. Maimonides, *Hil. Avadim* 9:6.

Many people are too immature to cherish freedom; they prefer security. Others might choose slavery in order to obtain bulk sums at the time of sale. The Halachah, therefore, did not outlaw the transaction. However, the man who voluntarily sold himself into slavery could not expect thereby to enjoy the looser standard of sexual morality; he was not permitted to mate with non-Jewish female slaves. He could not choose a form of family life less holy than a freeman. Moreover, if he sought escape from other moral and religious standards by becoming indentured to Gentiles, his family was compelled to redeem him.[14]

More common than voluntary servitude was the long-term wage contract. Here the conflicting values are freedom and the sanctity of the pledged word. To protect the first value, the contract could not extend beyond the three-year period; otherwise the employer-employee relationship might approach the master-slave relationship. In addition, the employee was permitted to quit at any time, even before the expiration of the three year term. The employer was bound for the full period.

However, favoring the employee so that he could quit at any time hardly induces respect for the pledged word of a party to a contract. For that reason, if as a result of the breach of promise the employer suffered an irreparable loss, the employer's promise to increase the wage because of the threat of a walkout is unenforceable.[15] Thus the employee's freedom did not become license to do harm.

These simple principles are also applicable to organizations of laborers. The law recognizes the right of workers to organize and bargain with employers. The majority in the group may bind the minority. The individual worker may leave the group, but if he accepts employment it has to be on terms fixed by his colleagues.[16] The duly constituted municipal authorities may exercise some power over the decisions of the unions to insure the fairness of their regu-

14. *Ibid.* 2:7.
15. *Bava Metzia* 75b.
16. *Bava Batra* 8b and 9a.

lations.[17] But in the final analysis the Law seeks to safeguard the freedom of the individual laborers and the groups they constitute even as it strives to make them fulfill their commitments to each other and to their employers where there is injurious reliance upon their pledged word.

The Legitimacy of Children

The Law was also concerned with antithetical values in the question of legitimacy. On the one hand, the level of morality was to be maintained. Since courts can hardly deal with anything but overt acts, and since most sinful sexual relationships are consummated in secret, these would normally lie beyond the reach of the Law's sanctions. For that reason the Law had to employ a different kind of deterrent —the fear lest the illicit intercourse yield a bastard. On the other hand, this might require the abuse of the innocent, and in justice, paraphrasing a biblical and talmudical dictum, it is inevitably asked: "Shall one enjoy the sin and another pay the penalty?"

Here again we have a conflict in values. To promote sexual morality, the Law induces the dread that the sinner will bear the burden of an illegitimate child. The same Law, however, eloquently ordains that no one shall be punished for another's sin. Talmudic texts and commentaries give abundant evidence of the delicate balancing of the interests involved here. The social stigma and ostracism, and the consequence of illegitimacy were magnified to the horror and chagrin of all sensitive souls, while at the same time the Law made it virtually impossible to prove that any one was a bastard, and frowned upon the publicizing of such rare instances as were conclusively established.[18]

In an interesting set of hypothetical cases the Talmud informs us by inference that the stigma attached to illegitimacy was so great that the mothers of illegitimate infants

17. See M. Findling, *Techukat ha-Avodah* (Jerusalem: Schreiber, 1945), pp. 119-20.
18. *Kiddushin* 71a.

212

would rather murder than abandon them.[19] If one came upon a foundling whose mother took precautions to insure the child's survival, though she was then and there abandoning it, the foundling was presumed to be legitimate, for if the child was illegitimate the mother would rather have sought its death. So successfully did the Law induce the dread of illegitimacy!

Yet how could illegitimacy be proved? Children born out of wedlock were legitimate. Moreover, children born of certain unlawful marriages were legitimate. Only such children were bastards who were products of incestuous or adulterous relationships in which no lawful marriage could ever be consummated between the parties, such as a child born of cohabitation between mother and son. But how could one prove that a child was born of an adulterous relationship when every husband was presumed to be the father of all children that his wife bore? Even if the husband was away for years, who could tell but that he came on a magic carpet in the dead of night to cohabit with his wife and impregnate her?[20] Or who knows but that the wife conceived artificially? Even the mother's admission that the child was illegitimate had no probative value. She was incompetent to testify. Her husband's testimony was also unacceptable for he was conclusively presumed to be the father. If he sought to deny paternity of his wife's child, his testimony would place his wife in jeopardy as an adulteress, and he was therefore incompetent to testify. A natural father might testify that a person whom he knows to be his son is illegitimate. But who would be so foolish as to volunteer such information! And who could ever be sure that a particular child was his! That the community may have doubts is not sufficient basis for the attachment of an adverse status to the child. The Law made this clear: only they whose illegitimacy is certain are bastards, not they whose illegitimacy is doubtful.

19. *Ibid.* 73a, b.
20. Comments of Tosafot and Asheri on *Kiddushin* 73a, and text cited by them from Jerusalem Talmud.

The ancients were no less sensitive than moderns to the ethical problem involved in penalizing children for the sins of their parents. In one talmudic text a method is indicated for the termination of a marriage by annulment instead of divorce, and as a result acts of adultery theretofore committed by the wife are no longer punishable. Since the annulment is retroactive, it follows that the woman was not wedded when she cohabited with men other than the one whom she once regarded as her husband and who now, as a consequence of the annulment, was nothing more than one of her many sex partners. The Rabbis, however, asked about the status of children that she bore during the period of the marriage before its annulment. The retroactive annulment would make all of them legitimate since there was no adultery whatsoever. Would not this be a way of subverting the biblical directives on bastardy? The Rabbis answered: "Would that we had equally effective ways of removing all illegitimacies!" [21] And they did expound other ways.

True, they never competely declined to use the stigma of illegitimacy as a deterrent for illicit intercourse. The only effective deterrent had to involve the suffering of the guiltless. Yet the Law also reduces the incidence of such sufferings to a minimum. It encouraged a minimum of notoriety when a judgment of illegitimacy was inescapable. The Rabbis would communicate the information to each other clandestinely once in seven years.[22] Even when the Messiah comes and reveals unto each and every Jew the name of the tribe whence one descends, he will nonetheless withhold all information about legitimacy and illegitimacy. If a bastard —concealing his identity—had managed to marry into a family of lofty status, and by imputation had acquired the same status for himself the Messiah will not betray him! [23]

It is typical of the Law's method that it first creates the badge of illegitimacy, and then mitigates the evil consequences. The Law has to do both in pursuit of the interests

21. *Shitah Mekubetzet, Ketubot* 3a.
22. *Kiddushin* 71a. The medieval rabbis were more vigilant.
23. *Ibid.* 71a, and Mishneh Torah, Hilchot Melochim XII:3.

214

it seeks to fulfill. Again we see how halachic creativity involves a continuous oscillation between conflicting values.

A similar dialectic can be found in innumerable folios of the Talmud dealing with virginity. To impress girls with the importance of pre-marital chastity, the Law makes much of the maidenhead. Special ceremonies marked the marriage of the virgin. The amount specified for her benefit in the Ketubah (marriage contract) was double the amount indicated for a widow or divorcee. Only a virgin was eligible for marriage to the High Priest. And the Law did not indulge the girl to pretend to be that which she was not. The husband could complain to the court that he had been deceived. In fact, the wedding date was fixed on the eve of a day when the court would be in session in order that the husband might make diligent application for the annulment of the marriage for fraud, or at least the reduction of the benefits due his wife because she was not a virgin.[24] On the basis of such texts alone, one might even be tempted to say that the Law was overestimating the value of virginity per se. This, however, is not the case. The Rabbis were concerned rather with the importance of sanctions that would encourage chastity. As in the case of bastardy, they simply wanted a threat that would deter. Yet, if a husband did come complaining, it was almost impossible for him to prevail. Virtually any facts the wife offered in justification were believed. She might even claim that she was raped after her betrothal (*kiddushin*) and she would lose naught unless she were married to a priest. She might claim accidental loss of virginity, in which case the marriage was not affected even though the amount indicated in her Ketubah might be reduced (some rabbis maintained that even this loss would not be sustained). In communities where between betrothal and the consummation of the marriage—the interval was usually a year—the bride and groom were permitted to see each other without benefit of chaperone, she could attribute the loss of virginity to her premarital intimacy

24. *Ketubot* 2a.

with her husband. Rare indeed were the circumstances where the husband's complaint was of any avail. The Rabbis gave the husband cause for even greater distress. If he did complain they cross-examined him as to how he had become such an expert that he was able to distinguish between a virgin and a non-virgin. According to one view they could flog him for having been so promiscuous as to become an expert! In the same passage the Talmud tells us of rabbis before whom husbands came complaining and who in each case managed to restore the confidence of the husband in his wife's chastity by convincing him that he had erred. The net result of the dialectic is that the Law accentuated the importance of chastity by creating the threat of embarrassment, but the husband could hardly ever prevail against his wife. The Law promoted the value of chastity but did not forfeit any of its dedication to the dignity of women.

In this connection an appeal must be made to Israel's halachic authorities not to become obsessed with devotion to one value at the cost of another. When they ponder, for example, the status of Karaites whose family law for centuries has deviated considerably from the standards prevailing in the rest of the Jewish world, or when they deal with Jews returning from lands of exile where frequently, without fault on their part, there was little observance of the requirements of Jewish law, and as a result, the halachic authorities must reckon with the legitimacy or illegitimacy of many persons born to these families, then the total law and all the values they sought to conserve should be considered. If the rabbis seek to achieve an equilibrium of interests, a more moderate approach will make a great contribution to their people and the Law.

The Law of Divorce

Interestingly enough, the values of freedom and morality suggested in connection with the law of slavery also play an important role in the Jewish law of divorce. To expand the freedom of the parties to the marriage contract requires the

216

broadening of the area in which their consent is the ultimate consideration. Furthermore, to expand freedom one normally dispenses with formalities. The cause of morality, on the other hand, is best served by formal procedures and by limiting the freedom of the parties to do whatever pleases them. The cause of morality also requires that divorces have some finality about them. Let us see how these values affect the legal rules and make the Jewish law of divorce more intelligible to moderns.

The Roles of Husband and Wife

The marital status is initiated when the groom performs a symbolic act of acquisition with the consent of the bride or her father. Similarly, to dissolve the relationship the Torah demands that he initiate the action. The husband must cause the bill of divorce to be written. Critics of the Law question this focus of attention upon the male. However, it is not difficult to accept the logic of the Halachah which requires that he who created the state of *kiddushin* should be the one to undo it.

The husband's active role in creating the marriage bond is derived from a premise that is present in all of Judaism —including the Kabbalah—that the male is regarded as the active principle in the universe and the female as the passive principle. In nature it is the male who actualizes the reproductive potential of the female. In wooing, too, Judaism regarded the male as the proposer.

Yet the consent of the female is considered most important. Without it the marriage may not be consummated. The Law magnifies the role of the wife's consent in sexual relations too. Ultimately, her consent to a divorce became one of the Law's requirements. The need for her consent was slower in coming only because the Law was more preoccupied with her protection against hate and abandonment, and assumed that it served no purpose to keep her wedded to a man who did not respect her. The Ketubah was created to discourage divorce. It obliged the husband to make adequate provision for his wife's maintenance throughout the marriage and substantial payments in the event of divorce or widowhood. This obligation reduced the incidence of divorce and shielded the wife against desertion by her mate. Subsequently, the consent of the wife became a legal prerequisite to its validity. In this way the Law virtually equalized the roles of the spouses in both marriage and divorce, although it was still the male who was to perform the necessary acts.

The substitution of a rabbinic tribunal for the husband as the initiating agent has been proposed as a solution to the present problems of the Jewish law of divorce. But it is not a solution that conforms to the spirit of the Halachah and the Jewish principle that only husband and wife shall create or dissolve the marital status. As long as the Law does not transfer the solemnization of the marriage—or most other religious acts—to a rabbinic tribunal, it does not transfer the power to divorce from the husband to a rabbinic tribunal. The emphasis, therefore, on the role of the spouses as individuals in the creation and termination of the marital status is an instance of the Law's concern for personal freedom.

Formality and Finality

Still other values remain to be reckoned with. First, the formal character of the act of divorce might be an added deterrent to hasty divorce action by the husband. Second, who knows better than moderns how farcical divorce proceedings can be when only the spouses' consents are required, and how adverse are the effects of such proceedings on the moral standards of the community! Formality and finality promote these standards.

When a divorce is consummated, a sacred bond is being dissolved. Many grave consequences flow from it: the eligibility of the wife for another marriage, and her release from all the prohibitions against adultery. Jewish law, which generally dispenses with formalities in connection with most of its civil law, is, therefore, meticulously formal with regard to the bill of divorce. In addition, the divorce must be of complete finality, or else it is invalid. Remarriage to another is permitted without exception, otherwise the divorce is meaningless. The legal status flowing from modern decrees of separation is not countenanced. Through marriage, the cause of family morality is to be advanced; divorce must not be allowed to place it in jeopardy. Separation agreements or decrees in modern times imply sexual continence; human nature being what it is, adulterous and extramarital cohabitation often ensues. Jewish law cannot permit such conditions. A husband (other than a *Kohen*) who had divorced his wife may remarry her on one condition. If the wife had married someone else after her divorce, and her second marriage was terminated by her widowhood or divorce, she may not marry her first husband. This is a significant deterrent to hasty divorces and also to the lawful exchange of wives by husbands who would make a mockery of the marital relationship. Divorces are thus given the effect of finality. For this reason cohabitation between a man and a woman after their divorce might invalidate the divorce. The Law glorifies friendship, but does not favor the "friendship" of divorced couples of which modern society has a notorious incidence.

Because divorce is so final, and in the case of *Kohanim* absolutely irrevocable, the Law seeks to impress the spouses with the awesome character of the step they are taking. Anything less than a meticulously formal procedure would cause people to underestimate the sanctity of marriage, mentioned in the husband's recitation of an ancient wedding formula, "Behold thou art consecrated unto me." The dissolution of an act of consecration requires the services of a scribe who will prepare a personalized instrument at the husband's request. The Rabbis added the requirement that the instrument include an exact rendition of the attendant circumstances of time and place. Interestingly enough, since the divorce severed all bonds between the spouses, the bill

219

of divorce must be a detached piece of parchment, an object whose very detachment from mother earth symbolizes the rendering asunder of two individuals.

Reformers in Judaism have made of divorce a matter of purely secular concern. The Rabbis would not tolerate a condition born of a solemn act of consecration to come to an end without the Law's involvement. Even animals once consecrated to Temple use cannot pass to another status without some formal act; even their death does not release them from their erstwhile holiness. How could the Law be less attentive to marital relationship! Talmudic authorities may have debated the validity of divorce granted by non-Jewish courts.[25] However, the weight of authority and practice supported the position that divorce, like marriage, must follow a Torah pattern.[26] Tradition prescribes how the divorce shall be written, attested, and delivered. The slightest variation might invalidate it.

The Conflict of Values

The formality and finality of the divorce are means used by the Law to insure a high regard for the sanctity of the marital relationship. Occasionally these means came into conflict with the ideal of consent which, philosophically speaking, is a badge of human freedom. Strict formal requirements in any branch of jurisprudence are usually the greatest hindrance to the fulfillment of the consent (or will) of a person. The Law has to veer between these values in many a situation.

If consent is all-important, then conditions ought to be permitted. Obviously conditions detract from finality. Conditions may or may not be fulfilled, and the divorce may or may not become effective.

The Law, however, does permit the stipulation of conditions. The conditions most often suggested in the Talmud are those benefitting the wife—conditions that would pre-

25. *Gittin* 10b.
26. See I. Porat, *Mevo ha-Talmud* (Cleveland: 1941), pp. 60-62.

vent her from becoming a "grass widow" or spare her the burden of the levirate law. In her interest the Law's concern for finality is compromised and the area of consent is expanded. However, the Talmud suggests that often conditions tend to make the wife even more the prisoner of her marital bonds. If, for example, a husband should grant a divorce conditioned upon his not returning home by a certain date, and he should be prevented from returning by unavoidable accident or duress, the condition ought not to be regarded as fulfilled. If so, no such conditional divorce would ever in fact emancipate a pious woman. She would always fear that non-fulfillment of the condition was due to duress or unavoidable accident. For that reason the Rabbis rule that duress or unavoidable accident does not affect the divorce. The Law makes the value of the divorce's finality more important than the value of consent. The husband is presumed *ab initio* to waive his right ever to claim duress or unavoidable accident.

For similar reasons, the Law sometimes compromises its concern for the rigidly formal character of the divorce and its manner of execution. In the event of an emergency the Law relaxes the strict requirements circumscribing the husband's designation of an agent to give his wife the writ. If the husband was en route to captivity and wanted to release his wife from the marriage bond, or if the husband was dying and wanted to release his wife from the ties of the levirate law, his authorization of the divorce could be most informal. In such a case the Sages expanded the area of consent and made it the overriding factor. Form was sacrificed.

Yet in other situations they did the very opposite. They restricted the power of the husband to revoke the agency he had created to give his wife a divorce. Their most revolutionary achievement was their use of force against the husband, compelling him to say that he consents to the execution of a divorce to his wife in such cases when they felt that the marriage ought to be terminated. The wife can precipitate such action in many instances. Sometimes she

221

might forfeit her Ketubah, but she nonetheless obtains her freedom. Here actual consent was ignored altogether and all the emphasis was placed on form.

How did the Rabbis rationalize their performance? They were loath to tamper with biblical requirements. But they presume that every marriage is consummated with the understanding that it is subject to rabbinic authority and that their will is the will of the spouses forever. The consent on which they rely is an imputed consent—indeed, imputed from the date of the marriage.

The conflict between the values of finality and consent is most evident in the later development of the Law's attitude toward conditional divorces. It has already been observed that to permit conditions in the granting of divorces is to magnify the area of consent and to diminish the element of finality. It is interesting that when the wife's consent to the divorce was not a prerequisite for its validity and there were few restrictions on the husband, the Law permitted the use of conditions in the hope that fewer divorces would become final. But when the wife's consent to the divorce became a prerequisite for its execution and delivery, (about 1000 C.E.), the granting of conditional divorces was generally outlawed. The communities could well afford to be more concerned about finality than consent, particularly since the special circumstances in which the use of conditions might be helpful to the wife could be handled differently. Yet until today some forms of conditional divorce are in use, as in the case of soldiers going off to battle who, following the precedent of King David's soldiers, divorce their wives conditionally or absolutely pending their return by a fixed date.

It thus appears that the Law's dialectic with regard to divorce veers between concern for the sanctity of the marital relationship and concern for the freedom of the parties.

The Present

It is with regard to divorce law that there is presently the greatest need for halachic creativity. Those who clamor for change make it appear that the Halachah is unfair to women. Those who resist change rest their case on numerous maxims which make one dread any tampering with the sanctity of the marital status. Neither group does justice to the Halachah. The former ignore the overwhelming evidence to be found in thousands of talmudic folios which deal with the obligations of a husband to a wife. The latter freeze the Halachah against further development by ignoring the dialectic which is the very essence of the halachic process.

True, the talmudic dialectic is not necessarily a quest for a reconciliation of opposites in a new synthesis. More often, it seeks the retention of the antithetical values and their fulfillment in the legal order. Thus, tradition continues to live on, but the future is not altogether determined by the past. The dialectic confirms the role of history while allowing for progress. However, he who takes one polar view or another all the time seldom equivocates. If the Israeli rabbinate were to follow this course in matters of personal status it would rapidly forfeit its exclusive jurisdiction in this area. Fortunately, it appreciates its grave responsibility. However, in its fear of, or respect for, the extremists it often fails to take the steps which it knows are required by the halachic process and consonant with its goals. Perhaps a candid articulation of the process and its goals would not only enhance the general appreciation of the Law and contribute to its development, but also relegate the extremists to peripheral status in the traditionalist Jewish community, where they can then serve in the role of vigilantes as in any social system. Certainly something must be done to prevent a recurrence of the late Chief Rabbi Herzog's sad confession that he had devised halachic means of promoting the equality of men and women in rights of inheritance but was prevented from implementing his decision by extremist colleagues in Israel.[27] The result was that the people of Israel ultimately had to ignore their

27. See I. Herzog, "Hatzaat Tekanot bi-Yerushot," *Talpioth* (Nisan 5713), pp. 36-37.

halachic experts and legislate, through their popularly elected Knesset, a law not based on Halachah but in fact closer to halachic axiology than that of the position of the Chief Rabbi's controversialists. It is important that the Knesset shall not be forced by rabbinic intransigence to act in matters of family law. The *Kulturkampf* in Israel would then be on in earnest and a hopeless schism would inevitably follow. The Israeli rabbinate can avert such a tragedy. It can further develop the talmudic dialectic and not freeze the law in one or another pole of the antinomies.

Chapter Two

ETHICAL NORMS IN THE JEWISH
LAW OF MARRIAGE

Do ethical considerations really play the dominant role
in the evolution of Jewish law? Many make the boast. Few
substantiate the claim. Even when they do offer isolated
illustrations of the manner in which moral values influenced
the Halachah, the illustrations are usually peripheral to the
mainstream of Halachic development. The consequences are
deplorable.

Jewish youth in whom we seek to induce a respect for
Talmudic learning is nurtured on generalizations, without
authentic illustrative materials. Even students in Rabbinical
seminaries are taught to become expert in the analysis of
Talmudic legal concepts without reference to their ethical
significance. Furthermore, while most Zionists, even secularists and laborites, agree that the legal system of the State
of Israel ought to be rooted in the lofty principles of traditional Jewish law, few scholars articulate the ethical and
moral postulates of that law. The hope of Zionists has inspired very little creative analysis and synthesis. Even the
religious parties have done very little in this connection.
Lastly, there is a decided trend today in the philosophy of
law to divorce ethical norms from legal norms. Austin in
Anglo-American legal thought, and Kelsen on the Continent,
gave impetus to this movement. Jewish apologists must
therefore be more convincing than ever that ethical consid-

erations should be of paramount importance in legal development.

This essay proposes to illustrate by reference to only one simple problem how rewarding the effort can be. The problem represents but one wave in the sea of the Talmud and all references are limited to a single tractate, *Kiddushin.*[1]

Kiddushin is still the principal source for the Jewish law of betrothal. Its folios discuss the manner in which a Jew takes a wife. The marriage status itself, and the rights and privileges thereunto appertaining, are discussed elsewhere. *Kiddushin* is concerned principally with the manner of bringing the status into being. However, one discovers early in one's study that though today all Rabbis—Orthodox, Conservative and Reform—require the groom, with the presentation of the wedding ring, to recite the same words to his bride, the Talmud itself is far less formalistic. The Talmud provides for considerable variation both in the words recited and the object given. What our sages sought to assure was not a rigid form for the ceremony but rather the unequivocal character of the parties' consent. *Marriage was to be consensual. This was the ethical value that the law sought to fulfill.* As a matter of fact, because of this preoccupation with consent, the modern law of contract in European and American law could have been, and was, derived principally from the Talmudic analysis of consent to marry.

That the Bible made the woman's consent to marry of paramount importance the Rabbis gleaned from the verse in Genesis which revealed that Rebecca was asked whether she wanted to marry the patriarch Isaac. Halachic exegesis, however, found a better source, a legal argument. In connection with the contract to marry, the Bible used the term *Kiha,* a term employed to describe Abraham's contract to buy land from the Hittites. Mutual consent is a prerequisite for a sale. It must therefore be a prerequisite for a marriage (2a and b).

Conceivably, this analysis might be challenged by point-

1. All page references are to the Tractate *Kiddushin.*

226

ing to the fact that Jewish law permitted a father to give his daughter away in marriage without her consent. Jewish law apparently did not deny the father all of the powers he enjoyed over his daughters in primitive society. This would imply that the woman's consent was hardly the ethical value to be conserved. It must be remembered, however, that in such a case at least the father's consent was a prerequisite. The father's consent then became the historical antecedent for the woman's consent when the father's rights over his daughter were virtually abolished. The abolition, though accomplished long ago, involved a slow process. The father's power was originally restricted to the daughter's minority— until she reached twelve and one-half years of age (3b). Then the Rabbis expressed their opposition to marriages before the daughters reached puberty (41a). The father's power was thus reduced to a maximum period from puberty to age twelve and one-half. Even the Biblical right of the father to sell his daughter as a slave when she was a minor was understood to be a step that would be consummated by the marriage of the daughter to the master. And this too was frowned upon, for the father who exercised this right was considered a sinner—his need to sell his daughter was regarded as the consequence of his non-righteous living to which a father would hesitate confessing (20a). Even when she was thus sold, her bondage lasted only until she reached puberty (14b). She was then completely emancipated unless she had wedded her master or his son. If, in the Middle Ages, the marriage of young children was reinstituted, it was, as the Tosafists explain (41a), because life was very precarious for Jews, and fathers wanted to see their children settled before poverty, exile, or murder overtook them.

That our sages regarded child marriages arranged by the father as the exception, rather than the rule, can be gleaned from an examination of almost all the illustrative case material of the tractate *Kiddushin* in which the woman herself, and not the father, is regarded as the contracting party. And so far as the woman herself was concerned, it can be said that it was her consent to marry that was the value our sages sought to advance. Thus, when the State of Israel recently made the contracting of child marriages a crime, and raised the age at which consent could be given, it fulfilled a Talmudic purpose. Furthermore, when a millennium ago Rabbi Gershom made the wife's consent a prerequisite to divorce, he was also extending a Talmudic value.

In view of the fact that the woman's consent to marry, as well as the man's, is essential, the Rabbis found that the law of sales was most relevant. It was not that they regarded women as chattels who could be bought and sold. It was rather, as already noted, that in sales of property one finds maximum insistence on mutual consent and understanding. That is why they chose to link the law of betrothal with the law of sales.

This can be gleaned from one apparently far-fetched hypothetical question discussed in *Kiddushin* (7a). The Rabbis had considered the possibility of applying to the contract to marry analogies from the law of consecrated things. In a sense, when a man takes unto himself a wife, she becomes consecrated to him alone, and forbidden to others. Thus she could be compared to things that had been consecrated to Temple service and could therefore be used only for restricted purposes. The rules of law pertaining to consecrated things—called *Hekdesh*—could have played a part in the development of the legal concept of betrothal as did the law of sales. The titles of the first two chapters of *Kiddushin* are revealing in this connection. The first chapter is called, "A Woman Is Acquired." The second chapter is called, "A Man Consecrates." Now, the Talmud poses this hypothetical question: "What if a man, using the correct form in every other respect, should nonetheless say that he consecrates only half of the woman?" If the law of sales is applicable, one can acquire half ownership in a thing. If, however, the law of consecrated things applies, then if one consecrates half of an object, the whole of it becomes holy and is subject to all the relevant prohibitions. And which rule shall be employed in the case of the betrothal of part of a woman? The initial impulse of any modern would be to

228

say that in the interest of womanly dignity one should avoid the concept of sale wherever possible and resort to the other more refined analogy of consecration. Our sages, however, ruled otherwise—and precisely out of respect for the ethical value of consent. Their decision was that the rules of sale would apply. Precisely because they respected the rights of women, they said that when the woman had consented to only partial betrothal, one dare not—without her express will—impute any more than that to her. Her consent must be real, not constructive. Therefore, having consented to only half marriage, we cannot automatically regard her as wholly wedded. However, since there can be no partial sale of a thing which cannot be shared by partners, and we know that two men cannot share the same woman, there can therefore be no partial betrothal at all and the whole act of the husband is null. Thus by the mundane-sounding law of sale, rather than the lofty-sounding law of consecrated things, a further safeguard was built around the woman's unequivocal consent.

Sales consummated by mistake with regard to the object sold or the price paid, or sales consummated on conditions which remain unfulfilled, can be rescinded. Marriages, too, which involve misunderstanding or unperformed promises, or unfulfilled conditions, were null and void. The parties must themselves be what they represent themselves to be, or must own what they represented they had, or do what they promised to do (49b).

However, parties might so take advantage of the great latitude permitted them with respect to conditions and representations that the institution of marriage may become very unstable. Two people might agree to wed on condition that the husband never absents himself from his wife for any prolonged period. They bear children and decades later the husband deserts. The marriage would be automatically annulled by this act. The children would be regarded retroactively as born out of wedlock. The wife would no longer be prohibited from marrying members of her husband's family, who heretofore, because of her marriage to her hus-

229

band, had been within prohibited degrees of consanguinity. She could now marry her brother-in-law or her father-in-law. The stability of Jewish family life would be in jeopardy if family relations were to be contingent upon conditions whose fulfillment was never certain.

Such considerations impelled our sages to formalize and institutionalize the marriage contract which heretofore could have involved whimsical and frivolous aspects. They had to impose limitations on the area of consent. They had to make marriage not only a matter of contract but a matter of status.

This is especially interesting because the distinguished legal historian, Sir Henry Maine, regarded the movement of progressive societies, as distinguished from static societies, as a movement "from status to contract." [2] Status signified personal conditions which were not the result of agreement. They flowed rather from the fact of family dependency. Members of the family remained tied to the family nexus dominated by the head—the father. However, with the gradual dissolution of family dependency and the growth of individual obligation in its place, we find that it is the individual who is steadily substituted for the family as the unit of which the law takes account, and arrangements entered into by individuals constitute contracts.

By Maine's standard, Jewish law was exceedingly progressive. At an early stage Jewish law changed the position of woman in the creation of a marriage from status to contract. However, Maine's thesis is presently regarded as faulty because in more complex societies there is often a reversion from contract to status. The law in modern industrial states tends to protect the right and duties of weaker groups by viewing them as if they were bound to "status" instead of free to contract as they please. The protection of labor unions in America, for example, required this reversion. In Jewish law, too, the protection of women required a reversion to the concept of status and a curtailment of the

2. *Ancient Law* (ed. Pollock), p. 174.

scope of the free contract. There had to be a limitation on conditions. And the process of limiting conditions—whose beginning the Talmud reveals—so developed in post-Talmudic times that the Rabbis ultimately prohibited all conditions.

The principal limitation on conditions which the Talmud prescribed was that they shall not negate Biblical requirements. If husband and wife stipulated that their marriage would obligate neither to cohabit with each other, the stipulation was null. Certain property rights which the marriage status involved could be waived, but never that which was of the very essence of the marriage relationship. Furthermore, purely whimsical conditions—"I thee wed if thou wilt ascend to heaven"—are null.

In addition to nullifying certain conditions the Rabbis decided that the language used in conditions must be given the meanings commonly held in the community. The parties could not argue that they had entertained unusual meanings. Even if a man contracted to marry on condition that he was wise or strong or rich, neither he nor she could maintain that standards of wisdom, strength or wealth, superior or inferior to those held in the community were intended (49b). Too much regard for the subjective would defeat the ultimate end of the definiteness and stability of the marriage relation.

On ethical grounds, however, two exceptions were made to this rule and the subjective was taken into account. If the man stipulated the state of his own mind as a condition to the marriage—his being a righteous man or a villain—the condition was null. If he stipulated that he was righteous, the marriage was valid even if he had the foulest reputation in the community. "Perhaps he had repented for one moment" (*ibid*). If he stipulated that he was wicked, even if he were a saint, the marriage was also valid. Perhaps he was an idolater in one of his thoughts (*ibid*). His subjective state could not become the basis for a condition. Its truth or falsehood could not be subject to legal proof. Jewish law would not require a man to prove that he was righteous or wicked. The privacy of states of mind was inviolable and conditions with respect to them were nullities. Even present-day America can use a reminder of the inviolability of states of mind.

Thus we see that while the ethical value of mutual consent was basic in the development of the Jewish law of betrothal, some limitations had to be imposed on the latitude which the parties enjoyed in creating the marital status to suit their own whims. However, the Talmud had already indicated at least two important areas in which conditions would be null and void. These areas suggest two added ethical postulates. First, a marriage cannot be contracted so that it does not fulfill its most natural aim—sexual gratification. Second, a marriage cannot be contracted the establishment of whose validity would involve the invasion of the privacy of a person's state of mind. The Rabbis simply ignored such conditions as if they had not been made at all.

To create a marital status, the declaration of intent to marry must needs be accompanied by the performance of any of three formal acts in the presence of witnesses. The formal act "clinched" the contract. (1) The parties could immediately cohabit. However, to do so with two persons present was hardly chaste and consequently this method was held to be morally objectionable. (2) The husband could deliver to the wife a written instrument constituting the marriage. Where there was a dearth of scribes, this method was not popular. (3) The husband could deliver to the wife an object of value. This became the usual procedure, culminating in the modern practice of marrying with a ring.

The object of value might even be an intangible delight. To such an extent did the Rabbis expand the scope of the object of value that they ruled that the marriage could be contracted even by the bride's giving of a gift to the groom. If the groom were a distinguished person and his acceptance of her gift was a delight to her, that delight would be sufficient to fulfill the requirement that she enjoy a gain. This is analogous to our modern situation when a famous person honors a university by accepting its honorary degree. Moreover, the instantaneous performance of a valuable service stipulated by the bride would be sufficient. The object of value was not necessarily a physical thing, but included any valuable privilege as well.

One's study of *Kiddushin,* however, reveals that while the concept of a thing of value was an exceedingly broad one in Halachic exegesis, the Talmud was equally concerned to eliminate a loan from the concept's scope. The groom could not create the marital status by waiving a debt due him from the bride (6b). Certainly the waiver was a gift she would appreciate. It requires little imagination to realize this. Yet, ostensibly because the bride received nothing tangible at the time of the marriage, no marriage was consummated. But why was not her delight in the waiver of her debt as good as other intangible delights which were held to be sufficient consideration? Many Rabbis in post-Talmudic times so held, but required that the husband make it explicit that the marriage was consummated with the delight of the waiver of the debt as the thing given. Maimonides, on the other hand, construed the Talmudic text differently and eliminated the debt altogether as a possibility for the consummation of a marriage. He does approve of the use of a debt as the consideration for the sale of property. The waiver of a preexisting debt by the purchaser to the seller is sufficient to pass title. Not so, however, for marriage. Was it not because the Talmud, without saying so, regarded a marriage predicated on the waiver of a debt by the creditor-husband as peonage? No more than a person could be enslaved for debt could a woman become bound in marriage for the same consideration. If the Rabbis frowned upon fathers selling their daughters because they were in debt, would they not also frown upon a woman contracting to marry, in lieu of paying her creditor? Furthermore, Maimonides derived from *Kiddushin* a prohibition to marry in consideration of the groom's loaning money to the bride. This resembled the taking of interest.

The modern law of contracts derived most of its concepts of *causa* and consideration from the Talmudic analysis of

233

the manner in which a marital status is accomplished. Even the Talmudic problem of pre-existing debts has its analogues in modern legal texts. But the legal systems of Europe and America which long tolerated the sale of a debtor for his debt, and ignored the Talmudic injunction against it, also found it difficult to grasp the implied taboo against peonage which the Talmud revealed in its folios on the marriage of women debtors to their male creditors.

One other important species of property could not be given by the husband to the wife in order to fulfill the requirement of a thing of value. These were things which neither the husband nor the wife could consume—things in which either might have a proprietary right but only for the purpose of giving them away to those who could consume them. For example, heave offerings due to the priests were items which a non-priest could not eat. The farmer who had set them aside could, however, name the priest who was to receive and enjoy them. Yet if he wanted to betroth a woman by transferring that privilege to her so that she, instead of he, could name the person who would become the owner, his act would be a nullity. The transfer of that privilege is not the giving of a thing of value—even if one would pay a considerable sum for it (58a).

This Talmudic ruling, however, reveals a philosophy of property which has profound ethical significance. Property generally might be defined in terms of rights for use and enjoyment. Or property might be defined in terms of power. Morris Raphael Cohen once defined property as nothing more than the power to exclude others. For that reason he regarded the concepts of property and sovereignty as kin. The owner exercises sovereignty over others by excluding them from the enjoyment of that which is his. Upon this type of lordship Jewish law frowned. Lordship over the earth and all its contents belongs to God. God gives man the right to consume and enjoy His bounty. Incidental to man's right to consume and enjoy is an almost unavoidable right to share and to give away. When, however, one's power over a thing is limited to its disposal, Jewish law hesitated to regard such power as property. That too closely resembles the exercise of lordship or sovereignty and man should not act the part of God.

The Jewish philosophy of property still begs for thorough analysis. Yet in *Kiddushin* we have one insight which only the Halachah can make clear. The emphasis in the Jewish concept is that of use and enjoyment and not lordship. *Property is intended to help make life more abundant and must therefore not be turned into an instrument for tyranny over one's fellowman.* Hence, marriage cannot be constituted by a transfer from husband to wife of a power which sustained his ego and shall now sustain hers.

Very few modern states permit marriage by proxy. In *Kiddushin,* we find not only that the Rabbis sanctioned such marriages, but also that they had the advanced conception of agency which prevails in modern law, a conception unknown to Roman law.

Roman law held that an agent who buys property for his principal is regarded as having made the purchase for himself. The principal acquires title when the agent resells to him. Precisely because Jewish law was broad enough in its scope so that it included matters religious, criminal and civil, and students of the Law became proficient in all its phases, it was easy to enrich each field with concepts borrowed from the other. And in the law of sanctuary offerings one finds a theory of representative capacity which is suitable for an advanced conception of agency. Moderns usually generalize that a system of law is primitive when it fails to differentiate between religious, criminal and civil law, or between divine, public and private law. Jewish law had all of these distinctions but regarded all as parts of the one Law.

The Rabbis thus remembered that the person who offers the Paschal lamb for his family group acts in a representative capacity (41b). His act for all is credited to each individually. This could, therefore, apply to any and all situations. Any man may choose to act through a representative.

235

What is particularly impressive is that the agent is a representative. Popular understanding to the contrary notwithstanding, a man's agent is not identical with himself. The Talmud was careful to point this out, for if the agent—when acting for the principal—is vested with the personality of the principal, then like the principal, he would be incompetent to testify with regard to the transaction. The Rabbis held instead that the agent's act is a representative act, while his person is not the principal's person. Therefore, he would not be incompetent to testify (42a). Furthermore, he can contract to marry a woman on behalf of his principal but may never consummate the marriage by sexual intercourse. That also explains, as later Rabbis have indicated, why a Jew cannot make an agent for himself to perform such commandments as involve the performance of a physical act—the placing of phylacteries on hand and head, the eating of *Matzoh* and *Moror* on Passover, or the taking of a *Lulab* on Tabernacles.

The conception that the agent is the principal's representative was borrowed by the canon lawyers of the Middle Ages and introduced into European law. In origin, however, the concept is religious. As in religious living Jews are responsible for each other, so generally they ought to have the capacity to represent each other. The concept also had political implications. The land of Israel, it was argued, was divided among the tribes with the head of each tribe acting in a representative capacity for his constituents (*ibid*). And thus even government of the people by their representatives has its roots in the same Talmudic discussion.

The most remarkable ethical insight to be gleaned, however, from the Talmudic discussion on agency is the exception to the rule. One cannot create an agent to commit a crime or a sin. The agent alone is responsible for his misdeed. The principal is not punished. Judaism recognized no accessory before the fact. Thus, if one hires another to commit a murder, only the actual murderer is tried for the offense. The rationale of the Talmudic rule is religious in origin. The agent is a free moral agent. He should not have chosen to ignore God's will and heed his principal's instead. Therefore, he alone shall answer to the law. And from the point of view of human behavior, this emphasis on the individual responsibility of the agent may have been a great deterrent to crime. Too often criminals conspire in groups and act in defiance of the law as they derive moral support and strength from co-conspirators. Jewish law reminded them that only he who consummates the murder or theft will be punished.

Returning to the law of betrothal, however, one finds marriages by proxy permitted, but not recommended (41a). A woman particularly should be protected from hurt and embarrassment. Her husband should see her before they are bound to each other. If a marriage is consummated without his having previously seen her, he may find himself wedded to one whom he will come to hate in his heart, thus creating a situation in which he will violate the Biblical injunction *to love one's friend as one's self*.

In *Kiddushin* a multitude of legal problems other than the creation of the marital status are discussed. Many of these pertain particularly to the law of persons, and warrant a separate analysis. In this chapter only one issue was examined—the formal manner of taking a wife. One would not have expected so simple an issue to evoke so much attention. Yet when ethical considerations absorb the jurist-theologian, he probes to fulfill the will of God for any act he undertakes to do and the taking of a wife is hardly one of the least important.

Chapter Three

HALACHIC PROGRESS: RABBI MOSHE FEINSTEIN'S
IGROT MOSHE ON *EVEN HA-EZER*

I

In contemporary halachic creativity rabbis are rarely daring. This complaint is often heard whenever Jews meet to discuss the present plight of Jewish law. It is, therefore, an event joyously to be hailed when so renowned a scholar as Rabbi Moshe Feinstein publishes a volume of responsa [1] which reveals not only erudition of exceptional breadth and depth but also courage worthy of a *Gadol* in an age of unprecedented challenge to our cherished Halachah.

It is well known that in no area of Jewish law is there now so keen and pressing a need for liberalism as in the area of family law. No other area involves hardships comparable to those which arise when a man or a woman cannot remarry because of the intransigence, insanity, or disappearance of a spouse. This is called the *Agunah* problem. It involves loneliness, and loneliness is a curse second to none. Our Rabbis explicity rate it as worse than death. For most American Jews the loneliness that is the consequence of commitment to Jewish law is no problem. They simply ignore the law. Enough Conservative and Reform rabbis are available to remarry them even when their first marriage

1. *Igrot Moshe* on *Even Ha-ezer*, New York 1961.

238

is not duly dissolved by a *Get* (divorce) or without proof of death adequate according to Halachic standards. Only the devout and observant now pay the price of loyalty to the law. And Orthodox rabbis are less able to help them today than ever before in Jewish history.

In the State of Israel at least some relief is afforded by the exercise of coercion against spouses who capriciously block the remarriage of another. What, however, can be done in a Jewish community such as America has—the largest in the world and completely voluntary! Persuasion often fails. Sometimes spouses even enjoy the exploitation of Jewish law for their own nefarious purpose and taunt their victims for their concern about a *Get*. No rabbi of experience has ever been spared the heartache resulting from his helplessness in the face of situations which beg for resolution. Rarely, however, does one undertake to do what Rabbi Feinstein has done. He has opened the door to relief in countless cases. Many will undoubtedly seek to close the door, but perhaps some will undertake to open it even wider.

This review will describe what Rabbi Feinstein has done and will also essay to describe why he is Halachically as well as philosophically to be sustained and encouraged. His effort, and that of Israel's Chief Rabbi Yitzhak Nissim in connection with the personal status of the Jews of India, are the first major breakthroughs for the exponents of a truly viable Halachah. Neither, alas, will be enthusiastically hailed by reactionary colleagues. Indeed, the emasculation of their decisions may come instead.

II

About one hundred fifty responsa are included in Rabbi Feinstein's volume. The overwhelming majority of them deal with family. One important exception is that responsum in which the author permits the purchase and ownership of shares of stock in a corporation whose activities involve desecration of the Sabbath. If the stockholder does not acquire control of the corporation and his power is limited to insignificant participation in the election of officers and directors, then he is not to be regarded as an owner of, or partner in, the business but rather as a potential claimant to profits, and no more. This is Jewish law accommodating itself to the modern economy and the desire of Orthodox Jews to invest in securities. A moral philosopher might well question whether, on the basis of cherished Biblical and Talmudic economic perspectives, Jewish law might not do better to curb the growth of corporations, the lack of social responsibility of their managers, and the speculative propensities of their shareholders. However, such a voice would be too visionary for our times, and, alas, even the religious parties in Israel are not ready for genuine Torah guideposts for the economic development of the new state.

In the area of family law, Rabbi Feinstein's accommodation to the facts of modern life is very much to be applauded. Liberalism in this sphere advances the objectives of the Halachah, which always sought to prevent the suffering of spouses who, for no fault of theirs, were denied the right to remarry. For that reason several responsa hold the wives of Nazi victims to be widows even though proof of death of the husbands does not meet the standards heretofore prevailing. The same ruling applied also to one widowed by an airplane crash.

Similarly, a definite ruling is given with regard to artificial insemination from a donor other than the husband: the child is held legitimate, and the wife is not regarded as an adulteress. Furthermore, she and her husband are permitted to continue their marital status.

The responsa that are of greatest importance are those which permit husband or wife to remarry without giving or receiving a *Get*. Orthodox rabbis have heretofore hesitated to suspend this requirement no matter how the marriage was first contracted—whether civilly or by an invalid religious ceremony. It was assumed that, since the two spouses lived as husband and wife and represented themselves to be such in the eyes of society and state, their marriage could not be dissolved without a *Get*. Rabbi Feinstein dissents. If the marriage was solemnized by a judge or even a rabbi who is not meticulous in his concern for the requirements of the Halachah, the marriage is a nullity, and either spouse can subsequently remarry without the Jewish bill of divorce. This decision is sound. Most Reform Rabbis, for example, have suspended the need for a *Get*. They assign divorce exclusively to the secular authorities. Thus Jews who enter into marriages according to Reform rituals are, from the very outset, creating the presumption that theirs is not a marriage according to the Halachah, and from the point of view of the Halachah their marriage should not be regarded as one that must be dissolved according to the Halachah. The State of Israel may one day have need of this decision. If the secularists succeed in introducing civil marriage and divorce in Israel, then the Rabbinate would do well to proclaim in advance that such marriages are not to be regarded as involving *Kiddushin* (consecration) but rather an exclusively non-Halachic status for the purpose of support and inheritance, and that consequently no traditional *Get* will be required for their dissolution.

There is abundant authority in earlier respona of great scholars for all thus far reported from Rabbi Feinstein's volume. However, he deserves our approbation for reaffirming the rulings in our contemporary situation when Orthodox rabbis have become so panicky about liberalism that they have "frozen" the law beyond the wildest expectations of more saintly forebears. But there is one area in which Rabbi Feinstein forges ahead of predecessors. He permits husband or wife to remarry without a *Get* when there is reasonable assurance that if either had known some important fact about the other in advance of the marriage they would not have entered upon the marriage. Rabbi Feinstein has revived the Talmudic notion of "marriage by mistake," and he does not limit it, as the Tosafists of the Middle Ages did, to the period intervening between betrothal and consummation of the nuptials. According to Rabbi Feinstein, the spouse may avail himself or herself of the fraud or concealment at any time after the marriage. Thus a husband may remarry without a *Get* if he discovered that his wife could not bear him children because of an affliction that existed prior to the marriage. Similarly, the wife may remarry without a *Get* if she discovers that her husband is incapable of sexual intercourse or that he was committed to a mental hospital for a period prior to his marriage and became ill again during the marriage. The presumption is simple: She would not have married him had she known all the facts.

What is especially noteworthy about Feinstein's desire to relieve anguish and pain is his readiness to ignore prior authorities when their conclusions are antithetical to his. Thus, with the zeal of a great humanitarian he cites the *Ein Yitzhak* who permitted a widow to remarry without *Halitzah* because he held the marriage of the widow to be a nullity, but he fails to cite the *Shevut Yaakov* whom the *Ein Yitzhak* cites and who unequivocally arrived at a conclusion opposite to that of Rabbi Feinstein in an almost identical case. Such is the power of *Heterah* (leniency) in the hands of a Talmudic giant! And we thought our generation was altogether bereft of them!

It is also noteworthy that the eminent Rabbi Weinberg of Montrieux ended one of his responsa, published in *Noam,* with a prayer that one day some rabbi will be bold enough to rule as Rabbi Feinstein has. He lived to see his prayer fulfilled.

III

There is no doubt but that the liberalization of Jewish family law can best be done through the broader exercise of the inherent power of a *Beth Din* to annul marriages for fraud or mistake. Of course, the consequence will be that the issue of marriages subsequently annulled will be regarded as born out of wedlock. But in Jewish law this does not mean illegitimacy—or even serious consequential stigma. Altogether, to solve the *Agunah* problem without annulling marriages is impossible. Even in Israel, where coercion against the recalcitrant spouse is feasible, the court may be helpless if the recalcitrant spouse is in another jurisdiction or escapes there before the court's relief is sought. Furthermore, in the event of the husband's insanity the wife is absolutely without a remedy even in Israel unless the marriage can be annulled. An insane husband is not competent to delegate his authority or power to the *Beth Din*. For these reasons, as well as others, the abortive attempt of the Conservative movement in the United States to solve the problem with an eye exclusively on the *Get* was unfortunate. It seized upon the least progressive alternative (as did some American Jewish journalists) and placed in jeopardy the course Rabbi Feinstein is pursuing.

The Talmud assumes in many of its tractates that marriages by mistake are void or voidable. Indeed, such marriages can be annulled not only because of facts known to one of the spouses before the marriage and concealed from the other, but also because of facts that no one could possibly have known in advance. Thus the Talmud queries why a widow who is childless cannot annul her marriage to her deceased husband on the assumption that she would not have consented to wed him had she known in advance that she would one day require *Halitzah.*[2] The answer is that we legally presume acquiescence on the theory that a woman prefers to be married even to a bad risk than remain a spinster. Yet this is a presumption as to a state of mind. And this state of mind is subject to change. Indeed, it has changed in our day. Most Jewish women today would never acquiesce to marriages which would ultimately involve them in an *Agunah* situation because of the husband's insanity, lack of masculinity, or recalcitrance to give a religious divorce. These are conditions which often exist potentially in advance of the marriage, albeit unknown to either spouse in advance. Certainly they are as much potential facts as is

2. The Tosafists would limit the query to deaths after betrothal but before the consummation of marriage. Rabbi Feinstein does not make the distinction.

243

the subsequent death of the husband without children when *Halitzah* is required, and but for the presumption with regard to an older generation of females who preferred any kind of marriage to none, our Sages would have waived the requirements of *Halitzah*. Now, however, women feel quite differently. The lot of the spinster is not as pathetic as it once was and is preferred to that of the *Agunah*. The *Agunah* is far more miserable, and her lot is far less enviable. Ours is the duty to reckon with the change.

Rabbi Feinstein hesitates to go so far. He did annul the marriage of a woman whose husband became insane after the marriage because he had been similarly ill prior to the marriage, and he so ruled even though the husband appeared sane at the time of the marriage and thereafter served for two years in the military establishment of the United States. Nonetheless, the subsequent development of the malady was enough to warrant annulment of the marriage. Insanity—actual or potential—is sufficient cause for either spouse not to want the marriage. Incompatibility, however, is not adequate. Sadism—even sadism in refusing to give a *Get*—is also not adequate. Why? We know now that almost all marital problems are due to one neurosis or another. The neurotic behavior and the circumstances that evoke it cannot be foretold. Insanity is only an extreme form. Yet if a marriage may be annulled because a woman does not want to cope with an insane husband, and, therefore, the presumption that she would prefer a bad marriage to no marriage no longer holds because the marriage is so bad, then in every case where it subsequently appears that latent neuroses make it impossible for the spouses to relate to each other as they should there ought also be a basis for decreeing that the marriage is annulled because of mistake.

The obvious reply is that if one adopts this position one is making virtually all marriages easily annullable and such liberalism might destroy the sanctity of marriage—one of Judaism's most cherished values and *desiderata*. Rabbis and laymen would raise a hue and a cry that marriage bonds in Judaism are made of straw. The stability of marriages would be adversely affected. Instead of being regarded as indestructible, marriages would be regarded as ephemeral. That is why our Rabbis in the past so hesitated to suspend the requirement of a *Get*. That is why they so formalized the procedure for a *Get*. This is also why they forbade conditions and the inclusion of capricious agreements in the original marriage contract.

However, there is another consideration to be reckoned with. The overwhelming majority of marriages will not be affected. Where the spouses continue to be decent, normal and humane, the *Get* is always available. The problem arises principally when one spouse becomes sadistic, vicious, or vengeful. And when we insist on the *Get* in such a case—despite the discovery of indecent, abnormal or inhumane behavior in the intransigent one—are we promoting respect for the sanctity of marriage or undermining respect for Jewish law altogether? This is the issue. Which end are we to safeguard? This brings one to a consideration of means and ends in Halachah generally. Respectfully it is submitted that more Halachic experts of our day ought ponder this problem.

IV

From a philosophical point of view, can it ever be said that correct ends do not justify wrong means? It would appear that there can be no such thing as an ethical objection to the use of so-called wrong means for correct ends, because nothing can be regarded as evil except by reference to the ends involved. If we refuse to adopt a course which we regard as evil—even to achieve a worthy objective—it is because the means are evil with reference to still another end which ranks higher than the end for which we are considering the controversial means.

This can be illustrated from the writings of two philosophers—one non-Jewish and the other Jewish. The former

245

is identified with villainy of the first order; the latter, with saintliness of the highest degree. They are Machiavelli, on the one hand, and Bachya, on the other.

In the history of political thought Machiavelli is regarded as the exponent of the notion that sovereigns may do anything—steal, murder, cheat and betray—in order to keep themselves in power. He is, therefore, often called the prophet of immorality—or amorality. However, this is not true. Machiavelli simply held that there were two ends that ranked higher than all other ends—the life and liberty of the country. Since there are no ends worthier than these, when these ends must be served one cannot be deterred by considerations of justice or injustice, humanity or cruelty, glory or shame. If Machiavelli had maintained that the life of an individual is as important as the life of the nation, a position very much supported by the Halachah, he might not have urged his Prince to be so "knife-happy" or "poison-happy." One must take issue with him not as to whether the use of foul means is proper or improper, but rather as to what are the highest ends. For that reason the philosophy of Halachah is so much sounder.

Halachic discussions are always with respect to ends. One asks: "Which end, which *Mitzvah*, ranks higher, so that a lesser one gives way or is even altogether disregarded?" We do not speak of ends justifying or not justifying means. Every deed and every thing serves some end. Even our involuntary breathing is related to an end—the *Mitzvah* of self-preservation. This end, however, may yield in one case to a higher end—as in the case of martyrdom for the sanctification of God's name—or it may not yield to that end as in the many instances when it is permitted to violate the law and save one's life.

Bachya makes this clear in a passage of his *Duties of the Heart* in connection with that incident in Samuel's life when God told him to lie to Saul in order to save his life (1 Samuel 16:2). When Samuel hesitated to go to Saul lest Saul kill him, God did not tell him to place his trust in the Lord; instead, He directed him to use a subterfuge. Thereby,

246

says Bachya, God gave His approval to the abuse of truth in self-defense, even though He could have admonished the prophet for his lack of faith in Him Who has the ultimate power of life and death over all of us.

The pursuit of truth is also a *Mitzvah*. Nonetheless, there are other *Mitzvot* to which it yields. In a similar vein one might interpret the two dissimilar prohibitions in the Torah not to lie. In Exodus the command is to keep one's distance from falsehood. In Leviticus the command is simply not to lie. It appears from numerous commentators that the Levitical command is a relative one; it yields in the interest of peace. God Himself lied to Abraham when He reported to the husband about Sarah's statement that her husband was old. In Exodus, on the other hand, the command is part of a code pertaining to courts of law. In courts of law there can be no compromise with truth. Witnesses must not conceal or doctor their testimony, no matter what the consequences.

The Torah's interest in justice is an interest so high in the hierarchy of interests that it would be defeated if witnesses could take liberties and revise their stories in the interest of good will or domestic tranquillity. To such an extent is unequivocal, absolute truth the *desideratum* in a court of justice that the ingenious author of the *Meshech Hochmah* explains that the reference in the ninth commandment of the Decalogue is to a false witness, and not to false testimony, because even if what the witness is telling is the truth, but the witness knows the truth only by hearsay and not because he saw the facts, he is a false witness: the testimony itself may be true, but the witness is a liar, for he is making himself appear as a competent witness when he is not.

Thus the Halachah never approved of the extreme attributed to Immanuel Kant that one may never lie. There are times even in a court of law, for example, when the obligation to tell the truth may be suspended—when the court of law is not one in which justice is really meted out. Indeed, there is one responsum among the many written by

R. Meir of Rothenburg to the effect that a Jew may not tell the truth in a non-Jewish court which is given to the persecution of Jews, when, thereby, damage would result to a co-religionist. For telling the truth, the Jew in such a case is held accountable to the aggrieved party; his obligation is to lie.

Professors Dewey and Tufts in their textbook on *Ethics* define moral experience as "that kind of conduct in which there are ends so discrepant, so incompatible, as to require selection of one and rejection of the other. . . . It is incompatibility of ends which necessitates consideration of the true worth of a given end; and such consideration it is which brings the experience into the moral sphere."

Thus, almost every time that a Jew exercises free will— *Behirah*—with regard to his performance of an overt act, he is having a moral experience. He is choosing between incompatible ends. Sometimes the ends are incompatible because one is God-given and the other Satan-inspired. Sometimes both ends are God-given, and the choice is dictated by Halachah. Sometimes the ends are God-given, and the Halachah enjoins one to make one's own choice.

V

This brings us to a further point. Does the Halachah ever bid one to exercise one's own moral consciousness to ignore one of its own norms because of an end also Halachically approved but for which there is no special rule calling for its possible violation—unlike the case of a positive commandment which is to be obeyed even if it involves a violation of a prohibition? There is authority for an affirmative answer.

Two such general instances are known to the Halachah. The first is based on the verse "When the time has come to act for the Lord, they violate Thy Torah." True, the authority given in this verse is dangerously broad. One should never exercise it without the greatest caution. However, the two historic instances cited in Talmud when this authority

248

was exercised are revealing. Rashi cites Elijah's sacrifice outside of Jerusalem on Mt. Carmel as a Biblical precedent. But this instance could have been a *Hora'at Sha'ah,* a crisis or emergency decision. The two historic instances were: First, to permit the use of God's name when we greet one another; for the end of peace—for the end of brotherhood— we violate the commandment in the Decalogue not to make needless mention of the Creator. Second, to permit the writing of the Oral Law, or more correctly as Prof. Czernowitz interprets the matter, to permit the use of written materials to teach the Oral Law. If this permission had not been granted, who knows whether Judaism would have survived except among a handful in every generation. The revolutionary character of this decision can only be fathomed in the light of the text that compares one who commits Halachic precedents to writing to one who burns the Torah (B. T. *Temurah* 14b) ! Nonetheless, the final ruling was that one may commit the Oral Law to writing.

One dare not spell out what powers are vested in rabbis of every generation in the light of these precedents. Of interest it must be that there was not always unanimity as to what type of conduct was called for by the mandate that one violate God's law when the time has come to act for God. There were differences of opinion among the Rabbis both as to when and as to how the prerogative should be exercised. One very timely illustration is found in the Babylonian Talmud (*Berachot* 63a) : Hillel the Elder said that "at a time of withdrawing one should scatter, and at a time of scattering one should withdraw." Rashi interprets this to mean that when Torah is being taught by *Gedolim,* lesser scholars should make themselves inconspicuous and not teach Torah; the value they are to conserve is that of personal humility. However, according to the Palestinian Talmud—as the Maharsha indicates—the lesser scholars are never under such a disability. They must always teach Torah. Their mandate to violate the law and avoid the teaching of Torah is only applicable when their superiors are similarly restrained—because Torah is held in low esteem. Perhaps this illustration is relevant to our day far beyond the scope of the problem of Jewish family law. It is cited only to indicate that policy differences there were with regard to the broad prerogative of the rabbis. Apparently the *Yerushalmi* felt that when Torah is well received, all of us, even young rabbis should not go into retirement but instead shoud take advantage of the opportunity and multiply scholars everywhere. Rashi, in his interpretation of the Babylonian Talmud, gives the young a more modest role. They can only teach when their elders have ghettoized themselves. Again, this instance is cited only to demonstrate that there have been, and will continue to be, until the Messianic era, differences of opinion as to politics and programs that properly come within the scope of the broad Rabbinic prerogative to vitiate one law for the advancement of another.

When rabbis as a group want to make decisions that are quite revolutionary and do so in the name of their historic prerogative, there is another principle that can also help them. This is a principle that constitutes an exception to the general rule that we do not ask one man to sin in order that another may thereby have a *Mitzvah*.

There is the classic instance of the slave who is half slave and half free. His master is forced to emancipate him. Why? Should the master be forced to violate a Biblical prohibition to emancipate Canaanite slaves only for the benefit of the slave who is already half free? Yet the answer given by the Tosafists is that this can be done when a *Mitzvah* for the collectivity of Israel is involved, such as the *Mitzvah* of public worship, or a *Mitzvah* of primary importance such as procreation. The Meiri argues that the Biblical prohibition is itself a minor one, because we are under no obligation to acquire a Canaanitish slave in order to perform the *Mitzvah* of holding him in bondage. In any event, the Halachah approves of such considerations as the relative significance of *Mitzvot* not only insofar as one yields to another, but even insofar as one Jew may violate a *Mitzvah* of lesser importance to enable another Jew to observe one of greater importance.

Thus the choice of ends involves not only one's own soul but the souls of others. Indeed, according to the great teachers of ethics in the last generation, this is the correct rationale for the prohibition that we may not blow *Shofar* on the Sabbath or take the Four Species lest someone desecrate the Sabbath because of it. Better it is for all Jews to forfeit the reward of the *Mitzvah* than that one Jew shall run the risk of suffering a penalty for his negligence.

Thus, according to the Halachah, one must sometimes—pursuant to its own norms—make bold decisions—for God's sake—for Halachah's sake—for the sake of *Klal Yisrael*.

In their own lives most rabbis have made such decisions. They will account to their Maker for both the wisdom and the motivation that were theirs. However, the time has come for them to act collectively in many areas on the basis of practical considerations, and they will have to ask whether this kind of action will truly advance their cause or undermine it.

Rabbi Weinberg of Montrieux and Rabbi Feinstein of New York have opened the door. A courageous *Beth Din* must now restudy the situation and make choices. The worldwide Jewish community feels less bound by Halachah than ever before in Jewish history. Bastardy is, therefore, rifer than ever, and Jewish communal organization with internal discipline is virtually non-existent. Which is the more important Halachic end to be pursued in the present situation—the preservation of an ideological commitment to family holiness which concerns only a few who will not be affected by liberalism in the annulment of marriages, or to prevent the greater incidence of bastardy against which there can be no real protection in so mobile and fluid a society as ours now is?

Needless to say, a minority among us will scream. But they need not suffer. Nothing will have been imposed upon them against their will. Jews always had small groups that were especially careful in matters of *Taharah* as well as family background. There need be no insistence on uniformity or regimentation. Let there be standards of excellence here as everywhere. However, one must help relieve a situation which begs for correction. Most Jews will hail the effort. That *Gedolim* in the past hesitated to act means only that they mistook the gravity of the situation. They simply erred. With their rigidity they did not save. This was even true in Europe. In America conditions have become indescribably worse.

What other alternatives are there? We can isolate all who are loyal to Halachah from the rest of the worldwide Jewry, outlaw their intermarriage with the rest of their coreligionists, and let those who suffer as *Agunot* because of their commitment to Jewish law resign themselves to their fate as the will of God. For those to whom these alternatives are not acceptable, the only available road is that initiated by two *Gedolim* of our day.

Chapter Four

A FUNCTIONAL APPROACH
TO THE HALACHAH

Philosophers explore the Halachic literature of Judaism for its ethical and moral insights. Theologians try to glean from its premises the core of a Jewish creed. Historians examine it for the facts it reveals about the social, economic, and political past of the Jewish people, and jurists analyze its dialectic for unique conceptions of property and obligation. However, many an anomaly which baffles students of the Halachah can best be understood by a functional approach, by asking not what the law is but rather what it did, or what it was expected to do.

Even if the substantive and procedural rules of the Halachah were never more than elements of a speculative discipline instead of an operative legal order, it behooves us to study it functionally, because its norms were meant to be applied and not to remain merely theoretical. One will arrive at distorted conceptions if one ignores this basic premise. For the Halachah is more than a system of rules and values; it projects a legal order and must be viewed within the framework of the legal order it projects.

It is the purpose of this essay to demonstrate, by a number of examples, how this functional approach can help to rationalize unusual Halachic rules. The propriety, for example, of indulging in self-help for the protection of one's legal rights is discussed in the Babylonian Talmud.[1] One may indulge in self-help if economic loss is threatened by another.[2] Even the destruction of another's life or the maiming of his limb is permitted when that other is presently menacing the life of a third human being, not alone the life of the person availing himself of self-help.[3] One may not, however, inflict bodily harm upon another in the course of righting wrongs already committed.[4] Yet in the event of an accidental homicide, Jewish law permitted the next of kin of the victim to pursue the killer unto death unless the latter sought asylum in one of the designated cities of refuge. One cannot rationalize this exception by blithely assuming that Jewish law indulged in human weakness and tolerated the vendetta. Such a rationalization is neither consistent with Jewish ethics nor with the Halachah's violent opposition to lynch law. Since Jewish ethics insists that only he who murders with malice and premeditation shall be executed, it would seem that the Halachah recklessly endangers the life of the man who kills accidentally. Furthermore, if Jewish law tolerated the hot temper of the blood avenger, as did many systems of primitive law, why was not the same consideration tendered hot-tempered husbands with regard to their adulterous wives, or irate fathers with regard to their daughters' rapists or seducers? Third, Jewish law made it almost impossible to execute even the malicious murderer by outlawing circumstantial evidence in capital cases. How can one reconcile this almost insane regard for the safety of the accused with the wanton abandonment of the accidental killer to the wrath of the murdered man's next of kin? What is more, one authority even makes it a religious obligation (*Mitzvah*) for the next of kin to pursue the killer.[5] This authority certainly did not hold that

1. Unless otherwise indicated, all references herein are to the Babylonian Talmud.
2. Baba Kama 27b.
3. Sanhedrin 73a.
4. Makkot 12a; Maimonides, *Mishneh Torah*, Hilchot Rozeah, I, 5.
5. Makkot 11b.

the Halachah was merely indulging human weakness when it permitted self-help for the purpose of vengeance.

The entire subject assumes an altogether different character when one approaches the problem from a lawyer's point of view—the functional approach. One then begins by asking how Jewish criminal justice was expected to operate. What were its provisions for the apprehension of criminals, the investigation of their offenses, their prosecution, and their punishment? The available sources indicate that the Talmudic scholars assumed that when a murder had been committed, the murderer, whether he killed wittingly or unwittingly, would flee to a city of refuge.[6] If he did not, he would have incurred the risk of being killed by the blood avenger. It would be the threat of the blood avenger that would make the law *self-enforcing*. That threat would solve the problem of crime detection. In the city of refuge the murderer could find peace. He could there confess his crime and thereafter be returned in safety to the site of the crime for trial, although in the trial his confession would be of no consequence whatever. After trial he might be acquitted altogether and restored to his home; or he might be found guilty of homicide by negligence so that he would be returned under safe escort to the city of refuge, there to atone for his sin; or he might be executed for willful murder—which was rare, if not impossible. In the final analysis, however, there would be little or no reliance upon a police force or district attorney. The threat of the blood avenger would take their place. It would be he who would set in motion the machinery of crime detection and punishment.

This would be the enforcement pattern in the event of murder. And that the law so intended can be gleaned from the fact that an almost similar system was used to stimulate the return of stolen property. Jewish law distinguished between *Gezelah* and *Genevah*.[7] The former was theft by one who revealed his identity when committing his crime. When apprehended he was expected to make simple restitution.

6. Makkot 9b.
7. Baba Kama 79b.

When, however, one stole without revealing his identity to his victim, he had committed the crime of *Genevah,* which might result in a severer penalty—not alone the return of the theft but in addition the payment of an equal sum or triple or quadruple that sum. The Talmud gives ethical reasons why the latter type of thief was punished more severely—he feared man but not God. Even the circumstances for quadruple and quintuple payments (commonly known as "four and five," including the principal amount of the theft) are assumed to have ethical implications. Commentators, however, overlook the fact that by providing a penalty for the thief who conceals his identity while none is provided for the more brazen criminal, the law is expediting its own enforcement. For any man who commits an act which is subject to a penalty (*a knas*), as distinguished from simple restitution, can confess to his crime and thereby be relieved of the penalty. He will be thus relieved even if witnesses subsequently establish his identity and prove the crime, so that his confession was not needed.[8] Nonetheless, his confession relieves him of the possibility of paying more than the gain derived from his crime. In effect, this was a bonus to the thief for his contribution to the detection of his own crime.

One may ask whether Jewish law was not indulging in the frivolous when it invited all who were subject to penalty to confess and be relieved of their penalties. Jewish law, however, provided a safeguard. The confession, to be effective, must at least obligate the criminal to some detriment to which he would not be subject without his confession. Otherwise, the subsequent appearance of witnesses might cause penalties to be imposed. To avoid the dire consequences of his testimony, the thief, for example, must at least incur the obligation of making restitution. In one case the detriment might even be to brand his ox as a goring animal, which might later increase his liability in tort.[9]

8. Baba Kama 14b and 74b.

9. See *Hagoot ha-Gra* on the Rosh, *Baba Kama* I, 20; and Ezekiel Landau, *Nodah Biyehudah,* 2d ed., Even ha-Ezer, Responsum 23.

Thus one finds here another instance of the law's concern with its own enforcement and the rationale for an anomalous rule providing a milder penalty for the thief who brazenly leaves a calling card than for the sneak who fears detection.

Another illustration is the use of the oath in civil suits. That the Halachah sanctioned the use of the oath as a form of proof has been cited as an instance of trial by ordeal in Jewish law. Again a functional approach to the Halachah is revealing. The oath was not regarded as a form of proof. If a plaintiff could not sustain his claim because he had but one witness and not the two required by the Torah, or if the defendant had made admissions which gave rise to suspicions, then the defendant was given an opportunity to clear himself by oath from the suspicions arising from his own admissions or from the testimony of the solitary witness. Thus, said the Talmud, all oaths required by the Bible are oaths to be administered not for the purpose of establishing claims but rather for the purpose of clearing the defendant of obligations alleged but not adequately proved.[10] Yet, what was the technique used to guard against perjury? Again the law provided for its own enforcement. Let a man be a proven perjurer, then in any lawsuit in which he might be obligated to take an oath, he would be denied credibility and his adversary—usually the plaintiff—would be privileged to take the oath in lieu of proof.[11] The plaintiff would then recover the amount that he pleaded as due. Thus anyone who would be reckless with oaths would make life intolerable for himself. He would place himself at the mercy of unscrupulous claimants who with proof adequate only to place upon him the burden of an oath find themselves prevailing in their causes by taking oaths themselves, since their victim has been precluded from clearing himself. In effect they acquire this privilege as a powerful weapon against him. This was the essence of the conception of the oath—a means of clearing oneself. The sanction to prevent

10. Shevuot 44b.
11. Shevuot 44b.

257

its abuse was not in the form of criminal penalties, which could almost never be imposed, but rather in the form of a rule of procedure which materially altered substantive rights. That rule was enough of a deterrent to insure the integrity of the man who swore.

It was not unusual in Jewish law to resort to this type of sanction. For example, a woman who had meager proof of her husband's death might be permitted to remarry. However, if her husband did appear after her remarriage, she suffered a disability exceeding that of the woman who had two competent witnesses to establish her husband's death and who subsequently remarried, only to be chagrined thereafter by the reappearance of her first husband. In the latter case, the woman could return to her first husband. In the former, she could live with neither the first husband nor the second. By imposing this penalty the law sought to insure the fact that she would exercise great caution before acting upon the assumption that her husband was dead. The law eased the burden of her proof in the first instance because it dealt so harshly with her in the event that she was proven to have acted recklessly with respect to her remarriage.[12] The same rationale applied to oaths. One could clear oneself easily, but woe unto him who accomplished it with perjury!

The functional approach to the Halachah is even more revealing with regard to the most famous of the so-called biblical ordeals—the ordeal of the *Sotah*. Let a husband suspect his wife of infidelity; let him warn her in the presence of witnesses that he does not want her associating with the alleged paramour; and let there be witnesses that she violated his wishes—then though the husband could not kill her, he could bring her to the priest who would give her a potion to drink. The results would establish whether she had committed adultery or had been merely indiscreet. On its face this appears to be as unequivocal an instance of trial by ordeal as can be found anywhere. However, the func-

12. Yevamot 88a.

258

tional approach applicable to our understanding of oaths in Jewish law is equally enlightening here.

The Talmud related the law of oaths to the law of *Sotah* [13] because the *Sotah*—the suspected wife—must take an oath as to what she and her paramour did. Yet, since the Talmud establishes as a major premise that oaths are only for the purpose of clearing a defendant, how can the oath be used to demonstrate the guilt of the woman with or without the potion? The Talmud admits that the failure of the potion to prove guilt is no proof of innocence, for if witnesses to guilt appear after the accused has drunk the waters they are believed.[14] The more realistic purpose of the so-called ordeal, according to the tenor of the Talmudic discussion, is to clear the wife of her jealous husband's suspicions. The law denied him the right of self-help; the Halachah gave him no pretense for vengeance in the name of a "higher law." If the circumstances, however, were suspicious, he could go to the priest who would urge the wife to confess her sin if she was guilty. No punishment would follow other than her divorce and the forfeiture of her property rights. If, however, she was innocent she had naught to fear from the drink. God had permitted His Holy Name to be inscribed on parchment which was placed in water, though He knew that His Name would thus be erased by the liquid. Yet he lent His Name to this abuse that He might be a party to the restoration of marital tranquillity. Therefore, if innocent, the wife was cleared and restored to her now-assuaged spouse. This was the law in operation, not in fact, for the law fell into disuse early in Jewish history, but the law as the Talmud visualized it in operation.

The utterly paradoxical view of the Pharisees with regard to the impeachment of witnesses also becomes more intelligible in the light of the functional approach. If two or more witnesses accused a person of murder and the latter was convicted and executed, the witnesses, when subsequently impeached, were not punished. If, however, they

13. Kidushin 27b.
14. Sotah 6a.

259

were impeached between the court's sentence and the execution, they must pay the penalty which they sought to mete out to their victim. The Sadducees justly complained that this was unreasonable.[15] Furthermore, one of the Talmudic scholars suggested that there was no reason why the impeaching witnesses should be more trustworthy than those impeached.[16]

The punishment of false witnesses with the same punishment which they sought to impose upon the accused is found in the code of Hammurabi. The rabbis, however, interpreted the biblical equivalent as a limitation, for in the final analysis why should the impeaching witnesses be more trustworthy than the impeached? The Oral Law understood *Hazamah* to mean the impeachment of the witnesses without any reference whatever to the accused murderer or to the victim. *Hazamah* meant the impeachment of the witnesses by reference to their being elsewhere on the date of the alleged murder. In effect, therefore, the impeaching witnesses were launching an independent suit for perjury against the witnesses in the murder action and in such an independent suit the newly accused must bring proof other than their own word. This is the Maimonidean view.[17] But Maimonides does not explain why the punishment of the accused in this new perjury action must be guided by the timing in the murder action that preceded it, so that if the accused in that action has already been executed, the perjury action must be discontinued.

Yet, from a functional point of view the rule makes sense. Law frequently involves a balancing of interests— sometimes its own. For the proper operation of any legal system it is necessary that witnesses tell the truth and that there be sanctions against perjury. It is also necessary that witnesses should not be deterred from coming forth to testify. To subject witnesses to an unrelenting threat that they may be impeached at any subsequent time would only deter

15. Makkot 5a.
16. Sanhedrin 27a, and Baba Kama 72b.
17. Maimonides, *Mishneh Torah*, Hilchot Edut, XVIII, 2, 3.

them from testifying in the first instance. Yet to relieve them of all punishment for false testimony would be equally unthinkable. Therefore, the institution of *Hazamah* becomes the lever. The witness is subjected to the threat of a perjury suit but only for the briefest possible interval—between sentence and execution—and only under very limited circumstances—in fact, the most limited conceivable: *testimony about themselves alone with regard to which they ought to be in the best position to defend themselves and obtain proof of their innocence.* A sanction against perjury is established but not one so severe that men will evade their biblical obligation to bear witness when they have knowledge of relevant facts. And so important was this sanction that if witnesses so testified that their testimony was not capable of being impeached by the method of *Hazamah*—e.g., they did not remember dates or places—then their testimony was rejected altogether. If they could not specify dates and places, how could impeaching witnesses prove that they were not at the scene of the crime but elsewhere!

It thus becomes apparent that to understand the rationale of many Halachic rules requires that the Halachah be regarded as a system of law projected for a legal order, and not as a detached body of rules each of which exemplifies no more than an ethical or moral principle. The study of any law—and the Halachah is no exception—requires a functional approach. Otherwise, one misses the very life of the law—its relation to purpose, including the purpose of its own enforcement.

Chapter Five

A CHALLENGE TO ORTHODOXY

I

A group of Israeli intellectuals, orthodox in practice and commitment, addressed an inquiry to one of the world's most pious and learned of rabbis. In their work and thought they had embraced scientific theories which appeared to contradict passages of the Bible when literally interpreted. The age of the earth was one example. From another rabbi they had heard that Orthodoxy requires that one believe the earth to be only 5728 years old. Were they to be regarded as heretics because of their disagreement with this view?

The twenty-five-page reply prepared for them is not yet published. Its author (who prefers to be unnamed) sought the concurrence of three colleagues who had occasionally expressed progressive views. One declined to become involved because of advanced age and poor health; another declined concurrence because of fear of what he himself calls "McCarthyism" in Jewish Orthodoxy; the third felt that his status in the traditionalist community was not yet sufficiently secure to be of any value to the scholar soliciting approval, especially since the latter himself enjoyed so much more prestige than he.

The reply—with copious references to authorities—indicates that Orthodoxy is not monolithic: it requires acknowledgment of the divine origin of the Commandments and

262

firm resolve to fulfill them; however, it also permits great latitude in the formulation of doctrines, the interpretation of Biblical passages, and the rationalization of *mitzvot*. It is not difficult to demonstrate that the giants of the Tradition held widely divergent views on the nature of God, the character of historic revelation, and the uniqueness of the Jewish faith. Not all of these views could possibly be true, and yet not one of them may be deemed heretical, since one respected authority or another has clung to it. The only heresy is the denial that God gave the Written and Oral Law to His people, who are to fulfill its mandates and develop their birthright in accordance with its own built-in methodology and authentic exegesis.

Often in the past, upon encountering new cultures or philosophical systems, Jewish scholars re-examined the Tradition and discovered new insights and interpretations. Their contemporary colleagues of a more conservative temperament resisted and attacked the creative spirits as heretics, though the impugned protested that they were deeply committed to the Tradition and had said nothing which was not supported by respected authorities who had preceded them. The resulting schisms were often no credit to the Jewish people and, in modern times, even yielded groupings among American Jews which are not based altogether on ideological differences.

Unfortunately, however, it is the reactionaries in Orthodoxy who bear much of the guilt for this tragic phenomenon. Their heresy, is that they regard their own Biblical and Talmudic interpretation as canonized in the same measure as the texts themselves—which was never true. They are repeating this heresy again, in Israel and the Diaspora, so that already Jewish sociologists detect the possibility of further schisms in Orthodoxy. At least four groups are even now discernible,[1] and the "rightists" are exercising pressure to brand the "leftists" as heretics and to force them either to create a new sect or to identify with Conservative Ju-

1. See Charles S. Liebman, "A Sociological Analysis of Contemporary Orthodoxy," JUDAISM, Summer 1964, p. 285 ff.

daism. The founder of Reconstructionism did break with the Tradition, and his views, insofar as they deny the divine origin of Torah and *mitzvot,* are heresy. But this was unequivocally clear to his own colleagues on the faculty of the Jewish Theological Seminary fifty years ago, and Solomon Schechter must have had him in mind when he poked fun at those who observe the *mitzvot* and yet deny their God-given character. However, this does not mean that all who have new approaches are *ipso facto* non-Orthodox and must affiliate elsewhere.

In more recent times Rabbi Abraham Isaac Kook, of blessed memory, was regarded as having expressed dangerous opinions. Dr. Joseph B. Soloveitchik and Dr. Samuel Belkin today are experiencing the same fate. The late Rabbi Aaron Kotler, dean of the "rightists," denied that those who receive a secular education can express authentic Torah views. The students of the Rabbi Isaac Elchanan Theological Seminary of Yeshiva University, whose graduates Dr. Belkin and Dr. Soloveitchik ordain, are taught by rabbis who are rightist, leftist, and centrist; and, while academic freedom is enjoyed by all, there prevails an uneasy tension among both faculty and seminarians which is also reflected in the rabbinical associations they subsequently join together with graduates of other Orthodox seminaries. Milton Himmelfarb has detected and written of this tension as it appears in the periodicals of Orthodox thought and opinion, like *Deot, Amudim, Jewish Observer, Tradition,* etc. It is even more pronounced in Israel in the sundry factions of several religious political parties and their daily, weekly, and monthly publications. The politicians there clamor for unity among the Orthodox, but the ideologists, especially in the religious collectives, insist that, before there can be unity even on an election slate, religious parties must at least unite on mutual respect for the legitimacy of their divergent religious views. But this is not forthcoming.

Two questions must needs be considered. Is the "right" correctly representing the Tradition? And is it wise even for them, from their point of view and certainly from the point of view of the survival of the Tradition, to deal with the "left" as they do?

One who undertakes to answer these questions must do so with fear and trepidation. Since he must deal with the totality of the law and creed known as Judaism, he ought not be so presumptuous as to regard himself as so much the master of the entire Tradition that he can offer definitive views on virtually every aspect. Furthermore, some of the views he must, of necessity, express will incur the wrath of colleagues and cause their exponent to share the fate of the very people whom he wants properly to reclaim as members of the community of the devout and committed. Like them he will be called a heretic whose ideas jeopardize the future and integrity of Torah.

Nonetheless, silence is not the alternative when one is convinced that precisely a measure of candor is the *desideratum,* not only because God wills that we speak the truth as we see it—for His name is Truth—but also because silence and its concomitant smugness are estranging Jewish intellectuals. Jewish intellectuals are becoming interested in the Tradition, but they will not accept the rigidity of most contemporary exponents of Orthodoxy. They crave more autonomy of the soul. Moreover, some effort ought to be expended to reaffiliate those who, principally because of the way in which Jews have organized themselves politically in Israel and socially and institutionally in the English-speaking countries, find themselves identified with groups whose ideology they do not truly share. For many reasons they cannot identify with the present leadership of Orthodoxy anywhere in the world, and yet they regard themselves as wholly within the Torah tradition. The time is ripe for a candid re-examination of fundamentals and a challenge to those whose principal claim to authority is that they have closed minds and secure their leadership by exacting a comparable myopia from their followers. One may not deny them their freedom of worship, but even as they want their views tolerated and respected so must they be prevailed upon to recognize that others are as devout and as committed as they, and the Tradition has always permitted a considerable amount of diversity in thought and action. It was never proper to consolidate ranks by substituting fixity for dynamic religious creativity, and certainly in the contemporary open society, with its emphasis on the open mind, it is hardly propitious to commit the error occasionally committed in the past when one group of Jews withdrew from their co-religionists, regarded the others as heretics, and sought to save themselves by severing contact with those with whom they disagreed.

Rightly or wrongly, one Jewish sociologist has named me as an ideologist of "modern Orthodoxy." However, one can hardly regard modern Orthodoxy as a movement: it is no more than a coterie of a score of rabbis in America and in Israel whose interpretations of the Tradition have won the approval of Orthodox intellectuals who are knowledgeable in both Judaism and Western civilization. None of the rabbis feels that he is articulating any position that cannot be supported by reference to authentic Jewish sources. None wants to organize a separate rabbinic body, and several have rejected an attempt to publish an independent periodical, because they did not want the remotest possibility that this form of separatism be interpreted as a schism in Orthodoxy. I, no less than they, deny any claim to innovation. Our choice of methods and values in the Tradition, our emphases, and our concerns, may be different. But the creation or articulation of shades and hues hardly warrants dignifying our effort with the terms "ideology" or "sect." We know that the overwhelming majority of Orthodox rabbis differ with us and that the faculties of most Orthodox day schools and rabbinical seminaries disapprove of some of our views and so instruct their pupils. It is not our mission to have them join our ranks. Rather do we seek to help Jewish intellectuals who are being alienated from the Tradition to realize that they can share a commitment to the faith which is acceptable to them and at least as authentic as the one they have received from their teachers but which they feel impelled to renounce. We reject the multiplication of dogmas and their precise formulation. Among Christians this notion is presently popular as "reductionism." In Judaism, however, "reductionism" is very ancient: the Midrash tells us of different prophets who sought to encapsulate the tradition in seven, three, or even one principle. Ours is a commitment which invites questioning and creativity in thought and practice, as applied not only to the Law but also to theology.

II

One must begin with the measure of freedom permitted in Jewish Law and commitment by the Tradition itself. When do one's thought and action place one beyond the circle of the devout? We discover that the range of diversity in creed, ritual, and law is so great that, no less than in a democracy, consensus is required on much less than is usually thought—in order to claim rightful status as an Orthodox Jew.

Must one who professes Orthodoxy be committed to the retention of the total Halachah insofar as it deals with civil law—the law of property and obligations, corporations, partnerships, sales, trusts, estates? According to the Halachah itself, there is a residual power to alter all property relationships in the *bet din* (court), and especially in a supreme legislative and judicial body such as the Sanhedrin once was and many hope will soon be reconstituted. The principle is known as *hefker bet din hefker*. A *bet din* has the power to declare property ownerless and in that way to divest a man of his rights, vesting them in another. This power was exercised whenever changes were made in the Halachah with regard to economic affairs. A man may thus be Orthodox and yet actively propagate changes in the law for the promotion of capitalism or socialism, bigness or smallness in economic enterprise, curbs on strikes, or greater freedom for organized labor.

The Halachah has many ethical norms and insights to offer on these subjects, but any Jew—committed to the

Halachah—enjoys, on the basis of his interpretation of the Halachah, unlimited freedom to propose changes; if he were fortunate enough to be a member of the Sanhedrin and to prevail on his colleagues to embrace his point of view, he would be the creator of new Halachah. There may be instances where the changes are so radical that resort would have to be taken to legal fiction. Thus, when Hillel saw that Jews were not lending money to each other because of the fear that the sabbatical year would nullify the debts, he could have changed the rule by exercising the power of *hefker bet din hefker,* divesting debtors of their money and vesting it in their creditors, but this would have been an unequivocal nullification of a Biblical mandate. Instead he instituted the *pruzbul*—a legal fiction whereby the debts incurred prior to the sabbatical year were transferred to the court for collection. Perhaps he also hoped thereby to keep alive some memory of the Biblical rule and that one day it would be revived in practice. To alter the Biblical rule of inheritance in order to establish the equal rights of daughters to inherit with sons, or to abolish the last vestige of primogeniture in Jewish law, may also require resort to legal fictions—as the late Chief Rabbi Herzog once unsuccessfully proposed. In any case, one cannot be regarded as a heretic because of one's dissatisfaction with the present state of the Halachah with regard to economic matters and one's determination to effect change and development. Such change and development have always been, and must needs continue to be, achieved.

Is the Orthodox Jew any less free in connection with criminal law? Whether he wants to diminish the number of crimes and mitigate punishments or whether he wants to increase them, he can do so within the frame of the Halachah. He must be most circumspect, it is true, with regard to capital offenses—but even here he is by no means without power. Again, there are residual powers in the *bet din* and even in the king (the executive authority) which can be exercised to safeguard peace and order and promote the general welfare. Centuries after capital punishment had virtually been abolished, the Jewish community protected itself against informers by reviving capital punishment. It also altered the rules of evidence to make convictions more feasible. A devotee of the Halachah, therefore—even as he tries to fathom its spirit and especially the enormous regard it has for human life and freedom by comparison with its lesser regard for the right of property—need not feel impotent to propose and press, in fulfillment of that spirit, for the adoption of a new criminal law for a modern state, even for a state that professes to be committed to the Halachah.

Nor need he feel inhibited as he seeks within the spirit of the Halachah to urge upon his fellow citizens the consideration of specific proposals for the constitutional structure of the state. He will be able to justify unicameral and bicameral legislatures, proportional representation, popular election of judges and their appointment by the executive, a parliamentary and a presidential form of government, and sundry other forms of government which may be found in modern states. The more profound his commitment to the Halachah, and the more preoccupied he is with what God would have willed for a new Jewish State, the more tolerant will he be of all the proposals and the more will he resort to the will of the people except when that will flouts basic norms and ethics with regard to which majority rule is not to be countenanced. Thus, as neither civil nor criminal law is fixed and immutable in the Halachah, public law in general is an area in which commitment to the Halachah requires no general agreement among the devout.

Israel's victory in the Six-Day War made this abundantly clear. Shortly after the occupation of the new territory, Chief Rabbi Nissim held that, according to the Halachah, it would be forbidden to negotiate for peace as the *quid pro* for the return of any of these areas. Rabbi Joseph B. Soloveitchik questioned this decision and indicated that perhaps for an enduring peace it would be necessary to relinquish some of the land and that statesmen might be in a better position to render such a decision which would be binding on rabbis precisely as the opinion

269

of a doctor is binding on a rabbi in connection with the breaking of a fast on the Day of Atonement. Rabbi Nissim countered with the suggestion that there are certain commandments for which martyrdom is required. He was certainly justified in making that suggestion, since almost every conquest in the history of humanity has involved the loss of blood, and Jews, too, have been commanded to conquer. (In at least one situation this was even a *mitzvah*.) In a recent essay, a pupil of Rabbi Kook, Rabbi Yehuda Gershuni, documented his support of Dr. Soloveitchik's view. In any event, it is obvious that on so historic an issue, one so vital to the future of the people of Israel, a radical difference of opinion prevails among giants in the world of Halachah. And who will deny that all are Orthodox in commitment and practice!

In family law we encounter a more circumscribed area. Yet here, too, as a devotee of the Halachah one can propose and agitate for changes that will nullify almost every rule of the past. It might be the sheerest folly to do so. But the question under consideration is not whether one should write a new code for Jewish domestic relations but rather whether the power resides in the duly constituted authorities to do so. And it does. Therefore, he who thinks that changes are in order and proposes them for promulgation by the *bet din* or Sanhedrin cannot be regarded as a heretic. As in the case of property, the Rabbis ruled that all marriages have an implied condition that their validity and continuance are based on rabbinic consent. Rabbis in the past have differed as to how extensive this power is, but one cannot be deemed a heretic when he agrees with the most liberal views heretofore entertained. Exercising the power that rabbis have, they may one day reintroduce the annulment of Jewish marriages and the abolition of the last vestige of illegitimacy (except in the case of unequivocal proof that the child was born of an incestuous relationship). They may find ways to legislate an Enoch Arden law and make the incidence of the levirate law impossible. There are some limitations; but for any Orthodox group to brand as a heretic one who feels keenly that changes should be made—within the Halachic frame and by its own methodology—is to define heresy as it was never defined in the past. One can argue with the proponents of change because of policy considerations, but one may not challenge their loyalty to the faith. Indeed, they may be its most passionate champions as they try to relieve human distress.

III

The areas of personal religious observance and congregational or temple practice are quite different. There the *bet din* is not so free to act as in other spheres of the Law. And he who would, for example, say that a Jew need not don the phylacteries or eat kosher food could be regarded as a heretic. However, one should not underestimate the extent to which rabbis may, in good faith, differ with each other within the frame of the Halachah without even recommending change. They may differ on policy considerations; they may differ on the steps that are required to nullify or modify earlier rabbinic legislation; they may differ on programs that are designed to guide people back to the Torah way of life. Even when they agree on what Orthodoxy requires in terms of normative practice, they can differ on policies and programs to achieve the goal they all envisage.

A few timely illustrations are in order. Should a rabbi use the microphone on the Sabbath in a synagogue where its use is required? The prohibition may be Biblical in origin. Others maintain that it is only rabbinic. Still others argue that the microphone may be used. Which is the better course for a rabbi to take—to rely on the more lenient view and serve the congregation so that it will not align itself with the non-Orthodox camp, or to decline to serve, thereby avoiding the compromise of one's own convictions and firmly presenting to that congregation a strict pattern of Jewish observance? In the final analysis, considerations of policy will dictate what one's decision will be, and Orthodox rabbis have been known to hold either view.

Similarly, Halachah dictates that men shall be separated from women in the synagogue. Some authorities hold that the most that can be Biblically supported is that they shall sit in separate sections. At least one authority holds that there is a Biblical requirement for a divider seventy-two inches high. But the Biblical rules are also sometimes suspended in the face of greater needs of the community, especially in times of stress. Most often the suspension is temporary, but not necessarily so. Perhaps this explains why some of the policy-makers at Yeshiva University's theological seminary permit rabbis to serve congregations with mixed seating, in the hope that these congregations may one day revert to the traditional practice. They may be in error, but they are acting within the frame of a well-established Halachic principle that for God's sake one sometimes flouts Torah mandates. They are not to be regarded as diminished in their commitment. On the contrary, they may be more prophetic, and as they venture they may reclaim many, while others are saving only a remnant.

My last illustration is perhaps the one on which rabbinic opinion is most sharply divided. Most prohibitions are rabbinic in origin—they constitute the "fence around the Law." In modern times many of these rules have become onerous, and often meaningless. There are many ways to modify and even nullify their impact. Some rabbis seek the re-establishment of a Sanhedrin to accomplish this desired result. Others rely on a well-known principle that when the reason for the "fence" has disappeared, the rule, too, automatically dies. What right does one have to question the integrity or commitment of an Orthodox Jew who proposes one way or the other? All have ample authority on which to rely. To what extent, for example, may electric power be used on the Sabbath, since the prohibition is at most rabbinic? Perhaps the use of musical instruments can also be liberalized. I personally may not agree, and in several instances I should like to see more "fences" added to safeguard Biblical rules (such as the prohibition against usury), but I cannot deny that there are reasons for modifying some established pro-

272

hibitions. One ought not, in any case, pronounce bans against those who are pressing for conclusions with which one differs, provided that they make their proposals out of their commitment to the Law rather than their rejection of it.

If heresy is to be found anywhere, therefore, it must be in the areas of doctrine and creed rather than of law and practice.

IV

Even with regard to doctrine, such a divergence of opinion has prevailed among the giants of the Tradition that only one dogma enjoys universal acceptance: the Pentateuch's text was given to the Jewish people by God. However, what its mandates are, their number, application, and interpretation—this is part of the Oral Law, also God-given, but its guardians were rarely unanimous on its legal norms and less so on matters theological. That a majority prevailed on any particular issue in the past does not necessarily mean that the minority view is heretical, for, while one must continue to fulfill the law as the majority decided, one may propagate the minority point of view in the hope that it will one day be accepted by a new Sanhedrin. Maimonides is less liberal on this point than his critical glossator, Rabbi Abraham Ben David, but even Maimonides accords this power to a Sanhedrin greater than its predecessors in quality and quantity. Therefore, how can one brand as a heretic anyone who in matters theological differs with his contemporaries and seeks to make normative a point of view once rejected or proscribed but for whose acceptance he continues to hope?

How many are the dogmas of Judaism? Maimonides said thirteen, but other scholars held that there were fewer. Even on so basic a point as to whether there can exist more than one divine law Albo differed with Maimonides. He denied that there is any evidence for Maimonides' contention that the immutability of the Mosaic Law is a pillar of the faith and opined that there may be a succession of divine laws, so that even Mosaic law is not beyond change or repeal.[2] Jews generally have agreed with Maimonides, at least until the Messiah will come, and upon his coming they believe with Albo that new divine laws may be promulgated. The collective experience of the Jewish people may warrant the conclusion that the Maimonidean view is the more prudent—pragmatically to be regarded as true—but who can gainsay the right of a dissenter to agree with Albo or even a modification or extension of Albo's view and yet regard himself as a member of the family of the committed?

Agreement or even consensus is still more difficult to find in connection with such matters as the nature and mission of angels, the character of "the world-to-come" and how it differs from immortality of the soul, the precise role the Messiah will play when he comes and what events will be the most dependable credentials of his legitimacy, the form final judgement will take in a hereafter and the reward and punishments to be dispensed, the transmigration of souls, and a score of other issues with which ancient and medieval scholars were concerned. One discovers in their writings virtually every opinion known to man, ranging from the purest rationalism to the wildest fancy. Few Orthodox Jews try to be specific in formulating their own creeds. They are content with a few generalizations: that God endows every human being with a soul, which is His eternal spark within us and immortal; the human being—body and soul—is responsible and accountable for his performance on earth; one day nature will be made perfect, and as God fulfills His promise to make it perfect He will also have to do justice to the dead, who are the most helpless victims of nature's imperfections. Details are not only avoided, they are unthinkable. Except in most elusive form these sentiments can hardly be regarded as dogmas; they leave too much room for the play of the imagination of the individual believer. Therefore, it is incredible that moderns, who are committed

2. *Book of Roots* I, 3, 25; III, 13-16.

to faith and the Law, should be excluded from the fold because of limited credulousness in this sphere. Indeed, it would be impossible for reactionaries to ignore the giants of the past who were equally skeptical. (Only recently did I come upon a note of Strashoun proving that the Talmud did not subscribe to Kabbalistic notions of the transmigration of souls.)

But the range of the diversity involves doctrines even more basic to the faith. To what extent, for example, is there any binding authority on the nature of God and His attributes? Here, too, Maimonides and Rabbi Abraham ben David differed so radically on God's corporeality that, were Jews prone to create sects because of doctrinal disputes, as Protestants do, each would have been responsible for a new sect in Judaism. Even with regard to so integral a part of Judaism as God's role as Creator, Maimonides retained an open mind. He believed that the correct interpretation of the Bible required a belief in *creatio ex nihilo,* but he admitted that if it could be proven conclusively—as Aristotle had failed to do—that this was impossible, one would then only be required to re-examine and correct one's interpretation of the Bible to make it consonant with the demands of absolute truth. Judaism is very much at peace with a host of antinomies regarding God's nature—His immanence and His transcendence, His prescience and His becoming, His absolutism and His vacillation. To deny that God is a personal God who communicates with all men, and especially with Israel, would be heresy according to Judaism, but any description of Him by rationalists, empiricists, intuitionists, or existentialists would hardly be without some warrant in the writings of the Sages.

Similarly, there is no substantial agreement with regard to the manner in which God communicated with Israel, its Patriarchs and Prophets. Somehow the Tradition preferred never to demand of Jews more than that they believe the text of the Pentateuch to be divine in origin. Otherwise, the widest latitude in interpretation was not only permitted but often encouraged. Even the authorship of the Five

Books of Moses was not beyond the scope of the diversity. Several Sages held that Moses himself wrote the book of Deuteronomy but God dictated its inclusion with the earlier books. Moreover, much in the earlier books started also as the work of man. In their dialogues with God the Patriarchs spoke their own words. Jacob composed his own prophecy for his offspring. Moses sang his own song of triumph on the Red Sea. In the final analysis, then, the sanctity of the Pentateuch does not derive from God's authorship of all of it but rather from the fact that God's is the final version. The final writing by Moses has the stamp of divinity—the kiss of immortality. So stated, the dogma is a much more limited one than one would be led to believe it is when one listens to many an Orthodox teacher today.

If this is the situation with regard to the Pentateuch, is it wise to add dogmas that the books of the Prophets and the Writings were all authored by the men to whom the Tradition attributes them? The Talmud itself was not dogmatic, but contemporary Orthodoxy always feels impelled to embrace every tradition as dogma. The Talmud suggests that perhaps David did not write all the Psalms. Is one a heretic because one suggests that perhaps other books were authored by more than one person or that several books attributed by the Tradition to one author were in fact written by several at different times? A volume recently published makes an excellent argument for the position that there was but one Isaiah, but must one be shocked when it is opined that there may have been two or three prophets bearing the same name? No Sage of the past ever included in the articles of faith a dogma about the authorship of the books of the Bible other than the Pentateuch. What is the religious, moral, or intellectual need for adding dogmas now when it is well known with regard to many such issues that there aways prevailed *noblesse oblige* among scholars? It may be heresy to deny the possibility of prophetic prediction, but it is not heresy to argue about authorship on the basis of objective historical and literary evidence. How material is it that one really believes that Solomon wrote all three

Scrolls attributed to him? Is the value of the writings itself affected? And if the only purpose is to discourage critical Biblical scholarship, then, alas, Orthodoxy is declaring bankruptcy: it is saying that only the ignorant can be pious —a reversal of the Talmudic dictum.

True, a pious man has *emunat hachamim,* faith in the dicta of the Sages. Yet Orthodox Jews do not rely on this principle in connection with their physical well-being. They are willing to be treated in illness by physicians who hold views that differ radically from those expressed in the Talmud for the treatment of disease. Certainly the Tradition condones this. Is it less forgiving of one who in his study of the Bible feels impelled to arrive at conclusions on the basis of evidence unavailable to his forebears?

No more than with regard to the authorship of the Biblical books did the Sages canonize interpretations of the Bible. For the purpose of the Halachah one interpretation may have to be followed until the Halachah, within its own processes, is altered; but the Sages recognized, offered, and delighted in many alternative, frequently contradictory interpretations which had significance for their spiritual living. Especially was this true when they interpreted narrative portions of the Bible. Maimonides was the most revolutionary of all when he held that most Biblical history is allegorical. Whether Jacob only dreamed that he wrestled an angel or actually did so was debated by sundry Sages. Nachmanides even held that it was God's intention that the *mitzvot* of the Torah were given for ultimate fulfillment in the Land of Israel, and our observance of them in the Diaspora is only preparation for our sojourn in the land of our fathers. Hardly any Orthodox rabbi agrees with him today —and perhaps none agreed with him in his day. Was he, therefore, deemed a heretic?

Even the historic fact of revelation was not specifically delineated. Whether God as much as spoke all the Decalogue so that everyone could hear it was controversial. One Rabbi dared to say that God did not descend to earth. Summing up the Talmudic and Midrashic texts available and the opinions of medieval philosophers, one modern scholar said that the best that could be said for the Jewish conception of revelation is that it is "elusive." Perhaps it is. But the net effect is a consensus on which the faith is founded. *Something* extraordinary happened—and the Jew begins with a text that is God's word. He may not always understand it. He may often question why God approved of much that He gave. Unlike Martin Buber, the Orthodox Jew does not reject any part of the text. If he finds it difficult to explain why the very God who ordered us never to take revenge also demanded the extermination of the Amalekites, he does not delete from the text the lines he does not fathom; he ponders them until divine illumination comes to him. He may discover that the Amalekites—unlike the Egyptians—merited destruction and continuing hate; he may regard Amalek as the symbol of militarism for the sake of militarism; or he may even conclude that what is meant is the id in every human being. Heresy begins not when interpretation is challenged but when the text is no longer considered divine. That is why Franz Rosenzweig did not consider himself un-Orthodox because of his theory of revelation but only because he could not bring himself to obey all the *mitzvot* until they spoke to him personally and became meaningful to his own existential situation. Unlike him, the Orthodox Jew obeys and does not wait. Obedience to God's will by itself is meaningful to his existential situation, and the more he obeys the more he discovers meaning and relevance.

If Jews differed with regard to their interpretation of the texts of Scripture, certainly they differed with regard to their interpretation of history. It has been demonstrated, for example, that Ashkenazim and Sephardim differed with regard to their positions on eschatology and the warrant that historical situations might provide for either activism or quiescence with regard to the coming of the Messiah.

Thus, even with respect to creed, the diversity is as legion as it is with respect to Law. To be counted among the devout and the committed never required unrelenting conformity in matters of the mind and heart. Judaism did not suffer as a result. On the contrary, it remained one of the most dynamic and spiritually satisfying of all religious traditions. In the last century and a half this magnificent Tradition was abandoned: in its encounter with the enormous diversity of the winds of doctrine prevailing in the modern world, Orthodoxy sought to guarantee its survival by freezing the Halachah and its theology. As a result, it now cannot realize its full potential in an age when more and more intellectuals are prepared for the leap of faith but hardly for a leap to obscurantism.

V

Are the "rightists" justified from a practical point of view? They argue that only the "freeze" will save Judaism and that it is better to weed out those whose outlook on the faith and the Law is liberal, to retain only the hard core of loyalists who never question. Some of them would even prefer to insulate their followers against all secular learning. If secular learning there must be, let it be held to a minimum, and that minimum should be restricted to "safe" disciplines such as mathematics, accountancy, business. Even natural science may be "safe." Social science is more hazardous; biology, psychology, anthropology and archaeology are most dangerous of all. Where possible, the loyalists seek to live in isolated, self-contained communities. For their right to do all of these things even the liberal must fight. Their freedom should not be curtailed because one disagrees with them. But one must question the wisdom of their program as well as the correctness of their perspectives. At the same time, one must demonstrate to them that Orthodoxy's future is bright if, instead of resorting to self-containment, it is true to its historic destiny to be ecumenical vis-à-vis the total Jewish community.

Perhaps the liberals have been too decent in their hesitancy to expose the sordid situation that prevails in the rightists' camp. Personal vilification and even journalistic blackmail are ruthlessly in vogue. An Anglo-Jewish weekly that consistently spoke the views of the reactionaries is attacked by a more extreme Hebrew monthly for being mildly sympathetic with the plight of the State of Israel. The same magazine heaped abuse on a day school that is Agudist, not even Mizrachi, in its orientation. Needless to say, it would be sheerest folly to expect that such extremists would heed an appeal to reason made by a rabbi whose liberal sympathies are well-known. However, the overwhelming majority of Orthodox Jews, who are not only devout and committed but also generous in their support of institutions dedicated to the survival of the Torah tradition, are decent people. They are not organized in any kind of "citizens' union" to cleanse their own movement, and they support no one party or publication. To them an appeal for Jewish ecumenism must be made. Jewish intellectuals also must be cautioned against identifying Orthodoxy with a committed but fanatical minority who, alas, because they were themselves in Europe the victims of so much hate, have lost the capacity to be tolerant and to love.

It is the nature of the extremist that he cherish extremes: the more extreme a position is, the better it suits his temperament and outlook. For that reason there are so many defections, for example, by more moderate Klausenberger Hasidim to the virulently anti-Zionist *Rebbe* of Satmar. For that reason also the most extreme group in Israel, which was never Hasidic—the *Neturei Karta*—affiliated with Satmar. If a *Rebbe* more extreme than the Satmar were to enter upon the scene, there would be many defections to the new "right." Would that be regarded as the new Orthodoxy, while the other Hasidic movements would be "conservative"? Jewish sociologists have studied with justifiable admiration what Hasidic communities are achieving, but they have respectfully ignored the strife, the hostility, and the unmistakable ugliness of the manner in which several of the groups react to others. However, unless the spirit of mutual respect and toleration is nurtured, deepened and propagated, many more Orthodox youth will not only detect the malaise of Orthodoxy but reject the entire Tradition precisely because it can breed such unhealthy psyches. This is a practical reason for ecumenism. One distinguished Israeli rabbi and popular author was so distressed by the bitter, almost savage-like factionalism that prevails that he initiated a movement for truth and peace. His effort aborted, and he was speedily silenced. If one talks about peace and truth and, above all, respect for differences, one becomes suspect and loses status in extremist Orthodox circles.

It would, therefore, be wise for Orthodox Jews frankly to reject extremism not only as ideologically inconsistent with the Torah tradition but as pragmatically untenable for survival. Moreover, there must be mutual respect if Orthodoxy is to mobilize all of the committed in a common effort to achieve adequate representation in the organized American Jewish community and in government circles. It is to the credit of Orthodoxy that on many national and international issues it has expressed original and courageous positions. There is a growing respect everywhere for its new strength and refreshing insights. However, its adherents still constitute such an amorphous community that its spokesmen are not accorded prestige positions or merited allocations from available funds by the leadership of the general Jewish community. The intolerance of Orthodox Jews vis-à-vis each other is matched by at least a comparable intolerance vis-à-vis non-Orthodox Jews, and the leaders of the general Jewish community cannot be gracious when their graciousness is less than reciprocated. Thus many of them, for example, who are profoundly impressed by what Yeshiva University has accomplished for both America and Jewry, still find it difficult to give as generously to it as they do to other universities—Jewish and non-Jewish—only because they equate the name "Yeshiva" with obscurantism and fanaticism. In academic circles, on the one hand, Yeshiva University's reputation continues to soar, while in the circles of Jewish federations and philanthropists there is resistance because of mistaken images.

Most important of all, only a liberal approach can help

youth who are groping to discover that Orthodoxy is an exciting quest and not always the oracle for final answers. Only the liberal approach can help them see that the quest is one which involves a creative partnership between God and man not only in the conquest of the earth but also in fulfillment of God's will for both nature and man. Youth are too sophisticated to believe that any man is the master of the ultimate. They are much more prone to accept the meaningfulness of process even in creed, not only in law, and will cherish the tension of the Orthodox who are profoundly committed to the fact of revelation at the same time that they seek to unravel that revelation and make it progressively significant for human thought and action.

With a respectful ecumenical approach Orthodoxy has much to gain. It is to be hoped that it will not miss its opportunity.

VI

In all fairness to those who share my views, it should be said that they are not alumni of any one Yeshiva but of virtually all. If half of them or more are alumni of Yeshiva University, it is only because half or more of all Orthodox rabbis ordained in America have studied there. They are all individuals who have not hesitated to expose themselves to the totality of humanity's accumulated learning. Indeed, they deem it an insult to the revealed word of God that the validity of what God gave can only be maintained by remaining oblivious of other disciplines. What is more, it is they who maintain that the Torah will be valid no matter what the test to which it is subjected and no matter what the circumstances in which one is called upon to live.

This is why they are most militant champions not only of a viable Halachah but also of the Torah's relevance to every issue one encounters in a modern state. They recognize that final decisions in many instances involve questions of policy, and often in policy questions the opinions of the knowledgeable laymen are at least as sound as those of the "doctors of the Law." In this way they also help to revive an ancient Jewish tradition that gives the layman a real voice in many matters confronting the Jewish community. They seek less of a dictatorship of the rabbinate and more the combined action of the community of the devout and committed. In an age when Hasidism is on the march, and thousands yield obedience to a chosen *Rebbe* or *Rosh Yeshiva*, their position can only be that of a few. But they are an influential few and do not want to separate from their brethren. Their brethren, too, should not cavalierly dismiss what need all have of each other, if Orthodoxy is to meet the challenge of the age.

SECTION FIVE

ISRAEL'S SANCTA

For the people of Israel many things are holy. But few have meant more to them in their millennial history than their land, their synagogues and schools and their prayerbook. No teacher of Judaism could possibly avoid involvement with them and in this section I deal with them—by no means exhaustively, but hopefully with some new and meaningful insights.

Chapter One

ERETZ YISRAEL IN
THE JEWISH TRADITION

I

It is well known that the three central ideas of Judaism are Torah, land, and people. However, what is not so well known is that the tradition derives all three doctrines from our patriarch Abraham. It was he whom God assured that through Isaac he would become the father of a great people. It was he to whom we are indebted for our monotheistic creed, and it was he through whom God made us the promise of the land.

Indeed, according to ancient sources, the land of Israel was originally bequeathed by Noah to his son Shem. Shem was dispossessed by his nephew Canaan but God had prom-

287

ised to restore the inheritance to Abraham's descendants, who were Shem's rightful heirs. In this way perhaps Jews sought to justify their conquest of the area from the Canaanites. Nonetheless, it becomes apparent how deeply rooted in the past is the concept of the land. It began with a promise to Abraham who traversed its length and its breadth; it was confirmed to Isaac who never separated himself from its soil; and it spelled home for Jacob all the time that he was in flight from Esau as well as thereafter when he asked his sons in Egypt to inter him in the cave of Machpela. Even for our forebears in bondage unto Pharaoh, and for their children who were liberated, the conquest of the land was the ultimate step in their redemption.

Why had God chosen the land of Israel for His chosen people? The tradition affords many answers. It was a land flowing with milk and honey as well as rich in mineral resources. It was a beautiful land, aesthetically exciting. The range of its terrain from high above to considerably below sea level made it a microcosm of the entire earth. Its wide diversity in climatic conditions strengthened the same conclusion. Last, but most impressive of all, is the suggestion that on the mountain peaks of Jerusalem, even before Abraham, there were scholars already searching for God. Theirs were the schools of Shem and Eber in which Abraham, Malkizedek, and their disciples found kindred spirits. This alone would have made the land holy, and it was conceived as holy even before it was conquered by Moses and Joshua.

With the conquest many centuries after Abraham, there came an added reason for holiness. The land was now the place where the Hebrews were to live and fulfill the mandates of Torah. Indeed, according to Nachmanides the Torah was intended to be nothing more than a constitution for the Jewish polity in Canaan. Whatever observance of the Torah there was to be elsewhere was only for the sake of keeping the people perpetually prepared for their return home. However, even those who differed with Nachmanides and ascribed to Torah a more universal significance readily admitted that scores of commandments were applicable only to the holy land. Not all the land may have been equally holy or had the same historical importance. The area to the east of the Jordan was not as holy as the area to the west. Some parts were conquered in Joshua's time; still other parts were settled in Ezra's time. Occasionally the boundaries were extended by a David or a Hyrcanus during the first or the second commonwealth. Yet no matter what varying degrees of holiness the Halachic rules may have assigned to the different parts of Israel, there are sections of the Torah that made of the land of Israel a factor of overwhelming importance in the law and life of our people. These sections involve the so-called "Mitzvot hatluyot ba-arez"—commandments applicable to only one particular area of the earth's surface, Israel.

II

The yearning to fulfill the commandments applicable only to the land of Israel was one of the most important factors making for the millennial hope of our forebears to return to their ancestral home after they had been exiled. In prayer and in study they described the joys associated with the service in the temple, which service they could not hold anywhere else in the world. Nostalgic expressions for these services are to be found in the liturgy for all Sabbaths and festivals. Even temple ceremonies for which there was no counterpart in the liturgy—such as the Simhat Beit ha-Shoaiva—were preserved in special celebrations among scholars and saints.

Of the system of tithes and heave offerings there was but one vestigial ritual in the Jewish home—the removal of "Chala" at the time of kneading dough. However, most of the concepts were transferred to the laws of charity. Thus it became customary for Jews to give at least a tenth of their incomes to charity. The earlier practices, applicable to the harvest and involving leavings for the poor—Leket, Shikha and Pea, constituted the legal precedent for a voluminous literature on philanthropy. However, at least one offering, that of Bikurim, the first fruits, was studied on every Pentecost festival and Jews were wont to dream of their own ascent to Jerusalem in the messianic era and their own reenactment of this joyous ceremony. Indeed, this ceremony has become one of the first to be reinstituted in the modern state of Israel by religious and secularist Jews alike. So popular was its appeal that earlier reformers—who had rejected the hope for a return to Zion as inconsistent with the universalist message of Judaism and the conception of Jews serving as a light unto the nations—felt impelled to retain the ceremony, although with a new dress and meaning.

Yet of all the commandments applicable to the land none captivated the imagination of scholars and saints in our millennial exile more than the system of land tenure and cultivation that involved the jubilee and sabbatical years. It was this system that was to help the land retain its holiness and save the people from being expelled therefrom.

To prove that the land was God's—sanctified by Him and reserved for His people—Jews were not to till the soil or sow the seed for one year in seven. Every fiftieth year there was to be not only no agriculture but a redistribution of the land to its original owners. The slaves too were to be emancipated then. That was the year when Jews "were to proclaim liberty throughout the land, to all the inhabitants thereof." The verse may be on the Liberty Bell of the United States; the texts may have inspired social reformers in every age; but the system was ordained for Israel—the holy land. God had promulgated special laws for a place that had special significance for Him. When Jews ignored their mandate, the prophet Jeremiah predicted their destruction and their loss of the land. These evils came to pass—not once, but twice. However, interest in the laws of the jubilee and sabbatical years never ceased. They constituted a unique pattern for a chosen people on a chosen land. The sounding of the Shofar at the conclusion of every fast of Yom Kippur was the annual reminder of the emancipation of slaves at the end of the Day of Atonement in a jubilee year. Yet,

Jews continued to count the years and with the restoration of a Jewish community in Palestine, and the reestablishment of a Jewish commonwealth, this aspect of the land's holiness was found to play an important part.

There are many in Israel who already want to observe the Biblical requirement that they desist from all agricultural enterprise in the seventh year. They do not want to wait for Israel to become more secure economically before indulging in this costly surcease from toil. Others would defer the observance until conditions within and without are more propitious, and temporarily they rely upon a legal fiction through which work may continue. Still others work but have in their settlements some reminder that it is the sabbatical year.

All, however, have reinstituted one historic ceremony that was observed in the wake of the sabbatical year—the ceremony of Hakhel. It is described in the Book of Deuteronomy. In the third week after a sabbatical year, with its reaffirmation of the people's faith in God, the people were wont to assemble on one of the mountains of Jerusalem. From a high platform the head of the state would read from the Torah and the people would pledge their allegiance once again to the King of all the earth and His immortal Law. This was also the festival of Tabernacles—the season of joy. Needless to say, having dreamed of all this pageantry for centuries, the Jewish people could have been expected to restore as much of it as soon as possible. And this they did. What the Bible had ordained for Eretz Yisrael had come to life again.

III

Yet, in addition to the involvement of Biblical history and Biblical legislation with the land, there is also a theological involvement. This is less easily culled from the sources. However, it appears that there is a special relationship between the very Being of God and the land of Israel. Once God had chosen the land for His chosen people, it became so charged with His holiness that it had to play a special role in the fulfillment of His ultimate purpose for all mankind. For that reason, for example, while idolatry, from Judaism's point of view, is a crime everywhere, it is especially heinous if practiced in Israel. The land itself cannot tolerate this effrontery to God. Furthermore, while homicide and sexual improprieties are unforgiveable any place, they are especially contaminating to the soil of the holy land. God's attachment to this land makes it necessary that higher moral standards prevail there. But, God's attachment to it is not only for purposes now discernible but also for the future destiny of humanity.

It is in that land that the messianic age will be heralded. On its mountains God will ultimately judge between the nations. Even for the resurrection of the dead which can only be realized in the age known as "Olam Haba," when nature will be perfect and her greatest evil—death—will be no more, the land of Israel will have a special quality. From this thought, too, was born the desire of Jews through a millennial exile to be buried in the holy land.

From the verse in Deuteronomy (11:12), "A land, with which the Lord thy God is concerned; perpetually are the eyes of the Lord thy God upon it, from the beginning of the year to the end of the year," the Rabbis derived the conclusion that God has a special relationship to the land. That is why it was a Mitzva to reside there—even if one could perform none of the commandments applicable to the land. By the mere act of residence there, one came physically closer to God. The land itself in its entirety was His altar. Even burial any place in the holy land was regarded as burial on an altar of atonement. Thus it was not alone the fact that the land was promised to the patriarchs, nor even the fact that the Jews resided there for centuries, that constituted the bond between the land and the people. Indeed, not even the Torah's many sections dealing with the soil, its produce, and the polity Jews were to establish there, were altogether responsible for the bond. It was God Himself who was part of the very atmosphere of that special area of the earth. We shall later see how important this perspective was in the literature of the mystics and the earliest resettlements in Israel centuries ago by Kabbalists. Suffice it to say now that the roots of this theological element are in the Bible and the Talmud.

Because of the holiness of the land, husbands and wives who resided in the Diaspora and could hardly otherwise coerce each other to change their place of residence, could force each other to move to Israel. Even a slave could run away from his master and take up his residence in Israel. All that the master could get from him was a promissory note for the amount of loss sustained by this act of self-liberation. If a man craved the holiness of a Nazarite he had to ascend to the holy land to fulfill his vow. Moreover, to buy land in Israel on the Sabbath one might use the services of a non-Jew, though this normally would constitute a breach of the Sabbath's sanctity.

The Talmud tells of Rabbis who were wont to kiss rocks of Israel and roll in her sands when they would approach the border en route from Babylon or other countries. Though Babylon had many great academies in the third and fourth centuries, and the Babylonian Talmud is understandably zealous in its regard for the prestige of these academies, nonetheless the Babylonian Talmud records with approval the prohibition that Palestinians should not leave the holy land to take up permanent residence even in Babylon. Perhaps a temporary sojourn there for the purpose of Torah study might be forgiven. Virtually the only reason justifying emigration from Israel is self-preservation. And he who emigrated was compared to him "who left his mother's bosom to cleave to the bosom of a strange woman."

Because the land partook of God's very Being, its waste was especially to be avoided. Whatever pagans ever worshiped as a god was, and still is, to be destroyed by Jews. Yet, the mandate did not apply to the trees of the land of Israel. These were presumed never to have belonged to pagans that they might create the taboo as if they had a proprietary interest in the soil and what is attached thereto.

To reduce the habitability of the land was a sin. Even to demolish a house in order to replace it with a garden was not permitted because one or more families were thus denied an opportunity to settle there. To such an extent did the Rabbis give expression to their passion for the preservation of everything in Israel that they ruled that, while outside of Israel one may occasionally remove a Mezuza from his door when changing his place of residence, one may never do so in Israel. Every home must be held in immediate readiness for someone to move in. Moreover, while outside of Israel one may wait thirty days before affixing a Mezuza—for the first thirty days in one's new residence one hardly regards one's self as settled—in Israel one must affix the Mezuza immediately. In the performance of the Mitzva of dwelling in Israel one never considers one's self a transient!

IV

The historical, legal, and theological significances of Eretz Yisrael as found in Biblical and Talmudic sources played their respective roles in the life and thought of Jews in the Middle Ages as well as in the modern period. The historical element was most important in the revival of Jewish nationalism, the renaissance of the tongue of the prophets, and the creation of the Hebrew literature of the Enlightenment. The legal element inspired many for whom Zionism meant a new opportunity to create the most perfectly just society on earth. To the theological element, however, must be credited the fact that there never died in the heart and mind of the Jew the hope for an Israel redeemed. Indeed, the miracle of a people that never forgot has its source in this religious commitment that never failed.

Perhaps a word about this miracle ought be said that its importance may be fully fathomed in the light of universal history. For many decades at the end of the nineteenth and the first half of the twentieth centuries "higher critics" of the Bible doubted that there ever was a destruction of a first

294

temple in 586 B.C.E. The entire tale of a people exiled by Babylonia and restored to its homeland fifty years later by Persia seemed spurious. It was attributed to the wild imagination of prophets who were always concocting fairy tales to induce loyalty to God. The Biblical confirmation of this narrative was regarded as inconsequential, for much of the Bible was supposed to be lyrical or allegorical, but certainly not history. Jeremiah's "Lamentations" was also deemed a dirge written long after the happening of an imagined event. Indeed, the Biblical texts themselves substantiated the mythical character of the story. For the Bible indicated that the king of Babylon exiled Jewish gardeners and what could be more preposterous than that the great Babylon, whose landscape architects created the miracle of her hanging gardens, should have need of the assistance of Hebrew horticulturists! Moreover, such things simply did not happen in history—a nation exiled never returns!

The arguments of the "higher critics" were all answered in the last few years. In fact, every detail of the Biblical narrative was confirmed including the name of one Jewish gardener, which was discovered by archaeologists. However, Professor William Albright, dean of all archaeologists of our day, made the comment at the conclusion of a lecture on this subject that his predecessors were not malicious when they doubted that the story ever happened. In universal history it hardly ever did. Yet, surprising enough, it happened three times in human history—only three—and all three times to the Jewish people—from Canaan to Egypt in Jacob's time and back to Canaan again under Moses; from Judea to Babylon in 586 B.C.E. and back to Judea again a half century later; from Israel to Rome and all the corners of earth in 70 C.E. but back to Israel again in our own day, with the restoration of the third Jewish commonwealth!

Historians cannot explain this. And theologians are not often respected. But if the thrice-repeated "miracle" happened only to Jews, then it must be explained either by reference to God's participation in the history of His chosen people or by reference to the people who refused to forget.

The least that must be admitted by skeptics as well is that through prayer to God the people kept their hope alive. In prayer they always gave expression to their yearning for "Eretz ha-Zevi"—the beautiful land—the land of their dreams.

Formal books of prayer are the contribution of the Middle Ages. But prayers giving expression to this yearning are found even in the Talmud and several were composed long before the destruction of either the first or second temple. These prayers had naught to do with the sacrificial cult in the temple and were not in lieu of animal offerings. Yet, after the destruction they took on added significance because the Jews then did not thank God for a land they possessed, but for a land to which they hoped one day to be restored. However, after the destruction many prayers were added specifically to plead for the return to Zion.

V

In two prayers whose texts are found in the Pentateuch itself we find special blessings for the land. One was recited when all the tithes and heave offerings were finally disposed of. The other was recited when the first fruits were brought to the temple. Indeed, a very interesting rule was applicable to the latter blessing. Even proselytes could recite it and thank God for the land which God had promised them, though they themselves were not descendants of Abraham to whom the promise was originally made. On the other hand, Jews who were unquestionably descended from Abraham could not recite the blessing unless they actually owned a tract of land in Israel from whose yield they brought the Bikurim offering. Mind you, to own a piece of sacred soil qualified one to recite the blessing while the fact that unsullied Jewish blood coursed in one's veins was not a qualification! So important was title to even the smallest plot in the holy land!

One other occasion for praying for the land is suggested

in the verse in Deuteronomy which ordains grace after meals. For that reason, the second paragraph of the grace after meals, recited until this day, thanks God both for food and for the sacred soil of Israel. Some people erred and assumed that the blessing ought to be for any tract of earth whence bread doth come. However, the Rabbis ruled that it shall concern itself exclusively with Eretz Yisrael and that is why there is a reference in the paragraph to God's covenant with Abraham which involved the promise of the land.

In an ancient prayer which the High Priest was wont to recite after the conclusion of the sacred service on the Day of Atonement, we also find reference to the land. Prayers for rain and dew in appropriate ceremonies are equally ancient. However, it is with the destruction of the temple that prayers for its restoration and the return of our people unto Zion became the most important theme of the liturgy. Even prayers for God's forgiveness are almost invariably linked with the thought that once we are forgiven our redemption will follow. Thus the retention of prayers for dew and rain which are chanted on the first day of Passover and the eighth day of Tabernacles, respectively, are only seasonal ties with Eretz Yisrael. But there were ties that were daily—thrice daily. In the Eighteen Benedictions, Jews pleaded for the privilege of beholding God's return to Zion with their own eyes and this entire prayer was recited by the Jew as he faced in the direction in which Jerusalem lay. On Mondays and Thursdays Jews recited special penitential prayers, known as "ve-Hu Rachum" and begged God to call a halt to their shame and restore His glory to His land and shrine. On New Moons, Sabbaths, and festivals, they recounted the offerings which Scripture had prescribed for the occasion. Many Jews even did this every morning and afternoon. With words descriptive of the temple service in days of yore they hoped to receive credit themselves "as if" they had personally brought the sacrifices. And in awe and trepidation, in the midst of "Kedusha," as they sang to God with words which the angels use in heaven to express God's immanence and transcendence, Jews wept, "When wilt Thou rule in Zion, soon in our own day, forever."

During the Middle Ages, the liturgy of our prayerbook was not only given a fairly definitive form but many hymns were composed which were later included in an expanded liturgy. In these hymns, too, the longing for a return to Zion found expression. None, however, was cherished by our people more than those composed by Rabbi Yehuda ha-Levi, immortal philosopher and poet, whose odes to Zion are among the world's classics. These poems were chanted at the close of the morning service on the fast day of Ab when Jews mourned the destruction.

This fast itself, together with at least three others, was directly linked with the mourning for the loss of the temple. The Fast of Gedalia, on the third day of the year, commemorates the blasting of the last hope for Jerusalem when Gedalia, who had been appointed governor of Judea by King Nebuchadnezzar of Babylon, was assassinated. On the tenth day of Tevet, Jews fasted because it was on that day that the siege of Jerusalem began, while on the seventeenth day of Tamuz the wall was cracked. On the ninth day of Ab, the temple went up in flames. All the special prayers for these fast days, and other fast days on the religious calendar of the Jew, focused attention on our sins because of which God still shuns us. Jews that did not use the prayerbook might have forgotten Zion. However, up until comparatively recent times such Jews were few and these assimilated altogether. Most Jews used the prayerbook and they could not forget Zion. It was writ into almost every page, if not every verse. And their dream of Zion restored was the dream of a messianic redemption—the end of all their sorrows, the recovery of their dignity in the eyes of the nations that loathe them, and their nestling once again in the land which was their mother, as God was their Father.

298

In the Middle Ages, there was literary creativity in areas other than liturgy. Philosophy, too, received the sustained attention of our great Rabbis, and the role of Eretz Yisrael in their writings merits consideration.

When one reads the classics in Jewish philosophy one cannot help but be impressed by the fact that two problems, which are of endless concern to moderns because of the intellectual climate of our own day, receive little or no attention from such luminaries as Saadia and Maimonides. They never tried to rationalize or validate the conceptions of chosen people and holy land. Since they were writing to meet the challenges of Christian and Mohammedan writers, principally the latter, they could assume the authenticity of the Bible which vouched for God's special relationship to the land and people of Israel. The only question that might arise is whether the Jews had not forfeited their privileged position by rejecting Jesus or Mohammed. The basic issue, therefore, was who was entitled to possess the sacred patrimony; and in the Middle Ages much blood was shed in wars and crusades to resolve this very question. Jewish blood was shed, too, by both of their challengers in Europe and in Palestine, but somehow there was not a year since the days of Joshua when the land of Israel was without a Jewish community. There are still many Christians and Mohammedans who regard us as pretenders and themselves as the truly chosen. However, the philosophical masterpieces of Saadia and Maimonides do not deal extensively with the unique position that the land and people of Israel hold in God's eyes. Saadia interprets all the Mitzvos as means to happiness and Jews were to bring these means to all mankind. For their sacrifice in this cause through the millennia they will be rewarded on the eve of the messianic era or at its very inception. Saadia's personal association with the holy land was virtually nil, except that he, in Babylon, once differed strongly with the Palestinian rabbinate on a matter involving the calendar and the fixing of a date for a festival, and he prevailed. However, he lived in many parts of the Middle East but never in Palestine. And he was so much the rationalist in his approach to every problem that his conceptions of land and people do not touch the heart.

Maimonides did live a brief interval in the holy land. The day of his arrival with his family was celebrated by them for years thereafter with feasting and prayer and the distribution of gifts to the poor. Indeed, this is one of the important precedents suggested by Rabbi Maimon, Israel's first Minister of Religions, to justify the ordaining of Israel's Independence Day—Yom ha-Azmaut—as a religious festival. In Maimonides' classic work codifying all of Jewish law he cites with approval many of the rules found in the Talmud concerning the sanctity of the land of Israel and the importance of residing there. Yet, in his philosophical classic, "The Guide to the Perplexed," he, too, was the captive of his own rationalism and one does not sense that the land is as central as it actually was in Jewish thought and hope. The same can be said of Albo.

The one philosopher who quickened the heart, while his colleagues were preoccupied with reason, was the same Rabbi Yehuda ha-Levi whose odes to Zion were already mentioned. He wrote his great classic the "Kuzari" at a time when his heart bled for the humiliation and destruction of his co-religionists at the hands of the Crusaders. He wanted to avenge his people's honor and one incident in European history provided him with the perfect background for the purpose. A Slavic nation, the Khazars, had embraced Judaism in the eighth or ninth century, and Rabbi Yehuda ha-Levi with creative imagination visualized that the king of the Khazars wanted to choose a religion for his people. He called unto himself a Rabbi, a priest, and a Mohammedan prophet. The three were asked to debate the merits of their respective religions and the king chose Judaism. From the dialogue between the king and the Rabbi one senses the writer's passion for the land of Israel. Indeed, he wrote with such deep feeling that he must have convinced himself to prove what the land meant to him and in his old age he made the trip. Legend has it that he reached his destination but upon embarkation was trampled in the sands he bowed down to kiss.

Let us examine his own words. The king of the Khazars said to him, "If this be so (all that you said about Eretz Yisrael), then you fall short of the duty laid down in your law, by not endeavoring to reach that place and making it your home in life and death . . . You believe that the Divine Providence will return there where it dwelt for 500 years. That is sufficient reason for man's soul to retire there and find purification near the homes of the pious and the prophets . . . Your bowing and your kneeling in the direction of Israel is either hypocrisy or thoughtless worship. If you really meant it you would go there. Your first forefathers chose that place as an abode in preference to their birthplace. They lived rather as strangers in the land of Israel than as citizens of their own countries. This they did even at a time when the Divine Presence had not yet revealed Himself and the land was full of unchastity, impurity and idolatry. Your fathers, however, had no desire other than to remain there. Nor did they leave it in time of drought or famine except with God's permission. Finally they directed their bones to be buried there."

To this the Rabbi replied, "This is a severe reproach, O King of the Khazars. Yes, it was because too many Jews failed to go to Israel from Babylon when the second temple was built that the Jews could not retain that temple forever. Indeed, the majority and the aristocracy remained in Babylon, preferring dependence and slavery, and refusing to leave their homes and affairs."

The King is right. However, there is more to the obligation to return than history and law. By returning to the land of Israel the Jew regains part of the divine soul that is his, for while the Divine Presence has gone into exile with His people, part of it remained in Israel. And the Jew cannot be himself altogether until he recovers that share of the divine spark within him that is the correlative of the Divine Presence in Israel.

Yet, if all Jews returned to Palestine, who would carry God's word to all the nations? Rabbi Yehuda ha-Levi says that Jews do not have to be missionaries. By living the perfect life in Israel we would render a service to all mankind. And by force of his own logic Rabbi Yehuda was driven to return.

VII

The question raised by the King of the Khazars was not easily answered but it troubled many. The Tosafists—who wrote brilliant notes on the texts of the Talmud and on Rashi's commentary—also dealt with the issue. One expressed the view that in their day it would be most hazardous to make the trip, wherefore the obligation to go is suspended. Another opined that since it was then impossible for reasons of survival to observe all the commandments applicable to the land, the Mitzva of residing there had lost most of its significance. This was a minority view but many Jews did feel that, rather than go to the land and find that because of sheer necessity they had to violate many of the rules applicable thereto, they should rather choose to observe the fewer Mitzvos that were theirs in the Diaspora.

What is important is that there was soul searching, and the seeds of modern Aliyah were sowed not in the late eighteenth century but in the twelfth and thirteenth. One of the first of these pioneers was the great Nachmanides who, in Jewish law, philosophy and mysticism, is the peer of Maimonides. The world at large may have found Maimonides' legacy of more universal significance. However, Nachmanides' thought was the more authentically and characteristically Jewish.

Nachmanides went to Israel after a bitter polemic with an apostate and in the three years that he spent there prior to his death he reorganized the Jewish community of Jerusalem. There he also wrote his immortal commentary on the Pentateuch, which is a veritable mine of materials on the holiness of the land of Israel. Thus, for example, on the

302

verse "And Jacob came in peace to the city of Shechem which is in the land of Canaan, after he had departed Padan Aram (in Mesopotamia), and encamped before the city and bought a parcel of land where he had spread his tent" (Genesis 33:18), Nachmanides said, "He did not want to sojourn in the city but he wanted to sleep on his own property his first night in the land of Israel. That is why he camped in the field but purchased the lot, thereby performing an act of possession in the land."

Another distinguished "displaced person," Rabbi Joseph Karo, went to Israel from Turkey almost three centuries later. He went to Safed as Nachmanides went to Jerusalem. There he wrote the great code of Jewish law known as the "Shulhan Aruch." However, both Nachmanides, Karo, and hundreds of others who went to the land of Israel were not the rationalists in the mood and style of Saadia and Maimonides, but mystics to whom must be credited the two greatest movements in modern Jewish history—Hasidism and Zionism.

The mystics were of the mood of Rabbi Yehuda ha-Levi and as their hearts panted for God, of whose reality they had an immediate sense awareness, so their hearts panted for the fullness of God which they could only sense in His land. All the texts of the Bible, Talmud, and Midrash regarding God's special relationship to the land were not only cherished by these mystics but became the basis for action—for Aliyah.

Love of God is enormously important in the life of the mystic—nay, the reciprocated love of God and man is enormously important, and the greatest manifestation of this love is between God and the people of Israel. The literature of mysticism is virtually a vast series of variations on this one theme. Now, God's gifts to the people were the Torah and the land. These were the gifts of the Groom to His bride. Indeed, with the giving of the Torah, He betrothed, and when the tabernacle was dedicated He consummated the nuptials. Therefore, to study His Torah and to dwell upon His land helped one to come physically as well as spiritually closer to Him. It was like attaching one's self to an extension of His Being.

You had to believe thus in order to appreciate the meaning of Eretz Yisrael to these people. Said Rabbi Nachman of Bratislava, "In physical reality one doesn't see any difference between the land of Israel and the other countries of the earth. But he who is privileged to believe in the holiness of the land of Israel can detect at least a bit of the difference." The rationalist has only what his eye doth see and his mind doth fathom. The mystic has a glimpse of reality by extra-sensory means—especially the grasp of faith. The same Rabbi Nachman observed, in his love of Eretz Yisrael, that the first commandment given to Abraham, our first patriarch, was to leave his home and go to the land of Israel. "Lech lecha" (go thee), said Rabbi Nachman, means to go by foot—not by mule and not by cart. Thus did he want to go to the land.

From the yearning of Kabbalists and their spiritual heirs, the Hasidim, came also the belief that the hour of redemption was nigh. That is why there were several instances in the Middle Ages and modern times when Jews believed that the Messiah had actually come. That these were periods of great distress for our people is not sufficient cause for this unique phenomenon in human history. It was rather that the people were prepared emotionally for the fulfillment of a promise—God's promise that could be delayed no longer. 'Twere as if the people were ready virtually to force the hand of God.

The rationalists and the legalists were less impulsive, and perhaps less passionate in their love of God and the land. But in their continued dedication to the Law they also nurtured the hope that would not die.

VIII

They sustained the hope by means direct and indirect. First as the curtain descended on the medieval period, and the modern period began to dawn, Jews and the Jewish community were governed less and less by their own law—the law of the Torah—and more and more by the law of the state in which they lived. Progressively, then, the study of the Torah became irrelevant to daily living. Its goal was either Torah le'Shma—Torah for its own sake—or Torah for a projected Jewish commonwealth, yet to be established. Indeed, the less need there was for Jewish law to be applied to real and existing problems, the more readily it could be idealized. Equity, rather than strict law, could be stressed and Rabbis in their communities were wont to stress the excellence of Jewish justice. Thus, on the one hand, Torah study in preparation for a third Jewish commonwealth was one indirect way of keeping the hope alive while the emphasis on Jewish conceptions of equity and justice paved the way for Jewish commitment to socialist ideals within and without the Zionist movement.

Furthermore, the study of the whole of Torah, including its vast literature on the laws applicable to agriculture, made many Jews aware of the abnormalcy of their economic existence in the lands of their dispersion. Many were overcome with a yearning for productive labor and an aversion for the types of enterprise in which most Jews were then engaged. From men who in their youth had been students of eastern European Yeshivot came the drives within the Zionist movement for a Jewish state that would, on the one hand, fulfill Torah goals of social justice and, on the other hand, transform the vocations and personalities of Jews. These men may have rejected Judaism as a creed and system of practice. But they did distill from their training in youth basic values which the Law advanced.

One group of Rabbis, including many who never identified themselves with the World Zionist Organization, and even opposed it, undertook the intensive study of those parts of the Torah which dealt with the temple service in days of yore. Despite their refusal to honor Zionist leaders who were not "religious," they felt that the new ferment signified that the messianic era was imminent. And they wanted to be prepared for the grand event with a mastery of all the knowledge that a rebuilt temple would entail. Much more than in the Middle Ages the Talmudic scholars of the modern period concerned themselves with that sixth of the Talmud known as "Kodshim"—"Things Holy." The ever growing group of Rabbis in Palestine itself also made a contribution in this direction. As the mystics were whetting the appetite for the land, and inspiring a movement homeward, the rationalists and legalists were preoccupied with procedures that would have to be followed.

Yet, the major contribution of the legalists—over a period of more than half a millennium—was to fashion and publicize the conception that every Jew has a share in Eretz Yisrael—every Jew, born and unborn. It was because of this conception that the singularly remarkable institution known to us as the Jewish National Fund was able to capture the imagination of Jews in every walk of life. The success of this institution whereby the land of Israel is bought by Jews to be held in perpetuity for the Jewish people is not the product of nineteenth century socialism, as so many mistakenly believe. Millions of Jews who responded to its appeal, especially on the Fast of Ab, were as removed from socialism as anyone could be. They responded because of a millennial conviction that every one has a share in Eretz Yisrael; that every Jew is a property owner, at least, in one area of the earth's surface. Aye, with soil of this land they even wanted to be buried. If their remains could not be transported there, then some grains of sand from there could be deposited in the casket no matter where interred.

Very interesting legal rules played their part in inducing the conviction. There is, for example, a manner of conveying title known as "Kinyan Agav." By this method one could transfer ownership to moveable things even when the objects sold were not in the presence of the vendor and purchaser. What one did was to sell one's land—a tiny piece of it—and with the land one sold the moveable objects as well. Title to both realty and personalty then passed simultaneously. But what if one had no land? The presumption was conclusive that every Jew had four square ells in the land of Israel. Even after he had sold it, he had more left. No matter how often he sold by means of the "Kinyan Agav," he could not expropriate himself vis-à-vis Eretz Yisrael.

This presumption regarding the inseparability of the Jew from his land became the basis for still another interesting rule which may now give comfort to the intransigent zealots in Israel who refuse to recognize the state of Israel, but which reveals the extent to which the conviction was nurtured that the Jew "belongs" to Eretz Yisrael and it to him. The general rule is that no matter where Jews live outside of Israel they must obey the law of the state which is their host. Jeremiah so ordained. There may be limitations. We need not obey the state if it promulgates immoral or discriminatory legislation. Generally, however, we must obey the law even if it contravenes the mandates of the Torah. Rabbi Nissim (14th century) expressed the rationale of the rule. We must obey the law of every host country because our residence there is conditional upon our obedience to its law. However, this is not true of the land of Israel. No Jew resides in Israel conditionally or by the grace of someone else. He has an absolute right to live there. And no king, president, parliament or other constituted authority can say to a Jew, "Either obey our statutes or go forth to exile." One cannot order a Jew out of the territory to which he has an inalienable right. The zealots in Israel today rely upon this insight of Rabbi Nissim to resist what they regard as an administration of sinners. Yet, the rule itself through the centuries induced in Jews a feeling of inalienability from the land.

The legal as well as mystical tradition reached a glorious climax in the writings of Rabbi Abraham Kook—peerless leader of his people in the critical years between the two World Wars. In one responsum he concerns himself with the manner in which a Jewish community shall take title to land. Shall it do so as a partnership? Are members of a Kibbutz who take such a title partners? Rabbi Kook observed that many people may view their community as a partnership—as a joint enterprise to improve the lot of every member of the group. However, a Jewish community in Israel is more than a partnership and its property is more than a partnership property. "The corporate entity of the Jewish community has a reality independent of the totality of its individual constituents." The Jewish community has a reality that transcends the present for the partnership is with those already born and those unborn. That is why it is a partnership that never terminates with death. Individual Jews may die; even individual communities may be wiped out. But the eternal mission of the Jewish people charges its very being and its land with a purpose and with holiness. Therefore, property owned by a Jewish community in Israel is not property in which every individual Jew has an undivided share. It is rather property that belongs to Klal Yisrael—the people that was, is and will ever be. It is therefore vested with the spiritual character of the Jewish community that exists metaphysically as a reality. To convey title to such land requires rules other than those applicable to partnerships. Martin Buber also distinguishes between a collectivity and a community. He too would like to regard a Kibbutz as more than a collective which is a group of individuals each of whom has a partnership interest in the group's property. A community, on the other hand, has a transcendent purpose and its property is charged with that purpose—"Zweckvermögung," the German legal philosophers call it. Indeed, the source for this conception can be found in the Mishna. Thus a conception which yielded the Jewish National Fund and the ownership of the land in perpetuity by the Jewish people has the deepest roots in Jewish law.

Yet, while the Law does much to give the land a position of centrality in the Jewish tradition, the Law requires the land for its fulfillment. No grander expression of this interdependence is there than in the rule that there can be no full "Smicha"—no formal ordination of competent authorities in the Law—other than in Israel. In the 17th century an attempt was made in Israel to revive this ceremony. The controversy that ensued is very relevant to the issue that Israel faces today: shall it reconstitute a Sanhedrin? Other than from Israel, there can be no final word on the Law. And howsoever Jews may now differ in their attitudes toward a central Rabbinic authority in Jerusalem, the fact is that other than in Israel there can be no such authority.

IX

Modern Zionism made the establishment of an autonomous Jewish state not so much a requirement of the Law for its fulfillment as the instrument without which the people could not live creatively in peace and dignity. Its roots were deep in the past but its very failure to be Torah-centered helped to attract to it countless Jews who were already committed to secularist conceptions of life and more particularly to secularist conceptions of nationalism. Many religionists forthwith became the movement's enemies and these included religionists of "rightist" as well as "leftist" orientations. Perhaps some German Jews craved an assimilation in which for them Berlin could be as sacred as Jerusalem and they objected to the convening of the World Zionist Congress in a German city. However, many Jews for whom Jerusalem could never be replaced as the eternal city also resisted the new movement. A number of orthodox Jews in Germany who were the spiritual heirs of Samson Raphael Hirsch were content to propagate Judaism in the Diaspora and wait for the miraculous intervention of the Messiah. They too regarded the universalist message of Judaism as inconsistent with parochial Zionism. Yet the overwhelming majority of Jews, especially those in eastern Europe, were not troubled by such considerations. Judaism always had its antinomies—and its universalism and nationalism were equally intensive and not exclusive of each other. The more important challenge for the devout, however, was whether they could cooperate with the irreligious in a sacred cause. Might it not be that the Zionist leaders were the agents of

Satan? And should not Jews wait for the coming of the Messiah? Had they the right to take the "Ketz"—the end-time—into their own hands?

The controversy in this connection was not between orthodox and reform Jews, but among the orthodox themselves. Indeed, the controversy still rages. The one man who dedicated his life and virtually all of his writings to the propriety of Torah-true Jews participating in the Zionist movement was Rabbi Reines. He was also the founder of the Religious Zionist movement which was first known as Mizrachi.

As the opposition among orthodox Jews to the Zionist movement revolved about a theological problem, the opposition among reform Jews was also based on theology. In America the anti-Zionists wrote the famous Pittsburgh Platform which read Zion out of Judaism but this unfortunate deviation from the overwhelming impact of the tradition was most unimportant. First, the number of reform Jews everywhere was small. Second, the most influential leaders of the movement were Zionists, Wise, Gottheil, Silver. Thus the fears and the alarms of the anti-Zionists in all groups could not serve as dikes against the emotional outburst of the people for the land of their dreams. The tradition of hope had struck roots too deeply throughout the centuries to brook any interference at a time when it appeared that the promise could finally be fulfilled. Indeed, in 1956 when the state of Israel undertook a defensive operation by invading Sinai, the worldwide Jewish community fulfilled its maximum unity in modern history. Never before were so many Jews aligned behind one cause as on that eventful day! The same situation prevailed during Israel's six-day war.

Not always, however, is there such unity. Apart from the different political and economic ideologies that are reflected in the programs of the political parties in the state of Israel and in the Zionist movement, there are differences that emerge from the differences among Jews because of their conceptions of Torah. The overwhelming majority of reform and conservative Jews who are Zionists are identified with either the General Zionist or Labor Zionist parties, both of which are committed to a policy which would virtually eliminate from the legal order anything other than the ethics of Judaism. Thus, for example, they would sanction civil marriage and divorce, an educational system that was completely secular-nationalist in orientation, complete freedom of transport on Sabbaths and festivals, and many other political, economic, and social patterns which offend the orthodox and right-wing Conservative Jews. The majority of the latter are in the Religious Zionist movement, which in recent years began to attract a growing number of Conservative Rabbis who delighted especially in the program of Hapoel Hamizrachi (Religious Labor). The collectives of religious Jews in Israel had a great appeal for them because they saw in these collectives the possibility of making Jewish law viable in a modern state. The more extremist orthodox Jews are to be found in the party known as Agudat Yisrael or its labor arm, Poalei Agudat Yisrael. Only a few hundred are so intransigent as not to recognize the state as anything but a machination of Satan.

The difference between the Religious Zionists and the Agudists is to be found in the degree to which they are prepared to permit a development in Jewish law that will meet the needs of an autonomous sovereign Jewish republic. The Religious Zionists, for example, are prepared to suspend the operation of the laws of the Sabbatical year during this critical period of the state's history. They till the soil in their colonies, sow the seed and harvest the crops. The Agudists refuse to do this.

What is involved is a difference in the interpretation of Jewish law with the greatest of scholars in the last one hundred years participating. The Religious Zionists rely on Rabbi Isaac Elchanan Spektor and Rabbi Kook who took a lenient view of the subject. Their adversaries were less bold with the tradition. And this difference in attitude toward the Law is to be found in many an issue. Even with respect to the celebration of Israel's Independence Day as a re-

311

ligious festival we find a contrast in point of view. Rabbi Maimon, Religious Zionist, chanted the Hallel with a blessing antecedent—thus giving the ritual a sanctity equivalent to that of Chanuka. The Agudists often hesitate to recite even the Hallel, and certainly frown upon the preface of a blessing.

X

Thus, alas, the Law which sanctified the land, and unified the people in their hope for its reclamation, has now become a basic cause for their disunity. The Talmud tells us that the second Jewish commonwealth was destroyed because Jews did not fulfill the mandate to love and respect each other. We cannot afford to lose the third for a similar reason. However, there is also a silver lining to the cloud.

Without the Law there would not now be land, people or state. But today, without the land, people and state, the Law would not have its greatest challenge to become the light unto the nations. For millennia the Law had a limited application. It pertained to very few areas of Jewish life. Because we had no state of our own, and no economy of which we were the masters, the Law did not affect these very significant aspects of our existence. With the restoration of "normalcy" to our people's existence in the holy land, the Law must prove itself capable of meeting the challenge on every front and, consistently with its historic and authentic conceptions, yield answers that will delight the religionist and the secularist alike.

There are those in Israel who do not regard the Law as equal to this challenge. There are those, however, who maintain that if the idea of Eretz Yisrael could play such a remarkable role in Jewish history, then certainly the Law, which is even more universalist in its significance than land and people, need not be abandoned so that only two ideas derived from Abraham would now survive.

Chapter Two

FROM SYNAGOGUE TOWARD YESHIVA

Institutionalized Cult or Congregations of the Learned?

The synagogue was once a building where men met to pray and study; today it is an "institution," often more social than religious. The rabbi was once a scholar-saint; now he is usually a "professional," a clergyman. Thoughtful Orthodox Jews in America have tried to resist the modern transformation of the rabbi into a religious functionary, but, paradoxically enough, they have often found themselves adding momentum to the new trend in the very act of seeking to reverse it. Orthodoxy, however, has shown a deeper appreciation of the true meaning of rabbi and synagogue in Jewish tradition than have Conservatism and Reform. Setting its face resolutely against the present cult of synagogue and minister in Jewish life, it is trying to recover for the rabbi his old primacy as teacher and man of learning, and through him and the Jewish school to restore Jewry to its old role as a "nation of priests and a holy people."

In its earliest beginnings (in Babylon) the synagogue was nothing more than a facility for group worship, a make-shift substitute, presumably, for the Temple which had been destroyed. But the synagogue did not disappear with the Temple's restoration. On the contrary, during the days of the Second Commonwealth there were four or five hundred synagogues in Jerusalem alone, and a chapel for prayer was

313

added to the new Temple itself. The synagogue of that day was owned by the city or village in which it was located and governed by the city's seven democratically elected elders. Title to the building was vested in the inhabitants of the city; the elders might sell or otherwise dispose of it only in the presence of the assembled citizenry, and provided that another house of worship had been made ready to take its place and the proceeds of the sale had been earmarked for the purchase of more sacred objects.

To "operate" it, this synagogue-building only needed the help of ten men whose job it was to be available at all times for a religious service when any worshiper came for prayer. Sometimes the community also provided a cantor and sexton; very rarely did it provide a rabbi. Though he might use the building as a member of the community, the rabbi was never a synagogue functionary. (In this connection it is interesting to note that the Israeli Ministry of Religions recently published a volume on synagogue matters in that country which, while it deals with everything from architecture to cantorial music, makes no mention at all of the rabbi.)

But the synagogue was not only a house of worship. Lectures and sermons were delivered there; it served as a school building for young and old, and as the courthouse where oaths were administered; notices of lost and found articles were posted in its halls. It was the place in which punishments were meted out, charity distributed, and the dead eulogized; public affairs were debated inside its walls, and travelers would find food and lodging there; occasionally it also provided the place for holding the circumcision ceremony.

The synagogue was indeed a "center"—but not a center where the secular-social rubbed shoulders uneasily with the ritual-religious as today; the social life of the community was also its religious life—religion and society were almost indistinguishably one. And what was the role of the rabbi in all this bustle and hum of activity? A strictly unofficial, almost casual one. Even when a rabbi participated in these

314

functions—and his presence was in fact indispensable to some of them—he usually did so as a volunteer. And indeed the voluntary character of the rabbi in historic Judaism is one of its noblest features.

The rabbi's role in classical Judaism was determined primarily by a need felt very early to prevent the surrogates of God from exploiting their position for personal aggrandizement. Abraham, Judaism's first teacher, suffered no man to feel that he "had made Abraham rich." All institutional religions of course face this problem, but Judaism was perhaps the first to recognize it and take steps toward its solution. The rabbi, however, came into prominence rather late in Jewish history. Originally it was the priests and levites who acted as religious ministrants, and through the institution of the tithe and heave offering, the Talmud hedged round all statutory gifts and taxes with so many conditions and restrictions that their delivery was in effect voluntary. A Jew was required to set the tithe gifts aside, thus learning the discipline of self-denial, but if he chose to let them rot, there was no one to stop him. Priests and levites were even prohibited from helping farmers at the harvest, lest the farmer feel morally bound to "pay" his helpers directly with the appropriate offerings.

But this was not the only measure taken to limit priestly power and privilege. Perhaps in reaction against the funerary role of Egypt's priests and their intense preoccupation with the dead, and fearful of priestly exploitation of the gullibility of the bereaved, Israel's priests were so completely excluded from participation in the funeral rites that they were considered unclean if they so much as ventured into a room where a corpse lay. The only corpse of a nonrelative that they were permitted to touch was that of a nameless, heirless pauper. Fear, too, of the extensive landholdings of the Egyptian priesthood—whom even Joseph could not expropriate—may have been behind the Torah's denial to the priestly caste of any share in the Promised Land. The fact that the priests were also expected to act as judges in matters of family law restricted their right to marry. Subsequently the Talmud imposed some of these same disabilities on lay judges who were not of the priestly caste. The priests did, however, get some benefit from animal offerings, but they could hardly grow rich on this since the gifts had to be eaten almost at once and under very restricted conditions.

A further safeguard against the evils of priestly privilege was the fact that Judaism was an exoteric rather than an esoteric religion, in which the law was promulgated, taught, and interpreted by all. Would that every man in the camp of Israel were a prophet, exclaimed Moses.

But in the course of time these safeguards proved inadequate to the task for which they had been designed. Particularly in the exercise of their judicial function, the priests contrived to overcome their legal disabilities, and we find them being denounced over and over again by the Prophets for aligning themselves with the rich and against the poor. Nor did they remain content with priesthood alone, but attempted to usurp political power as well. Moses, in assigning the priestly office to his brother Aaron and the "secular" military leadership to his disciple Joshua, had implicitly declared his opposition to a merger of these two functions. But perhaps the most serious consequence of the growth of priestly power and influence was that it led the priests to neglect their duty as custodians and expounders of the Law. It was mainly for this reason that the rabbi came into prominence, inheriting not only the responsibilities of the priest but his disabilities as well. From the beginning, the rabbis were clearly determined to guard against the tendencies that had corrupted the priesthood; they especially made it clear that learning was of the essence—a bastard with learning, they declared, ranked higher than an ignorant high priest. Moreover, the rabbis refused to arrogate to themselves even the few privileges which the priests had enjoyed. They ruled that no one must profit by his pursuit of Torah. If the rabbi did perform a ritualistic service, he could lawfully be compensated only for the time he had given and for the loss he had sustained by being taken away from his non-rabbinic vocation, whatever it might be. The same rule also applied to cantors or readers of the Law, who, because their service to the congregation was rendered on the Sabbath, could only be paid for such time as they spent in preparation prior to the Sabbath.

Centuries before the Protestant development of the idea of a non-professional clergy, Judaism was putting it into practice. This idea found its most vivid expression later on among the Jews of Eastern Europe. Every Jewish community in East Europe supported at least one rabbi, but in each there were scores of others, also ordained and equally learned in the Law, who chose not to make the Torah their "trade." The yeshiva student, preparing himself for the rabbinate, looked forward to nothing better than to devote his life to study for its own sake (*Torah li'shmah*), rather than for the sake of a livelihood.

The Talmud mentions no fewer than a hundred rabbis who were artisans by profession. In fact, the Talmudic rabbi was "the true successor of the Judean prophet and the Pharisaic scribe, retaining absolute financial independence." During the Middle Ages, rabbis occasionally were able to become influential advisers or counsellors in the courts of kings, but their more learned colleagues did not on that score hesitate to deny them rabbinical authority. Generally, the Jews objected to the office of "chief rabbi" (a creation of the state), and they regarded holders of the office as government agents seeking to strengthen royal control. The claim of a rabbi to leadership, they felt, should derive from his learning and personal piety, and on these points they preferred the judgment of the people (sometimes expressed through elected representatives) to the judgment of the state. The Jewish community was always democratically organized—even by modern standards. Men of wealth and learning, of course, were prominent among community leaders, but there were carefully established voting procedures, and the lay leaders who chose the rabbi reckoned only with piety and scholarship. Moreover, while sanctions, whether of a religious or secular nature, could be

317

invoked against the rabbi for malfeasance in his judicial character, his *spiritual* authority was based principally on popular confidence. There was no trace of the professional or charismatic priesthood in the rabbinate.

Even more unequivocally than Protestantism, Talmudic Judaism rejected the distinction between laity and clergy. A rabbi could do nothing prohibited to a layman, nor could he ignore any of the obligations binding on the layman. In his official capacity, he had no greater powers than any layman learned in the Law—that is, he could give instruction in a particular situation, but always on the basis of his knowledge of the Law. Rabbis seldom conducted religious services—even a funeral was not regarded as a service. Daily and Sabbath services were led by laymen—cantors or readers. Very often the rabbi did not even attend the synagogue: a quorum of men would come to his house and pray there. Nor did rabbis ever *solemnize* marriages, for marriage in Judaism was not a sacrament requiring a cleric's participation. The groom and the bride and the witnesses were the only necessary parties, provided they knew what to say and do during the ceremony. The only power entrusted to the rabbi which was denied the layman was the power to ordain other rabbis, but the latter's competence extended to matters of Jewish law alone and a rabbi's authority ultimately depended on its acceptance by the community. Even in litigation the parties to the suit might stipulate that the judges need not be ordained rabbis or scholars, and in general many a layman would resolve questions of Jewish law for himself, trusting to his own familiarity with the sources.

Everywhere we look, then, we find that for almost two millennia to be a rabbi meant nothing, or nothing else than to be a pious Jew learned in the Law. Like anyone else, a rabbi might lead the services, but this would be determined by his singing, not by his position. Similarly, he might deliver sermons, but only because he was a skilled preacher. His principal functions, and the only ones for which his ordination constituted *prima facie* evidence of qualification, were to teach the Law and to resolve legal questions for those who *voluntarily* sought this guidance. To help him fulfill these functions a community or a congregation might retain him in an official, salaried capacity, but even then he regarded it his major responsibility to establish a school—a yeshiva—in which he himself taught. Of course, the rabbis to whom historic religious questions were referred, or whose religious decisions (*responsa*) had a vital bearing on community affairs, sometimes became involved in the political, social, and economic strife of the community. But their major role remained that of the teacher. While the best of their students may have become rabbis who in turn founded new yeshivas or succeeded to the leadership of the already existing ones, the majority of the students returned—whether ordained or not—to Jewish community life, taking their place as learned citizens. And they, too, devoted their leisure time to study.

The change that has occurred in the rabbi's character and functions in modern times was preceded by a change in the nature and place of the synagogue in Jewish life. Diaspora Jewry was always faced with the problem of what constituted the "Jewish community." Was it all the Jews living in a particular city, or only those who made up a given congregation? In the United States, where one could choose not to affiliate himself with any religious group at all, it was inevitable that the congregation should replace the community at large as the nucleus of Jewish organization, for only through the positive act of joining a congregation did one identify himself as a member of the Jewish community. The synagogue thus became the focal point, almost the determinant, of community membership, instead of the simple community facility it had been.

With the synagogue now so important, the American rabbi found himself responsible for its success, which was conceived in terms of its ability to "make Jews" out of more and more people—that is, to increase its membership. As the head of an institution, the rabbi's duties became more numerous, the talents he required more diverse, his motives more worldly, and his Jewish learning less impressive. As a professional group, rabbis measured up to other professionals in versatility and erudition, but unfortunately they found themselves reduced to ministers who were forced to covet the loyalty and good will of the laymen they served. Public relations became an integral part of their job, and pastoral work and social service an integral part of public relations. The sermon became their principal instrument of attracting attention and support; membership drives and building expansion were necessary for greater emoluments of office; even schools for the young became bait for congregational membership. Everything seemed to be subsumed under this one overriding, tyrannical responsibility of public relations.

That the synagogue in America has become an institution catering more to social than to religious needs does not mean that it is performing a function entirely inconsistent with its traditional character. After all, it is not at all the social role *per se* of the synagogue that is the trouble, but the feebleness of the overall religious purpose and meaning that should suffuse the synagogue's social functions. Moreover, according to Jewish theology, the preservation of the Jewish people *qua* people is itself a religious value—a point Marshall Sklare overlooks in his excellent study *Conservative Judaism*—and the modern synagogue helps to do that. What demands criticism, however, is the damage done by the modern synagogue to the role and personality of the rabbi who is the sole surviving carrier of the religious heritage in most congregations. And it seems distressingly clear also that the synagogue is dropping Jewish law overboard like so much ballast in order to save itself as an institution. To sanction driving an automobile on the Sabbath because more and more worshipers living in suburban areas find it impossible to walk to *shul* is to sacrifice the Sabbath to the synagogue.

To prevent the institutionalized synagogue from turning Judaism into a temple cult and the rabbi into a public relations man, Orthodoxy today is transferring its prime

320

emphasis from the synagogue to the school—preferably to a yeshiva. This shift of emphasis is in part a kind of holding operation, aimed at re-creating an elite of scholars who will preserve Judaism through a period of agnosticism and non-observance. But the more immediate hope of the program is to train a substantial body of people literate enough in Torah to demonstrate by their way of life that a fully traditional Judaism can stand up to the intellectual and emotional challenges of our day. Such a program represents a clear-cut departure from the aims of those reformers who made the synagogue and its rabbi the Jewish counterpart of church and minister. If a significant number of Jews do not respond to this attempt to restore them to their traditional role of active participants, as a "holy people" of scholars, in Jewish religious life and leadership, if they are content to remain a passive, more or less ignorant flock superintended by their pastor in a narrowly limited religious sphere, and "superintending" him in all other spheres, then Judaism must eventually find itself transformed into an esoteric body of doctrines: in other words, it will become the very kind of religion that it repudiated so forcefully in its own beginnings and throughout its history.

The question of primacy as between synagogue and school is not a new one in American Jewish community life. There have been occasions when American rabbis even opposed the establishment of Jewish day schools in their communities for fear that these yeshivas would reduce the registration of their own Hebrew schools and thus deflate synagogue membership. Today, however, though the day schools seek the cooperation of neighboring synagogues, they do not hesitate to assert their superiority to synagogues in the hierarchy of Jewish institutional life.

But there is another factor at work here as well. The largest Orthodox rabbinical seminary in America will soon graduate about fifty rabbis every year, and even if many Conservative synagogues employ these new rabbis, at least half will almost certainly enter the teaching profession or Jewish social service. Hundreds of such teaching rabbis will be available for supplementary work as spiritual leaders of small neighborhood synagogues in every section of the country, and it will be to their interest to encourage the process of decentralization and to resist the transformation of their own modest synagogues into mammoth enterprises. As leaders of small synagogues, they will be able to maintain closer relations with their congregants, and because the size of the membership, it is hoped, will no longer be the measure of rabbinical "success," they will be free to exert a much more challenging and effective spiritual influence than the rabbi who must say nothing that will offend his congregation. They will be volunteers serving in the synagogue without pay or at token salaries—a fact which will eliminate the pressure, this time from the rabbi's side, for the large membership needed to provide him with a "professional's" salary. Instead of using the school maintained by the synagogue as bait for membership, these new rabbis will be free to persuade parents to give their children the best, most extensive Jewish education available, such as no synagogue school can hope to provide.

The tendency toward small synagogues is already evident in America. Orthodox leaders seek to establish such synagogues wherever a minimum of ten families desire it. Moreover, it is Orthodoxy's hope and aim to fill these synagogues with men and women whose background in Torah will be virtually on a par with the rabbi's, even though they are engaged in business, medicine, law, engineering, accounting, or what have you. There are already several modern Orthodox synagogues in New York which boast a dozen ordained rabbis in their lay membership and scores of others who have spent ten or more years studying in yeshivas.

The conflict between the rabbi as scholar and the rabbi as preacher was resolved for a long time among American Jews in favor of the preacher. A generation ago the distinguished pulpit orator was called to the largest congregation and commanded the highest salary. But in our own day there has been a renewed tendency (fostered partly by the

322

fact that so many congregants are college graduates) to esteem a rabbi for his learning rather than for his eloquence.

Among the Orthodox, rabbinical leadership is passing out of the possession of the rabbis of the big synagogues into the hands of those who direct the institutions of learning. And it is the avowed purpose of the heads of the yeshivas to train Jews expert in Bible and Talmud. If he is not to forfeit his leadership, the rabbi who stands at the head of a congregation made up of such members must be a scholar himself. These congregations, in keeping with their orientation toward learning and scholarship and away from the institutionalized cult, are rebelling against the practice of making the synagogue an exclusive center of American Jewish religious life. The synagogue's displacement of the home would be as fatal to Judaism as its displacement of the school. Ideally, the synagogue is the place in which one seeks personal communion with God, and discovers one's identification with *klal Yisrael*, the community of the Jewish people. But there is a whole range of religious experience and obligation which is embraced by the home and the home alone. This crucial side of Jewish life is fast being forgotten in America as more and more homes are de-Judaized and the synagogue clumsily strives to substitute for them.

There is one real hazard in the shift of primacy from synagogue to school. Will it only hasten and promote the divorce of Jewish law from the needs of contemporary life? Will it end up by making Jewish law entirely a matter for schools and academies and unworldly scholars remote from the actual lives of American Jews? The modern synagogue, with all its faults, is part and parcel of the people's life. Can we say the same of the Jewish academy?

It remains to be seen if the yeshiva movement can cope with this danger. The ultimate authority to change and develop Jewish life rests with the people—with all those who are committed to a belief in the divine origin of the Law. Rabbis, as I have pointed out, derive their authority as interpreters of the Law from the people, but this authority can only be conferred by a public literate enough to recognize who is worthy of it. As more and more yeshiva graduates come forward who are both Judaically literate and worldly enough to fill positions in all walks of life— who, that is, are qualified to appreciate the demands of Jewish law as well as the needs of life in the present—a Jewish "general will" may develop, and from this general will those "scholar-saints" who possess the religious penetration to perceive the unity of life and Law can derive their authority as the Law's doctors. Such men have appeared in the past. They rose to prominence not because they were rabbis of synagogues or presidents of rabbinical associations or heads of great fund-raising campaigns. Most often they were both rabbis in the communities and teachers in the seminaries. Orthodox Jewry the world over has thus far succeeded only in transferring leadership from the preacher to the scholar; it has still to produce such "scholar-saints."

Now that the passion of the postwar American Jewish community for building "fine edifices" has almost exhausted itself, it may not seem petulant to suggest that the architecture and decor of synagogues are not as important as their spiritual organization. The Talmud, which prescribes meticulously for every phase of personal and social living, is relatively permissive with respect to the establishment of synagogues and the hiring of religious functionaries. Perhaps the Talmud recognized that synagogues are only a means, and divine law does not attempt to fix means in the same way as ends. Precisely for this reason Judaism is not saddled with fixed institutional patterns for church and clergy. And in an age when so much of the antipathy to religion is an antipathy to its bureaucratization and institutionalization, the Jewish rabbinate, by taking up again its old non-institutional role as teacher, can demonstrate how Judaism favors the modern point of view on this as on so many other matters.

Chapter Three

ARROGANCE OR HUMILITY IN PRAYER

I

There was a time when the most striking difference between the Orthodox Jew and the "reformer" was that the traditionalist prayed with covered head. According to one Hassidic interpretation, this time-honored practice reminded the Jew of his intellectual limitations. As the wearing of clothes was symbolic of man's modesty with respect to his procreative capacity, so the covering of the cranium symbolized his modesty with respect to his mental faculties, for the brazenness of man's mind can be as immoral as his physical nudity. Unfortunately, too many of our co-religionists, even among those who have not discarded the millennial practice, approach Judaism with an arrogance that is unworthy of them who would walk in the way of religion.

It is with regard to the traditional prayerbook of Israel that one discovers the greatest contrast between the attitude of the traditionalist and that of his critics. The Orthodox Jew is simply too modest to tamper with the "Siddur." He knows that it was compiled by saints and sages whose religious fervor he wishes he could match. The secular humanist is equally modest. He will not tamper with that which was composed by believers, for he respects the sincerity of their commitment. Those, however, who would rewrite what time has sanctified, approach the prayerbook with their characteristic worship of man and try to make it fit their new religion in which, as has already been said,[1] God is an "It" instead of a "Thou." And the "It" is usually "I"— a man.

II

The traditional prayerbook, for example, often refers to the animal sacrifices that were brought in the Temple at Jerusalem. Orthodox Jews do not presume that they understand the significance of these sacrifices. The many rationalizations of Maimonides, Nachmanides, Karo, and Hoffmann leave much unexplained. But because they do not comprehend they do not feel that they are privileged to reject. They do not know, but they believe. They believe not only in God but also in the wisdom of their forebears. They are not certain that they know better than their ancestors. They are never so certain of their rationalization of the Biblical ordinances on animal offerings that in reliance upon it they feel entitled to disdain those who preceded them. Professor M. M. Kaplan has even been said to resort to the ugly quip, "Would we convert our synagogues into slaughter-houses?" However, Orthodox Jews are too modest to feel that their religious yearnings are superior aesthetically or philosophically to those of prophets, who approved of the sacrificial cult. And on close examination, Orthodox Jews discover how ill-considered are some of the blithe assumptions of their adversaries.

These adversaries assume that prayer was ordained by progressive prophets as a substitute for sacrifices, and the synagogue as a substitute for the Temple. They ignore the overwhelming evidence in talmudic and midrashic sources that prayers were recited at the same time that the sacrifices were being offered, and that even in Temple times, when animal offerings were the rule, there were not only hundreds of synagogues in Jerusalem, but there was a synagogue in the

1. A. J. Heschel, *"The Spirit of Prayer,"* Proceedings of the Rabbinical Assembly of America, XVII (1953), 162.

Temple itself.[2] True, the prophets criticized the hypocrisy of those who brought offerings and thereby hoped to propitiate their Maker for crimes which they were committing against the widow and the orphan. But the prophets were equally critical of those who spread out their hands in adoration of God when their hands had been instruments for theft and bloodshed.[3] Does this mean that the prophets were opposed to prayer?

It may be that sacrifices were offered by some primitive peoples to propitiate their gods, but an Orthodox Jew cannot ever forget chapter nineteen of Leviticus—that immortal chapter which contains the mandate "And thou shalt love thy neighbor as thy self." That same chapter contains the fundamental rules with regard to the validity and invalidity of animal offerings. Now, if the chapter is God's mandate, who would dare presume to edit it and delete any part of it! But if it was written by a man, as is alleged by the non-orthodox, who would presume to say that the religious genius who conceived of the magnificent ethical prescriptions contained therein was at the same time such a barbarian as not to appreciate, at least to the extent that Dr. Kaplan does, how offensive animal offerings are to genuine religious experience! The Orthodox Jew is willing to give either God or His gifted servant the benefit of the doubt, and while the Orthodox Jew does not presume that he knows the overall significance of animal offerings, he also does not presume to reject them as hallmarks of barbarism. Indeed it must never be forgotten that Jews retain in their religious calendar until today one souvenir of the sacrificial cult of old—the Seder service—and that is, by far, Judaism's most widely observed and beloved ritual.

Liberals and Reconstructionists are wont to cite one passage in Maimonides as justification, by inference, for their elimination of all references to sacrifices in the prayerbook. But how honest are they when they ignore Maimonides'

2. See Eliezer Levi, *Yesodot Ha-tefillah* (2nd ed., Tel Aviv: Betan Hasefer, 1952), 74.
3. Isa. 1:15.

explicit statements that when the Messiah will come, the entire sacrificial cult will be reinstituted! Moreover, they cite the fact that Rabbi Yohanan ben Zakkai in the year 70 prohibited the bringing of animal offerings, but ignored his expressed rationale—to prolong the mourning for the destruction of the temple. He decreed many similar prohibitions, such as the prohibition against festive weddings,[4] which was later suspended with the substitution of the breaking of the glass at the end of the ceremony as the reminder of national grief.

III

The arrogance of moderns with respect to forebears in their attitude toward animal sacrifices is matched only by their feelings of superiority in the realm of chivalry. The Orthodox Jew again does not presume that he is more chivalrous than his ancestors; and if in Judaism in general, and in the prayerbook in particular, there are factors that offend women, he does not reject—he simply wishes that he knew more. As in the case of animal sacrifices, so with respect to women the Orthodox Jew does not blithely dismiss the tradition as unfair, but probes the sources for more light. Instead of emending the prayerbook, he turns to talmudic folios to study more and more about the subject. He assumes that he knows too little, and that he is not as saintly as the creators of our great ancestral heritage were, for modesty must be the hallmark of a religious man.

True, there are many texts that one can cite from Talmud and Midrash which illustrate in what low esteem some rabbis held the intelligence of women. One can cite an equally effective number to prove the reverse. The rabbis also differed as to who were more chaste—men or women.[5] But generally speaking the Law was markedly progressive with regard to women's rights, in and out of marriage, even if equality was never the rule, then or now. (Few courts

4. *Sotah,* 49a; *B.B.,* 60b.
5. See, for instance, *Kiddushin,* 80a.

anywhere have yet undertaken to award husbands alimony.) In Judaism, however, the status of woman from the point of view of religious observance, prayer, and synagogue or Temple functions, warrants more philosophical analysis than it has ever received from those who in haste seek to proclaim themselves as her emancipator. With regard to the overwhelming majority of commandments, women were as much subject to the Law as men. And their capacity was hardly different. Any ten women could conduct services as men did. And women could be called to the Torah. They themselves preferred to be inconspicuous—unlike their present-day counterparts who may clamor for equality with respect to the conspicuous role of ascending a pulpit for an honor but have not yet been heard to request equality with respect to the inconspicuous duty of donning phylacteries and prayer-shawl in private meditation, which the Law might permit them to do.

From the point of view of rituals, women were not obligated to perform many commandments. They were permitted to perform them, if they so chose. But whenever the commandment (and there were exceptions here too) involved a limitation in time, they were exempt. It was for this reason that they were relieved of the obligation to don phylacteries and prayer-shawl, because even men need only don them by day and not by night. And the exemption was not at all related to woman's so-called "uncleanness." One authority did suggest that this regard for time was prompted by the fact that women's household duties could not yield to the exacting time requirements of these *Mitzvot*. However, many moderns concluded that this was the only rationale, and since it was no longer applicable they assumed that the rule could be changed. A more modest—and scientific—approach would have made them less impulsive with conclusions. For women are never busier with household chores than on Passover and the Passover they must observe precisely as men do. They must eat *Matzoh* and, needless to say, avoid the ownership or even possession of any *Chametz*.

A careful examination of talmudic sources reveals that the Law's differentiation between men and women was based on nature and natural function, and not on social or economic considerations. Now, nature has not endowed males with any "built-in" apparatus for measuring time. In order that man learn to sanctify time, the Law ordains for him many commandments which are governed by a calendar and a clock. Women, on the other hand, by the very nature of their physical constitution and the requirements of the Law with regard to their menstrual periods, needed little more to make them aware of the sanctity of time. Their natural periodicity has been geared to holiness by the Halachah. A modern novelist sought to explain why man "is forever trying to escape his instability through conquest" while woman is "reconciled" to her "earthbound fate." For woman "the pattern is in time with the seasons of the earth." In her own body she reproduces "the pattern of the evolving earth." Perhaps it was some such insight that the tradition had captured in the Law.

All the prayerbook indicated, however, was that man should be grateful that he was subject to the whole Law. That is why he thanked God for having made him first a Jew, and then a man. It is interesting that the author of these blessings was Rabbi Meir, whose wife was not only his beloved, but also his peer—a woman who was so scholarly that her view in opposition to the majority of rabbis is cited by the Talmud in connection with a very difficult Halachic problem (and her view prevailed!). She was one of the many to be credited with the literature of the Mishnah.

And when an Orthodox Jew recites the blessing Rabbi Meir composed, he hesitates to emend it and make himself appear more chivalrous than the great sage, and more appreciative of his own wife than Rabbi Meir was of his.

IV

However, it is with respect to God—more than with respect to either women or sacrifices—that the Orthodox

Jew must find himself most modest. The Orthodox Jew may not fix the scope of God's omnipotence. He does not know how or when God will resurrect the dead, but he does not therefore place the possibility beyond God's power. In fact, God *must* resurrect the dead if He is to exercise His omnipotence in the fulfillment of His attribute of charity. For as Dr. Joseph B. Soloveitchik argues,[6] the highest rung on the ladder of charity involves the giving of help to those in greatest need, to those whc are *most* helpless. And who are more incapable of self-help than the dead! Therefore, if God's attributes of Power and Charity have any significance whatever, they must spell the ultimate resurrection of the dead. The dogma is not easily embraced, but the dogma is no more supernatural than most of the teachings of the prophets that nature will become perfect, that death will disappear, that the moral order and natural order will both reflect at one and the same time the ultimate design of their Maker. Only with the leap of faith can one make any of these basic prophetic teachings meaningful.

Agnostics are consistent. They do not claim that progress is real or that there is such a thing as perfection. But those who still reverberate the prophetic ideas—despite their supernatural character—but deny God the power to bring an actual Messiah or to do justice to those who through no fault of their own were born before the age when death is no more, must try to be more consistent.

Reconstructionists especially have sought to read all the norms of modern naturalism into Judaism. The traditional prayerbook has many references to natural law. "He established (the planets) forever; He fixed their law which none shall transgress." [7] But with the Psalmist, the Orthodox Jew regards the natural as miraculous and to this mood the prayerbook gives expression. No natural scientist ever presumes to give the complete explanation of any phenomenon. Even if he did, the explanation would still be a mystery, for

6. Unpublished lecture at Yeshiva University, N.Y., during the summer of 1953.

7. Ps. 148: 6.

the phenomenon explained may yet be more awe-inspiring than the unknown. It is even as the explicable is comprehended that man confronts a miracle in nature. However, to take away from the Creator His power to interfere with natural law is not only to deny God His omnipotence, but also to deny that element of chance in nature which scientists have established by sense experience and philosophers of pragmatism have been rationalizing since the days of Peirce.

What is fundamental in Traditional Judaism is the worship of God as Creator, and the companion dogma that no created thing is ever to be worshiped. To conceive of God in human terms is virtually to substitute a creature as the object of worship instead of the Creator. For this reason any tampering with one blessing of the traditional prayerbook—the first blessing before the *Shema*—was most unfortunate, for in its original form it has a special message. That prayer, a paraphrase of Isaiah 45:7, was introduced originally as a protest against Zoroastrianism, which subscribed to the belief that good and evil, light and darkness, were represented by separate deities. To affirm the unrelenting opposition of Judaism to this view, Jews were called upon each day to hail God as "The Creator of light and darkness, the Creator of everything," Who everywhere is regarded as holy by created things—even by the heavenly hosts. This is the essential meaning of the first blessing before the *Shema*. Later, this blessing was expanded.[8] On Sabbaths and festivals, and especially on High Holy Days, it is the one blessing to which there were additions of major importance (also eliminated from non-Orthodox prayerbooks). The net effect sought is the death of every kind of idolatry—not its survival. Nothing created was the measure of God. And few who understood the prayers were misled to conceive of God in human terms, even if anthropomorphic figures of speech were used. But in the zeal of moderns to banish every anthropomorphism, they substituted anthro-

8. Levi, *op. cit.*, p. 144.

pocentrism. Instead of anthropomorphic figures of speech, they presented a God created in the image of the crown of His creation—man. What man could not conceive God to do, was *ipso facto* assumed to be beyond God's power to do. That is why God was presumed not to have revealed Himself at any time anywhere. That is also why God could not have chosen anyone or any people to be His special kingdom of priests.

V

And here too moderns sat in judgment on forebears and not only accused them of being anthropomorphic, when the critics themselves were doing worse, but also of being egocentric, by believing in their chosenness by God. A modicum of modesty should have prompted moderns to understand that the truly endowed religious spirits of the past, those who composed the traditional prayers, were in many cases the very people whose miserable lot in life must have made them question whether they were really the Chosen People. Needless to say, to thank God "for having brought us near to Him," as the Reconstructionists pray, can be just as offensive as thanks to Him "for having chosen us." If the latter implies that He chose us by rejecting others, then the former by the same logic implies that if we are near, others are far. Nearness can have no meaning other than a relative one. And if the other nations can also elect to come near Him, so can they elect to be chosen. That is precisely what Jews felt. They also chose to be chosen. God had indicated [9] that He is sanctified by those nearest Him—from the nearest. He expects maximum fulfillment and exacts maximum obedience. And Jews were to be commandos in the struggle for the realization of God's Will in the universe. In this struggle Jews learned from many non-Jews—from a non-Jew we even took the opening verse of the daily service. But a religious personality with the basic virtue of modesty

9. Lev. 10: 3.

would hardly aggrandize himself by making it appear that he is a true universalist while his forebears were guilty of xenophobia. On the other hand, he would seek the better to fathom the mood of those who as commandos for God's Will were ever prepared to make the supreme sacrifice.

That the non-Jewish world reacts negatively to the concept of "Chosen People" hardly justifies our seeking their good will at the expense of the integrity of the reputation of many who can no longer defend themselves. Indeed, if we are to worry excessively about the misunderstanding of non-Jews, then the Reconstructionists ought most certainly abandon Zionism, and even the Seder service which the non-Jew cannot possibly fathom—a service, plus a sumptuous meal, plus children's pranks, plus humor, plus much that is so unbecoming the mood of a "religious" observance!

VI

Most Jews would not now eliminate Zion from their prayers, but they concur that to pray for a "return" there is hypocritical. Since they do not believe in a personal Messiah who will gather the "exiles" from the widely scattered scenes of their "punishment," and since they are sufficiently enamored especially of life in America, they would alter the traditional prayerbook to suit their present-day "at-homeness" in Western civilization.

One should not argue with those who feel that the millennium has come. It might even be cruel to dispel the bliss of their ignorance. But most Jews are still realistic enough to appreciate that if the doctrine of Isaiah with regard to Israel's role among the nations as a suffering servant ever had validity, the measure of that validity has only been increased in our day. Jews have been the litmus paper of civilization in every capacity imaginable—as individuals, as a people, as a religious community, and now finally with the emergence of the State of Israel as a sovereign state. Nothing has changed very much. It is only that now worldwide Jewry has created a new instrument—a state—with which to try the morality of the United Nations, the Soviet Empire, the democratic West, and even the Oriental traditions of India and China. Alas, that vis-à-vis Israel all have demonstrated an almost congenital inability to render that justice of which the prophets dreamed. And Jews continue to serve as the prophets said they would and they continue to pray for the day when the return to Zion will represent the triumph of absolute justice on earth. As Zion was the place whence that prophecy once came forth, so it continues for Orthodox Jews to be the place on whose mountains God's anointed will administer the Law for men and nations that are free under God.

However, for traditionalist Jews the prayer for a return to Zion is also a prayer for a more comprehensive return to God. This more comprehensive return they can fulfill now only in a limited sense. It cannot possibly be fulfilled *in toto* until both the State of Israel and the nations of the earth are on the threshold of the Messianic era. Until that day there is much work to be done everywhere—if what the prophets taught is still valid. Some may choose to do it in Israel and others in America. All are keenly aware of Judaism's and Jewry's roles in the advancement of social justice. But to the traditionalist Jew, Zion stands for more than a geographic location. It is the Holy Land. As the world must be made right for the right, Israel must be made right for Judaism. And as in earlier periods of Jewish history, both functions must be performed by Jews at home and in exile. That some of us, by choice or force of circumstances, serve in one place or another is consequential, but does not detract from the significance of prayers for a complete return, when all the world will know the just, and the Jew will come home to enjoy greater communion with God and to experience more of His Holiness as he observes the whole of Torah—all of its 613 commandments.

Again it may require a leap of faith not only to believe that this will come to pass but also that total communion with God is the ultimate desideratum. But that alone is the religious ideal. The professed ideal of the so-called religious humanist—and Liberals and Reconstructionists think no differently—is to achieve social justice, freedom, equality and plenty, so that man can develop himself. The ultimate goal is man, beyond whom there is nothing else. And when the Messianic era will have come, man will be able to do the maximum for and with himself. For what?—one is tempted to ask. The secular humanist is candid enough to say that he does not know for what. He presumes to know little of life, and he lives it as he finds it. But those who would lend to their doctrine the adjective "religious," and end the quest with man's maximum potentialities, owe us an explanation: When man has improved to the maximum, what then? At least the traditionalist affirms that the end is fulfillment of God's maximum will—the Torah. Man is the crown of creation but he is nonetheless a created thing, and it is to the Creator and His will that we crave "return."

VII

The traditionalist not only directs his prayers to the future. His prayers also give him a sense of history, and he links himself with his past. Just as his prayers for rain and dew in Israel link him with the economic needs of his coreligionists there in every age, so his retention and recitation of prayers that now appear to be anachronistic link him with his forebears. He does not hesitate to pray for the schools of Babylon, which no longer exist. Nor does he hesitate, in his prayers, to take note of the fifteenth day of Ab to which he gives a festive character only because it makes him mindful of the ruling promulgated long ago that the twelve tribes might intermarry with each other—a revolutionary step towards national unity out of our distant past.

Liberals and Reconstructionists would eliminate the anachronistic. They would rewrite the prayerbook to spell out more recent or current historical situations. But why? In literature they are not impelled to destroy imagination. Must prayer be altogether without it? To appreciate Shakespeare's "Hamlet," no one suggests the need for substituting a president for a king. Cannot one also pray for schools in Babylon, and thereby bring the impact of their historic roles to bear upon the present, having in mind the schools of today? Must the sins of the atomic bomb and Nazi and Communist cruelty be spelled out? Who but fools would not think of Hitler and Stalin as they read the verse in the Haggadah, "Pour forth Thy wrath upon the nations that knew Thee not!"

VIII

Indeed, as the traditionalist does not want imagination in prayer to atrophy, so he does not want to ignore the aesthetic element. But aesthetic considerations, which have prompted Liberals and Reconstructionists to make of synagogue worship a soothing experience, must not become the primary values. If the principal purpose of religion is to induce peace of mind, then perhaps a violin may be more suitable for the synagogue than a shofar whose irritating sounds are to serve as goads to more spiritual living. To shorten the reading of the Law because the modern Jew is bored by it is to challenge a basic Jewish conception that the study of Torah is a more important channel to God than prayer. A proper regard for authentic Jewish values ought prompt us to spend more time on the Torah readings each Sabbath. If the rabbis do not want to interpolate comments, at least the congregants ought to be provided with the necessary materials and stimulated to spend the hour in study. Indeed, nothing represents a graver Christianization of the Jewish service than yielding to the suggestion that the time spent on Torah readings be reduced to a minimum.

That traditionalists continue to stress the primacy of Torah study over prayer is indicative of the fact that it is the traditionalist, and not his adversary, who stresses the role of intellect in religion. Indeed, nothing induced a critical approach in Jews more than the traditional system of education. Children were taught a verse of Scripture and goaded to ask a question. When first exposed to Rashi's popular commentary, they were told that they must always seek to discover first what troubled Rashi that he should bother to comment. The same critical approach marked their instruction in Talmud and Codes. Nothing ever said by the greatest of sages was beyond questioning. There was no blind adoration, although in modesty the traditionalist Jew was certain that if he would read the sources critically, he would after great travail discover the answer to the question he posed. He rarely rejected what a forebear said. That he had a question meant only that he must grope the harder for light. Thus, there was a critical approach to the old; there was a readiness to question from the cradle to the grave. But the critical approach was that of men who were modest. Today moderns are arrogant, and even believe in their own omniscience. And that is the principal reason for the inadequacy of the prayerbook. It is not that the prayers have no appeal, but that prayer itself has no appeal. Immodest men simply cannot pray. Immodest men have no sense of awe. Immodest men are rarely grateful. And to pray requires both a capacity to stand in awe and to feel thankful. This is the heart of the issue.

On the Day of Atonement, when the Orthodox Jew spends the entire day in prayer, he recites a hymn in which he expresses his thankfulness unto God for even wanting the praise of mortal man. Instead of complaining—as many moderns do—that the tradition requires us to spend so much time glorifying our Maker, the humble, pious supplicant expresses his gratitude that so glorious a God deigns to crave the adoration of His finite creatures. This is the mood of the truly religious person whose appreciative heart reflects his feelings of unworthiness as he confronts God—his feeling of modesty in prayer.

SECTION SIX

THE CONTEMPORARY SCENE

A traditionalist may live *with* the past, but he lives *in* the present and must cope with many more challenges than others precisely because he wants to preserve the past in a rapidly changing world. The essays in this section reflect continuing preoccupation with the contemporary scene, some insights with respect to it, and even a view to future challenges.

Chapter One

AMERICAN ORTHODOXY—
RETROSPECT AND PROSPECT

The earliest Jewish settlers on American soil brought with them the only Judaism they knew—Orthodox Judaism. Two centuries later Reform Judaism took root and still fifty years thereafter Conservative Judaism was born. Under the circumstances, one would have expected that Orthodox Judaism would be the first to meet the challenge of the American scene, ideologically and institutionally. In fact, it was the last to do so. Paradoxically enough, it is only in the last few decades that Orthodoxy seriously came to grips with the problem of its own future.

For too long a time Orthodoxy relied upon the fact that the preponderant number of American Jews professed to be its adherents. Majorities supporting the status quo in many social situations often rely upon the force of their numbers and their inertia, while well organized and dedicated minorities make gains for change. The Orthodox Jewish community once was such a majority. It was slow to realize the extent to which it was losing its numerical advantage. Second, the ranks of American Orthodoxy were ever replenished with thousands of immigrants from abroad. The new arrivals more than compensated for the defections to other groups. Now the loss of the European reservoir of Jews has caused American Orthodoxy to become concerned. It must find the way to command the loyalty of American-born Jews. Third, Orthodoxy by its very nature compromises less easily with new environments and new philosophies, so that it could not avail itself of that flexibility which aided the growth of the Reform and Conservative movements. The challenge of the American scene had to be met differently and the solution was later in its formulation and implementation. Nonetheless, significant and many were the contributions of Orthodoxy to our dual heritage as Americans and as Jews.

It fell to the lot of Orthodoxy to establish the legal status of Jews and Judaism in American democracy. To the ever-lasting credit of our pioneering forebears it must be said that they were not content with second-class citizenship in the United States. George Washington confirmed this attitude in his now famous letter to the Orthodox congregation in Newport, Rhode Island. However, the false dictum that America is a "Christian state" must be challenged again and again, even in the twentieth century, and while the battle is now waged by all Jews, and especially the defense agencies, it is usually one Orthodox Jew or another who creates the issue. The right of Sabbath observers to special consideration where "Blue Sunday" laws are in effect; their right to special treatment in the armed forces; their right to unemployment insurance benefits when they decline employment because of religious scruples—these are typical of many problems that Orthodox Jews raise in the hope that their resolution will insure maximum expansion of the

American concept of equality before the law. In many instances, bearded Orthodox Jews who retain their eastern European dress are also a challenge to the sincerity of most Americans who boast that their way of life spells respect for differences. The resistance of many of our co-religionists to the leveling character of American mores and its inevitable discouragement of diversity are healthy contributions to our understanding and practice of democracy. Altogether too often American Jews require the reminder even more than American Christians.

In the same spirit it was American Orthodoxy that bore, and still bears, the lion's share of the resistance to worldwide calendar reform. Though all Jewish groups have co-operated, it is Orthodoxy alone that regards any tampering with the inviolability of the Sabbath day fixed at Creation as a mortal blow to Judaism, and in the name of the religious freedom of minorities it seeks to alert the American conscience to desist from prejudicial action.

It was, however, in the establishment and construction of thousands of synagogues throughout the country that Orthodox Jews made manifest not only their loyalty to their ancestral heritage but their appreciation of their grand opportunity in this blessed land of freedom. How truly pauperized immigrants managed, in cities large and small, to rear beautiful edifices for worship is a saga worthy of more attention than it has heretofore received. What is particularly noteworthy is that no central agency guided or financed the movement. In every case it was individual Jews who banded together and performed the feat, a remarkable tribute to the effectiveness of our tradition in inducing in individual Jews the capacity to act on their own initiative for the greater glory of God. Even today no central body guides or directs the establishment of Orthodox synagogues. Orthodoxy's synagogue organization—the Union of Orthodox Jewish Congregations of America—is still totally ineffective in this kind of work. The initiative must always come from Jews who desire an Orthodox synagogue, and not from any resourceful, missionary, national or international

343

body. In part, this is also one of the weaknesses of Orthodox Judaism which its leaders want to correct on the threshold of its fourth century on the American scene. However, it remains to be seen whether it will be the Union of Orthodox Jewish Congregations or Yeshiva University that will blaze the new path.

The extent to which Orthodox Jews gave of their worldly goods for the establishment and construction of synagogues was exceeded only by their willingness to sacrifice for the cause of Jewish education. Their first venture in this direction, even before the era of the public school, was a Jewish all-day school under the auspices of Congregation Shearit Israel in New York. The more usual approach to the problem, however, was via the Talmud-Torah, the afternoon school in which children spent from five to ten hours weekly. In some instances the Talmud Torahs were successful, and many distinguished American Rabbis and scholars received their earliest instruction in Judaica in such schools. Yet altogether too often because of incompetent instructors, bizarre methods, and inadequate facilities, the Talmud Torahs failed to induce either a love or an understanding of Judaism. In the twentieth century, therefore, Orthodox Judaism countered with the Yeshiva movement. This movement has enjoyed a phenomenal growth. In the ranks of Conservative Judaism, too, it is receiving sympathetic attention and support, and even among Liberal Jews one occasionally hears it suggested that the all-day school is the most effective answer to Jewish illiteracy.

Three organizations of Orthodox Jewry now propagate the Yeshiva program and supervise the establishment of new schools. The Vaad Hachinuch Hacharedi of the Mizrachi Organization of America also deals with Talmud Torahs, while Torah Umesorah, whose program and goal were conceived by the saintly Rabbi Faivel Mendelowitz, is concerned with Yeshivoth alone. The Lubavitscher Hasidim have their own unit for identical work. The Vaad Hachinuch Hacharedi is more Zionist in its outlook than the last two groups; the last two groups even regard the knowledge of

Yiddish as important for the survival of Torah. Together, however, they stress the importance of a thorough background in Bible and Talmud at the same time that secular studies more than meet the standards of the American public schools. With the increase in the number of schools on the elementary level, there came also an increase in the number of schools on the secondary level. Beyond the high school level there was also established a network of schools which ordain Rabbis. At one time the Rabbi Isaac Elchanan Theological Seminary in New York (still the largest) and the Hebrew Theological College, founded by the late Rabbi Saul Silber of Chicago, were the only two Orthodox seminaries in America. Now there are at least a dozen. Unfortunately, however, these schools are not even federated with each other; there is no joint action whatever. Even their graduates are not affiliated with one Rabbinic body, although the Rabbinical Council of America has the largest percentage of all the graduates, while the Rabbinical Alliance of America, and the oldest of all, the Union of Orthodox Rabbis of the United States and Canada, get a fair measure as well. These three Rabbinic groups have recently sought some areas for joint action but as yet the results are meager. And this is perhaps the greatest weakness of Orthodox Jewry—its inability to consolidate, or even coordinate, its educational institutions and their alumni.

Nonetheless, the enrollment of about thirty thousand Jewish boys and girls in the all-day schools constituted Orthodox Jewry's proud achievement at the close of the third century of American Jewish history. The financial burden has been indescribably great. And the financial problem will be insoluble in times of economic depression. For that reason many supporters of the Yeshiva movement hope for state support of parochial schools. Heretofore Jews have been quite unanimous in their support of the defense agencies' position on the complete separation of church and state in America. However, with most welfare funds denying aid to the Yeshivoth of their own communities, or at best making niggardly allocations, one can predict that in

345

the not too distant future, the sponsors of the Yeshivoth will be desperate enough to join with representatives of the Roman Catholic Church in an effort to obtain state or federal aid. Such a move may make for a further cleavage between Orthodox and non-Orthodox Jews. But Orthodox Jews feel that they have more than vindicated the right of the Yeshiva movement to be hailed as a major contribution to the survival of Judaism in America and that the time has come for welfare funds to abandon their hostility to the cause. New York City's Federation of Jewish Philanthropies, for example, has only begun to see the light.

One interesting by-product of the Yeshiva movement has been the remarkable financial success that publishers have enjoyed in their republication of classics in Judaica. The Union of Orthodox Rabbis republished the Babylonian Talmud about thirty-five years ago. Thereafter business firms have done it profitably several times and they have added many other works. Orthodox Judaism does not yet adequately subsidize its scholars nor provide for the publication of their original contributions to scholarship. Yet enough of a demand for books has been stimulated to make many a reprinting financially worthwhile.

Another interesting by-product of the Yeshiva movement has been the effect of the presence of a Yeshiva in many a mid-western city upon the Orthodox group within that city itself. Within the Orthodox community, where only chaos and anarchy reigned before, the Yeshiva became the great cohesive force, and the Yeshiva leadership inspired greater control over kashrut supervision, the construction of better facilities required by Orthodox Jews for all ritualistic observances, and even more cooperation in fund-raising for local and overseas religious needs.

How the Yeshiva movement served more than the cause of Torah, narrowly conceived, can be gleaned from the fact that it was a Yeshiva, led by the brilliant and visionary Dr. Bernard Revel, that established on American soil the first Jewish college of arts and science; later it became America's first Jewish University. More recently it undertook the construction of a medical and dental school. Furthermore, that Orthodoxy in America was prepared to abandon its historic indifference to the education of women, was made manifest not only by the fact that a large percentage of the children enrolled in the Yeshivoth are girls, but that Yeshiva University, headed by the resourceful and indefatigable Dr. Samuel Belkin, now has a secondary school and college for them.

In the area of overseas relief Orthodoxy was always impatient with the general agencies because of their neglect of religious institutions, and as a result during and after World War I the Central Jewish Relief Committee and Ezrath Torah Fund were organized to bring aid and succor to European Yeshivoth. The Union of Orthodox Rabbis deserves special commendation for this achievement. With regard to Palestine, too, Orthodoxy was preoccupied with religious development. Within the framework of the World Zionist Organization, American Orthodoxy advanced the program of the Mizrachi and Hapoel Hamizrachi parties. Rabbi Meyer Berlin (Bar-Ilan), who was also the founder of the Teachers' Institute which became affiliated with the Rabbi Isaac Elchanan Theological Seminary and later was one of the larger schools of Yeshiva University, was the ideological spokesman and administrative head of every phase of the work. With the new wave of immigration immediately prior to, and after World War II, the separatist Agudath Yisrael party gained an appreciable following in the American Jewish community and created a very marked cleavage between the traditionalists who hoped for some synthesis of western thought with our ancestral heritage and the traditionalists who hoped to reestablish on American soil replicas of Eastern European Jewish communities. The former are also more cooperative with non-Orthodox Jewish groups and participate in the work of the Synagogue Council of America even as they are represented in the Commission on Jewish Chaplaincy of the National Jewish Welfare Board and organizations like the New York Board of Rabbis. The profound ideological differences between the

347

two groups came to the fore with respect to the issue of the conscription of women in Israel. However, the same lack of unity that has weakened Orthodoxy's achievement in the fields of synagogue and Yeshiva organization has also undermined the esteem in which Orthodoxy's significant achievements for Israel ought be held. Nonetheless, it is American Orthodoxy that has always borne the brunt of the responsibility for the preservation of almost all of Israel's religious life.

Orthodox Judaism has maximalist objectives not only for religious education in America and abroad but also with regard to religious observances. Unfortunately, in this area too it has failed to achieve any measure of unity or coordination. Kashrut supervision for example, is under the aegis of no central body, and even the cooperation of states that have laws on the subject has not eliminated the anarchy that prevails. The most progressive step forward was taken by the Union of Orthodox Jewish Congregations, in cooperation with the Rabbinical Council of America, when it registered its "U" as a guarantee of kashrut and made the label available to firms that meet the strictest requirements. This helped to popularize Kashrut and the Union not only advertised the products it endorsed but published brochures on the significance of the dietary laws generally. The ultimate hope is to divest individual Rabbis of the right to act on their own for personal gain. The resistance of members of the Union of Orthodox Rabbis is great and even the Rabbinical Council of America had to pass resolutions censuring its members who flout the policy and give *Hechsherim* as individuals. In the area of Sabbath observance there has been less success although the number of professional and business firms that observe the Sabbath has been increasing. The Young Israel movement has helped to find employment for Sabbath observers and it has sponsored the establishment of many orthodox synagogues everywhere. Modern Mikvehs are being built in many communities and though the laws pertaining to *Taharat Hamishpacha* have suffered the greatest neglect, Orthodox Judaism has sought

348

to improve the situation by constructing more attractive and inviting facilities for their observance and by publishing literature on the subject in English.

In the area of English publications and public relations generally, Orthodox Judaism must meet new challenges. Its Halachic and scholarly journals, such as *Talpioth,* of Yeshiva University, have a limited circle of readers while most American Jews have only the vaguest notions of the nature of Orthodoxy and its spiritual and intellectual vitality. True, within the ranks of Orthodox Judaism there are many to whom the modern scene and western thought constitute no challenge. These elements are to be found principally among the recent immigrants to the United States. And they often intimidate the more progressive Orthodox elements who recognize that Jewish law was always dynamic and that Judaism never required an ostrich-like indifference to currents of thought that prevailed in the world about. A sad illustration of the dangers of such intolerance was recently afforded Orthodox Jews when an Orthodox Rabbinic Journal—which was never noted for its progressive approach, and even delighted in attacking the young Rabbis of the Rabbinical Council of America—found itself under attack by an even more "rightist" journal because it published an article suggesting that the redactors of the Babylonian Talmud did not see the Palestinian Talmud! The tendency to canonize each and every view of the past with absolutely no critical or historical evaluation is strong among these "rightists." Some of them even favor the social and economic isolation of Orthodox Jews. They propose the establishment of Orthodox Jewish communities with Sabbath-observing professional and service personnel, etc.

The position of these "rightists," however, is not typical. Most American Orthodox Rabbis are not isolationists. They admit that for at least another generation or two most American Jews will not be observant. Nevertheless, they want these Jews to appreciate their moral obligation to support the totality of their ancestral heritage as Jews that it may be transmitted intact to later generations whose knowledge of Judaism and whose spiritual climate may be more conducive to the development of Judaism in consonance with its historic philosophy and pattern rather than as a compromise with Jewish illiteracy and the materialistic, "sensate" values of the present era. The prevailing values of our day are antithetical to most of the values of Judaism. They, therefore, believe that to adjust Judaism to the values of today is to forfeit the role of religion as a goal and aspiration for a more spiritual tomorrow. Our posterity should not be prejudiced by us and receive from us only truncated conceptions or patterns of Jewish thought and practice. With this approach, most Orthodox Rabbis are urging even the non-observant to identify themselves with Orthodox synagogues and send their children to Yeshivoth. Serious problems do arise when such children are confronted with the contrast between what they are taught in school and what they see at home. However, the leaders of the day-school movement are trying to solve these problems through their publications, their conferences with parents, and their day-by-day contact with the children.

Most Orthodox synagogues now have English-speaking Rabbis who preach in English. Prayerbooks and copies of the Pentateuch with English translations are the rule, not the exception. Especially noteworthy among the English translations of the traditional prayerbook is Dr. David de Sola Pool's, recently sponsored by the Rabbinical Council of America. Under the auspices of the Union of Orthodox Jewish Congregations, Dr. Leo Jung edited a number of excellent volumes on Jewish information. Several of the essays have become classical expositions of Orthodox Judaism. At least one, "Study as a Form of Worship," by Professor Nathan Isaacs of Harvard University, has gained a worldwide currency among Jews. Rabbi Herbert S. Goldstein translated selections from Rashi's commentary on the Pentateuch for family use on the Sabbath, and more recently a linear translation was made available by a commercial publisher.

Orthodox Judaism is endeavoring to recapture the loyalty of American Jews. However, it cannot "adjust" to the American scene. The term "adjust" too often implies man's right to trim religion to meet his personal desires. Such a right Orthodoxy denies any Jew, and notwithstanding even Dr. Kinsey, the sixth commandment of the Decalogue is binding no matter how high the percentage of spouses who flout it. Nonetheless, most American Orthodox Rabbis recognize that there have always been, and still are, different modes of Orthodox Jewish thought and practice, and that Orthodoxy has always admitted a great measure of innovation. The innovation, however, is always within the Halachic process and pursuant to its revealed norms. The result, therefore, is organic development of God's will, not man's.

In order to communicate this point of view to American Jews, Orthodoxy must have leaders who are not only articulate in English but also masters of western thought and its temper. That is why Yeshiva University and the Hebrew Theological College advocate the mastering of all western thought in order to create an ultimate synthesis with Jewish learning. This goal will be achieved as more of the graduates of these schools and other Yeshivoth become expert in the natural and social sciences.

There already exists a society of Orthodox Jewish scientists which is dedicating itself to the solution of problems created for Orthodoxy by modern technology. Many a Halachic point of view is receiving support from the natural sciences, and what is more important, these scientists are demonstrating that there is no conflict between natural science—which has abandoned the notion that it can attain any absolute truths whatever—and religion which calls for faith in given absolutes. The greater challenges to Orthodoxy, however, come from the social sciences, and an impressive group of Orthodox leaders, lay and Rabbinic, are coping with them.

Orthodoxy's position vis-à-vis the Higher Criticism of the Bible is one such area. While Orthodoxy is committed to no one conception of Revelation, all Orthodox Jews regard the Pentateuch as divinely revealed. Moses wrote it while

351

in direct communion with God. Moreover, with Moses too, the Oral Law had its beginnings and its process was ordained by God. German Jewish Orthodoxy perhaps made more progress in its defense of this position than has American Jewish Orthodoxy to date. However, Orthodoxy relies heavily on the fact that modern archaeological research has bolstered the historicity of the Biblical narrative and Orthodoxy is confident that further progress in philology will precipitate the same kind of retreat from anti-Orthodox viewpoints that the Bible's erstwhile plastic surgeons have suffered. Rabbi Chayim Heller, at Yeshiva University, stimulated both the confidence and the type of research necessary to sustain the Orthodox position. Moreover, many Orthodox thinkers believe that with a retreat from humanism generally, humanism will no longer be the vantage point from which the revealed Word of God will be arrogantly evaluated. Man will not be the measure of God.

The greatest challenge of all, however, lies in the realm of Halachah; first, the importance of its study, and second, the importance of living by its prescriptions. Is the Halachah viable in the modern age? Can it and does it enrich our spiritual existence? Is it relevant to our yearnings and aspirations and can it edify and fulfill them? Only a small percentage of even Orthodox Jews are content with the mandate, "The Law is the Law and must, therefore, be obeyed." Philosophical approaches to Halachah and philosophical analyses of the Halachic process must be articulated. The undisputed leader of the Orthodox Jewish community in this domain is Dr. Joseph B. Soloveitchik, of Yeshiva University, who is now also Chairman of the Halachah Commission of the Rabbinical Council of America. In addition to his brilliant resolution of many involved Halachic problems of the modern age, and his equally masterly analyses of Talmudic texts, he is demonstrating the viability of the Halachah, the relevance of its insights to abundant and adventurous spiritual living and the intellectual harvests to be reaped from preoccupation with its study. Most of the great Halachic scholars who adorn the faculties of

America's Yeshivoth, and most of the distinguished Orthodox Rabbis who founded and still lead the Union of Orthodox Rabbis of the United States and Canada, deserve credit for their benign influence upon the loyalty of thousands of American Jews to our ancestral heritage. But they have done little more than transplant the Orthodoxy of Eastern Europe on American soil. It is to Dr. Soloveitchik, his co-workers and students, that American Orthodoxy looks for the ideological content, the techniques and the conclusions required to stem the tide of defections to other groups by making it abundantly clear that Halachic Judaism is eternal and has naught to fear from the challenges of western thought, present and future.

First, however, it wants to stimulate a renascence of Torah learning on American soil. Orthodoxy feels that until Jews are learned they cannot be pious. It insists that it sustained its greatest setback in America because of Am ha-Arazuth, Torah illiteracy. For more than two and a half centuries America could not boast of a score of men learned in the Law. How could Orthodoxy then achieve here that synthesis that was once the glory of Spanish Judaism? The first task, therefore, is to spread the knowledge of Torah. As tens of thousands become masters of the Halachah, the Halachah will have a new birth in the new world.

Second, Orthodoxy does not believe that the modern contribution to progressive revelation can come until the modern age recaptures basic religious experience. The commitment of our age to material values has deadened our capacity for religious experience. Yet, there is evidence that as we face the atomic era in human history, there will be a resurgence of religious values and a reawakening of religious experience. In such an atmosphere, Judaism will thrive. Particularly will Halachic Judaism thrive as more and more Jews seek to apprehend God's will rather than merely indulging their own.

Chapter Two

IS JEWISH–CHRISTIAN DIALOGUE WORTHWHILE?

Israel's crisis galvanized the American Jewish community precisely at a time when the religious organizations were girding for a bitter controversy. The debate pertained to dialogues between Christians and Jews. Orthodox rabbis had asked that the dialogues be limited to social issues with no confrontation whatever on matters of dogma or doctrine.

In May, 1967, the Synagogue Council of America, which comprises delegates from all three Jewish groups, and Christians jointly sponsored a conference held in Boston. It dealt with conscience in our time. The two orthodox constituent organizations of the Synagogue Council of America —the Rabbinical Council of America and the Union of Orthodox Jewish Congregations of America—had raised no objection and had even agreed to participate. Shortly before the conference opened, however, they withdrew because of the pressure of leaders of the Union of Orthodox Rabbis.

Notwithstanding, several orthodox rabbis attended. Before their defiance and the generally embarrassing behavior of the orthodox groups could become the subject of sad incriminations and recriminations in the community, Israel was confronted by the armed might of the Arabs and all the energies of Jews were focused on unity and help for our beleaguered brethren. Now, perhaps, as Jews united, one

354

may with less passion and more reason give the entire issue a new look.

What is meant by "dialogue?" What form is it expected to assume? What do its proponents hope to accomplish? What do its opponents fear? And last, but not least, did we learn anything from Christendom's response to Israel's plight and victory that we may the more realistically appraise what Jews can expect from Christians in any crisis? Is that which we can expect worth another conflict among Jews?

It is inevitable that in American society there will be communication between Christians and Jews. And who will undertake to supervise and control what individual Christians and Jews discuss with each other! This is dialogue in its original meaning—talk on a "one-to-one" basis. Certainly the controversy cannot pertain to this kind of interpersonal relationship.

What is meant must, therefore, not be dialogue at all, but organized confrontations between leaders of both groups. If the themes for discussion are not theological, there is no objection whatever to the confrontation. If the themes, however, are theological, then one must ask several practical questions. Will only Jewish theologians participate? If so, can we who are three per cent of the population provide enough theologians to enlighten ninety-seven per cent who are Christians with that which they seek to know about Judaism? Of necessity, most Christians will have to learn about Judaism from books and not from face-to-face encounters. Perhaps Jews will not use professional theologians but laymen—presidents of synagogues and B'nai B'rith chapters. Visualize their Jewish knowledge pitted against the erudition and forensic skill of a Jesuit!

Perhaps on a limited scale, in great citadels of learning, there could be dialogue between the intellectual giants of both religious traditions. And for what? Do such giants resolve any issues in their conferences—no matter how learned—without the subsequent publication of their papers, critical rejoinders by those who differ with them and ongoing debate in periodicals and books? If this is what is meant by dialogue, then it always was and always will be, so long as freedom of the press endures. The face-to-face encounter is usually only frustrating in such situations. One needs the precise formulation of a paper to begin with, and time within which to formulate an equally precise reply.

Indeed one such exploratory conference was held at Harvard University. It was most impressive, yet at the one seminar devoted to theology it became apparent that there could be no dialogue. The distinguished chairman—a world-renowned Christian theologian—in virtual exasperation asked at the conclusion of the seminar, "Is there naught upon which Christians and Jews can agree?" Fascinating it was that the orthodox, conservative and liberal rabbis present were all agreed on that which united them—a common history that determined even their theology—while it was precisely history that Christians wanted either to ignore or to transcend. They had no answer to the chairman's query. And if Jewish theologians at such a conference felt frustrated, what form shall the dialogue assume, as visualized by its proponents?

In the final analysis, it is not the face-to-face encounter of intellectual giants that is being proposed but rather public sessions where less knowledgeable Christians and Jews will talk it out. But again let us be practical. Do Jews have the qualified manpower for such enterprise? Do Jews have the manpower in the Midwest, the West, the South and the Southwest? And it is precisely in those communities where Jews are so anxious to find favor in Christian eyes. It is there, too, that the threat of Jewish assimilation is greatest. Are we wise to accelerate that process by having more Jews enter churches to hear sermons by priests and ministers, and then to organize social activities which are the inevitable prelude to, and aftermath of, any kind of program to which the public generally is invited?

Many American rabbis who were chaplains during World War II will recall how active they were both in military installations and in the so-called "good-will" programs under the auspices of the National Conference of Christians and Jews. They appeared together with priests and ministers on programs promotive of brotherhood. Their collective experience was that those who attended the meetings were those who needed no convincing. And no one could tell who, among even these, would have had the courage to take a stand on behalf of a Negro when a lynching impended or on behalf of a Jew if the star of another Hitler began to rise.

The chaplains were convinced that nothing short of legislation could help protect the rights of minorities. Today, we wonder whether even legislation is enough and whether anything less than drastic social, political and economic action will accomplish the desired result. But public rallies for good will, for toleration, for brotherhood are deemed an utter waste of time and energy. Even the National Conference of Christians and Jews has abandoned the approach.

Is this, then, what the dialogues shall now become? Will it make a difference that today the dialogues will deal with theology while a generation ago they dealt only with the dignity of man and the right to be different? On the other hand, who knows better than theologians how little influence a man's doctrines have over his deeds and how little professions of the mouth reflect one's behavior in time of crisis?

By all means, in social action, Jews and Christians, whites and Negroes must not only have dialogue but joint planning and implementation as a team. To this kind of enterprise there is no objection whatever. The Boston conference was conceived with this in mind. But because it was made to appear unwittingly and erroneously that the conference was an indirect response to the call for ecumenism between Christians and Jews—and some might have deemed the participation of orthodox rabbis as a blanket endorsement of the total program including confrontations on theological levels—a number of orthodox rabbis panicked and forced their more reasonable colleagues

357

to withdraw. From every point of view what happened was embarrassing to all Jews, especially orthodox Jews. However, this is the time for conservative and liberal rabbis to ask whether the broader dialogue makes sense.

Do Christian theologians need the dialogue to learn about Judaism? Isn't there enough available in books and periodicals for their edification? Do we need to face them to learn about Christianity? And if the dialogues are for our lay Jews—young and old alike—have we done enough to make them knowledgeable vis-à-vis their own faith that we must now expend our limited resources on teaching them comparative religion?

Perhaps it is Israel's crisis, more than anything else that has happened in the last five years, that ought to pinpoint the bankruptcy of any program designed to get Christendom to revise its attitude toward Jews, Judaism and the survival of both our people and our heritage. What help Jews received in our present crisis was not due to Christendom but rather to political realities—to the desperate need of the United States to keep the Soviet Union at bay in the Middle East, to a very satisfactory trade treaty to Israel with Rumania, and to political leaders in Europe whose Christian loyalty is superficial. (The weakness of Christianity in Scandinavian countries is too well known to require documentation.)

Did the Pope react to the threats of the Arab world against Israel with even the concern he made manifest for the Vietnamese people? Can he and organized Christendom anywhere pretend that they knew nothing of the desecration of cemeteries and the demolition of synagogues in Jordanian Jerusalem with their representatives living alongside these sites of sacrilege? Did only Moslems use the driveway to the hotel through the Jewish cemetery? Were the Lutheran sponsors of schools in old Jerusalem and the Christian tourists in the hotels there or even the patrons of the Helen Keller institutes—were all of these blind Christians who had naught to say when Jewish holy places were violated but became concerned like "His Holiness" only when

Jews took charge? Isn't this precisely how Christendom behaved in Hitler's day? One finds it difficult to forget that German S.P.C.A.'s took care of the pets of Jews while the owners were taken away to death camps.

True, there were a few Christian theologians who signed pleas for Israel even as there were a few heroic Christians during World War II who saved Jews. Who will gainsay that there are righteous people among the Gentiles now as there were then! One of them did regret his compassion once it became apparent that Jews were no longer the underdogs. And this is the heart of the matter.

The continuing existence of our people is a fact which the Church cannot reconcile with its historic theology. The restoration of Israel—the fulfillment of the prophecies of the Prophets for us and not for a Christian Israel—is more unacceptable to Christianity than unequivocal proof that we never committed deicide. And public debate will not change the Church's position.

A few liberal Protestants do not so hold. With them Jews already work well in many areas of social action. With the others, too, we should seek to work in the same areas. Let all of us do this in the name of God each of us serves. But we do not have to define that God for each other in order to toil for the amelioration of the lot of all His creatures. On the other hand, let us respect each other's right of privacy—in this case, the privacy of one's religious commitment and covenant and in that way help society achieve even knowledge of the tension between collective action and individual belief. Moreover, what we must know about each other's theology will always be available in books.

In the final analysis, it is only thus that we will fulfill the meaning of dialogue in its loftiest sense. Dialogue is more than communication. Years ago when I would sit down with members of the Communist Party to discuss ideologies, I had the peculiar feeling that it was not dialogue in which we were engaged. There was always a desire on the part of my adversary to manipulate me. For there is a difference between communicating with another in order to sell and communicating with another because you really crave to understand each other, to fathom each other's motivations and yearnings so that your love of each other may grow because of a deeper understanding of each other's souls.

This is dialogue. When East and West sit down at the table, it isn't dialogue. We know that they sit down with mutual suspicion. There is a desire in each to destroy the other's power system.

And between Christians and Jews there cannot be dialogue in the correct sense of the term until there is a basic recognition that all the participants are equals and what each group seeks is to maintain its own spiritual heritage, not absorption or assimilation of the other. Until it is recognized that I am an absolute equal whose Jewishness the other party is as anxious to see continued as I am, it is not dialogue.

To be sure, there can be unison with each other on levels where there is agreement, but this cannot possibly involve theology if the Church is to be true to its own commitment. I cannot have dialogue with one who feels that he is bound by his own religious commitment to change my convictions and the pattern of my commitment. Thus the dialogue between Catholics and Jews can never be on the theological level, and if it can't be on the theological level then we ought to be frank and say, "When you Catholics are engaged in theology—it's not our business."

You have to do what is right for your theology. You have to do what is safe for your covenant. We cannot be involved any more than we can invite you into our covenant. On the social action level, however, there can be dialogue.

American Jewry is presently more united than ever. Let us not rock the boat for a mess of pottage.

Chapter Three

JEWISH AUTHORS AND JEWISH VALUES

I

Several generations ago Jewish intellectuals abandoned Judaism principally because of their discovery of Marx. More recently the defections were due to Freud. Today, however, the idolization of avant-gardist Jewish authors has become one of the gravest causes for the alienation of Jewish youth not only from their ancestral heritage but more particularly from their people.

The threat from Marx was serious enough but somehow the ideas of international socialism and Jewish peoplehood were reconciled. Especially in Israel was the peace achieved. In the foreseeable future religion and communism may lie together like the lion and the lamb in the post-messianic age. In much of Europe the entente is now a fact and Israeli communists will not languish far behind. The threat from Freud is also losing its momentum. Freud himself confessed late in life that he craved his Jewish roots—his sense of belonging to the Jewish people. Social psychologists have advanced far beyond Freud, and religion, in general, and Judaism in particular, are becoming allies of the very science whose founder once dramatically subscribed to God's obituary. Not so easily met, however, is the challenge from modern literati and more consideration must be given this challenge if Jews and Judaism are to survive.

II

A fact it is that in our generation the number of Jewish authors that have achieved recognition and fame exceeds by far the proportion of Jews in the general population. Ofttimes Jews note this fact with pride; equally often they deplore the bizarre image of Jews and Judaism that these authors convey. However, critics continue to ponder why it is that so many of one minority group are in the forefront of modern belle lettres, irrespective of how their own ethnic group reacts to them.

One reason is commonly suggested. The sensitive, intelligent Jew gives expression to his own alienation from his past and his God and it is this alienation that is the dilemma of modern man. Yet, if this dilemma is well-nigh universal, why is it that Jews preponderate in giving expression to what so many others also experience and suffer? Daniel Stern, in the *Saturday Review,* suggests that Jews are preserving the important questions even when they cannot answer them. But that does not explain why the questions are more poignant for Jews that especially they should become the vigorous, creative spokesmen of all the perplexed of our day.

As a rabbi, and not as an expert in English literature, I want to suggest that the questions come forth devastatingly, particularly from Jewish authors, precisely because it is the ancestral heritage of the Jewish author that provides him his stance. Even when he is not the master of that heritage, its quests and its values are so deeply rooted in the Jewish environment in which he was reared that he cannot possibly avoid their impact. They come to him almost as if with his mother's milk and they account for his passion and his protest, his venom and his despair. Indeed, they are the fundamental values of the values system of Judaism and Jewish authors, and the multitude who idolize them would do well to ponder and respect the source of all this soul-searching: the unusual religion which millennia after its founding still has the component of prophecy and the capacity to address all mankind on the most vital issues of human experience. Certainly the questions come from that heritage and even if the answers of the past do not satisfy everyone in the present, at least two items ought be kept in mind. First, because of the quest it inspires, the heritage itself merits more respect than it is being accorded. Second, the answers of that heritage might still have validity which a more sympathetic and penetrating analysis reveals.

III

The most recurring conviction in Jewish life and thought is that human existence in general, and Jewish existence in particular, must have meaning. The Jewish position contrasts boldly with that of other Oriental religions. And Jews not only shared the conviction but of necessity had to communicate it ardently and effectively to their progeny. Jews always had to explain to themselves and to their children the fact of their separate existence, its significance, and why it was worth the price in anguish that it exacted. They had the alternative to change the character of their existence by apostasy and assimilation but refused to do so. This denial was an affirmation of some meaning. When Hamlet asked "To be or not to be," he may have been emotionally disturbed. But Jews were always similarly conflicted with regard to their Jewishness. They could opt out of their faith. And when they chose instead to rationalize and justify their selfhood, their identity, they endowed their lives with a stature and meaning that constituted self-fulfillment. In Tevye's words in "Fiddler on the Roof," everyone knew who he was and what God expected of him.

Non-Jews were never so hard put to search for the meaning of existence. They had fewer goads to engage in the quest. They could accept life naturally and be content with the naturalness of the processes of living and dying. They could take so much for granted. So little had to be explained or rationalized. Perhaps they too encountered challenges which might have precipitated the quest. But the tragedies which nature had wrought for them were few by comparison with the very precarious situation of the Jew at all times. The Jew simply could not survive unless he grafted meaning and purpose on his existence and suffering.

Thus for the Jew the search for meaning and purpose was a perennial and millennial one. All that happened in the modern age was that for the Jewish author the search became more universal and less parochial in character. He asks why he lives altogether and not only why he lives as a Jew. He no longer finds the traditional answers adequate but he has no new ones either. Yet his need to ask is inescapable. It is part of his patrimony.

Therefore, from this point of view it is no accident that a committed Jew, Victor Frankl, should be the founder of a school of psychotherapy which makes the search for a meaningful existence central in the treatment of emotionally disturbed persons. Frankl made his discovery in the German concentration camps where with millions of other coreligionists he was forced daily to ask basic whys and wherefores. Jews always had to do this throughout their history. And they found answers in the written and oral law, in legends and homilies, in chronicles and prophecies. They could not have survived unless their existence and their suffering had a purpose.

In the liturgy of the High Holy Days one also finds the question and the answer explicit and implicit everywhere. But for God, what would man's existence mean? But for the mission which God gave the Jewish people to make every creature mindful of Him, what would our suffering signify? God, the King, Whom we crown each year anew, is concerned about His creatures. Despite His infinitude, He craves the worship of finite man! What stature is ours that He needs us! Our life is precious; we want its continuance on earth, and not only in heaven. And He superintends our this-worldly living. The deafening music of the spheres and its constellations does not drown out thin, small voices— the voices and the deeds of men, which have worth in His eyes. He takes account of them and our striving is not lost in the vastness of the universe.

However, if God has died, or never was, one has only the question and no answer. Jewish authors who almost congenitally ask the question thus give expression to the malaise of modern man. The non-Jewish world was never similarly obsessed with the question and when they now have it they cannot verbalize it with the anguish of ages.

IV

The Jewish tradition and its values system had still another obsession: an inordinate emphasis on unity—the oneness of God, the oneness of body and soul, the oneness of past and present. Holiness was wholeness—integration. Philosophical theories which permit one to bifurcate experience and assign different categories to different realms of reality were almost congenitally unacceptable. The antinomies of good and evil, truth and falsehood, beauty and ugliness, exist but their co-existence must needs be explained in the light of one Creator in whose absence there would be only chaos.

Albert Einstein was wont to say that the monotheism of Judaism impelled him to search for one formula which would unify all of reality. In the final analysis this is a matter of faith. Dualists find it much easier than monotheists, for example, to resolve the problem of evil. Christianity also, because of its Greek component, could juxtapose spirit and flesh and evaluate accordingly. For Jews everything emanated from one God and was good. All must be made holy in fulfillment of His will. He is not only the principle of explanation but the unifying principle for all that is.

Certainly no theme of the High Holy Day liturgy is more eloquent than that of the unity of creation, including all mankind. Even non-Jews have been impressed by the universalistic mood of the prayers and the aspirations they express. Fervently we beseech the advent of that day when in peace all nations will hail God as their Creator, when heaven and earth and their hosts will sing His praises, when all will constitute one symphony—the waves of the waters, the vales and the forests, the beasts that inhabit them, and especially the race of man.

Now, when God—in Whose Being all is united—is no longer there, the resulting disintegration of reality is far more frightening and disastrous for one who was reared in an environment committed to that unity as a good, than for one who was committed to dualism or pluralism. Therefore, the Jewish author far more than the non-Jewish author is overwhelmed by the forces in our day making for disintegration and annihilation. His world collapses more readily and he gives most eloquent expression to his sense of panic and his obsessive need to rediscover some new principle that might save from chaos and restore unity. With alienation from God, unity goes the way of meaning.

V

This leads to still a third value fundamental in Judaism. For an answer to a vital question to be acceptable to the Jew it must be sustained by the very warp and woof of God's design. It cannot be self-deluding for the purpose of escape. Nor can it be aestheticism alone. The Greeks were content with philosophies of escape but the Jewish tradition has always insisted that the only values worthy of pursuit were those that were firmly and inextricably rooted in the will of God. Their law was an expression of His will, as Professor Carl Friedrich once observed. Even their ethnicity or peoplehood was *His* choice.

That a mode of behavior was natural—that, in and of itself, was insufficient warrant for its propriety. Certainly the pragmatic or utilitarian test was not the ultimate one, and to live by "as if" philosophies was unthinkable. Whether or not God had willed a course of conduct was the litmus paper of validity. God's will might have been revealed in Mount Sinai, or in nature, or in history. Man's duty was to discover and fathom that will but Jewish ethics had to be rooted in it.

The High Holy Day liturgy invites us to confront God with an account of our behavior. Blasts of the shofar not only accompany the coronation of God as King but stimulate reflections on His revelation, his unique and ongoing relationship with the Jewish people in history, and the vision of the Messianic era when justice will reign supreme. Pursuant to the Law, which unites Israel and God in the past, present and future, we review our own personal performance and are judged to be righteous or evil men. How awesome is the standard by which we are measured!

To most non-Jews the Law was never central in either practice or belief. Correct faith meant more to Christians than good deeds, and salvation was dependent upon the former rather than the latter. The antinomianism of Paul made mystic communication with God more important than the fulfillment of His will. It became easier to detach ethics from religion and especially from ultimate reality. The demise of God, for Christians, therefore, does not affect human behavior very much, any more than His existence did earlier.

But the Jewish author seems conflicted between a passion for a very substantial sense of the right—as rooted in reality—and the absence of a God Who is its source, Who constitutes the standard and provides the barometer. The anguish of this conflict seems to emerge from their writings —their ambivalence with regard to right and wrong: on the one hand a passion for the right and yet a realization that a humanistic philosophy can yield only relativism in ethics. Yet subconsciously they have a need to seek and champion absolutes even when they worship no Absolute—with a capital "A" or "G."

VI

A fourth value of Judaism involves the notion that sin represents the failure of the individual, and not the failure

367

of God, the group, environment or forebears. Atonement is never easy; damage is rarely reparable; punishment is this-worldly; and heaven is principally in one's heart. That is why Jewish authors are so critical of their characters, so introspective, so demanding, and so unforgiving. Their heroes suffer not from fate but from fault. And atonement can only be the consequence of the recognition of fault and personal responsibility.

It would be insulting to a reader to document this value from the High Holy Day liturgy. This value is the corner-stone of our observance of the New Year and Day of Atone-ment. Man has free will; man chooses life or death; man redeems himself or perishes. No religious tradition ever vested man with more control over his own destiny. The Jewish author has this value as part of his patrimony; yet because of his knowledge of modern psychology and its com-mitment to determinism, he finds himself in a conflict be-tween antithetical notions than can only evoke powerful, explosive, treatments of human beings and their behavior.

VII

Several important conclusions may be derived from the essentially Jewish character of the disaffection of Jewish authors and the malaise to which they give eloquent expres-sion. Perhaps one may thus explain their hostility to the tradition. It is not only that unwittingly they are in its grip but it may be that subconsciously they resent what makes them so exacting in their criticism and so frustrated that they are unable to accept what other contemporaries find acceptable.

But the intelligentsia among Jewish youth idolize these authors. With them they abandon the tradition to a greater extent than Christian university students abandon their re-ligious heritage, and with the authors they too ask funda-mental questions which can only be answered by acceptance of the total commitment which Judaism requires. It is comparable to an "all or nothing" situation. Either God is nothing, or He is the Source of all meaning, the unifying principle of all that is, and the Absolute in ethical aspiration and performance. Earlier generations of Jewish intellectuals did occasionally embrace partial answers—socialism, Zionism, humanism. Their descendants, because of the very Judaism they reject, cannot be content with anything less than an all-inclusive and all-pervasive philosophy of existence. A leap of faith they hesitate to make but without it they are the most perplexed of all Jews in our millennial history. It would be self-deluding not to reckon with this fact if we sincerely crave the survival of Jews and Judaism.

Yet the exacting values of the tradition are at the same time the basis for optimism with regard to Jewish survival. In my broad experience with college youth I have come in contact with a small but dedicated number of Jewish youth who are rediscovering their ancestral heritage and with a leap of faith are making Judaism meaningful to themselves even as they will ultimately produce the thinkers and the authors who will write new guides to the Jewish perplexed of the twentieth and twenty-first centuries.

The faith of these young intellectuals does not have its inception in any kind of mystic experience. On the other hand, it flows from reason. They observe that the road taken by those alienated from Judaism does not yield meaning or purpose. Nor does it altogether ennoble the existence of the alienated, ethically speaking. Indeed, in many instances the alienated crush those nearest to them. Their individual worth is not enhanced and certainly personal integration is not achieved. The road of alienation thus proves to be self-destructive and it is not only one's Jewishness that is forfeited but frequently one's humanity as well. Reason dictates, therefore, that a course that proved successful through the centuries should be tried again. And many are seeking to do precisely this.

They find that their complete involvement with Judaism not only provides strong ties with family, community, and

369

people, but at the same time a noble stance for involvement with all mankind, with nature, with history, with past, present and future. Somehow Judaism makes possible microcosmic and macrocosmic experience without one's becoming schizoid. The heritage simply integrates both. Can one explain how? Perhaps not, but this is what being Jewish implies.

Because they are Jewish, these young intellectuals are not shattered by the vastness of the universe. Long ago Jews were taught that worth was not related to size. Quality is not affected by measurement, which by its very nature is quantitative. God had chosen the Jewish people, according to Deuteronomy, though they were the fewest of all nations. And despite their fewness the Jewish people achieved so well for themselves and all humanity in matters of the spirit. Consequently they want as Jews to make this insight available to all mankind in the space age. Nor is the "chosenness" of the Jewish people regarded by them as the hallmark of the primitive character of the tradition they cherish. And though many misunderstand the concept, it is not to be abandoned any more than one abolishes sex because some practice sodomy. A distinguished sociologist, Will Herberg, writes of Jewish "chosenness" as sustained by history. Even archaeology supports the conviction as William Albright and Nelson Glueck frequently suggest. However, the young committed Jewish intellectuals are also discovering the "transhistorical" character of the Jewish people. The Jewish people are simply not bound by so-called historical laws, if any such exist. The very emergence of the state of Israel after the most savage attack on the Jewish people in recorded history appears as a miracle that is as inexplicable in the present, from the point of view of historical laws, as the exodus of a people from a land of bondage was inexplicable thousands of years ago. For these young people the words of the Bible are not simply great literature and the object of literary criticism, but the record of revelations from God which speak to man in every age. Even the Talmud and its dialectic reflect a continuing con-

370

cern to discover God's will and its viability in all circumstances.

Sometimes these promising students surprise many of their elders by insisting that even their appearance be distinctively Jewish. In action, as well as in thought, they are affirming Jewish self-identification. And they are militantly Jewish on university campuses for Jewish observances. Their affinity for Israel is strong but they are not tolerant of Israel's aspiration to be like all nations. On the other hand, they empathize most with Israel's religious collectives and their ideologists.

These young intellectuals are not organized. They are to be found in every country where Jews live and are creative. They have no one organ but in many publications one spots an essay, a story, a critique, that may well represent the wave of the Jewish future. They are not preoccupied with "modernizing" or "liberalizing" Judaism—which in the final analysis was only a technique to make possible acculturation and ultimate assimilation. Of this they want no part. On the other hand, they want the authentic tradition to address itself to them as Jews and as human beings—living apart as Jews but yet living in one world with all mankind. Franz Rosenzweig, even when they have not read him, is much more their spiritual father than Martin Buber. But what they are thinking and saying and doing is emerging from their inner need to discover themselves both as Jews and as men from within a God-given Jewish frame. Sometimes their views appear to be heterodox; when was there no witchhunting when youth was in ferment? But essentially they are traditional in the best sense of the term—they seek in the tradition the roots and the poles by which they can be creative in the present and the future.

Perhaps as the State of Israel emerged as if from the pyre of six million dead, so a new school of Jewish thought is emerging from the overwhelming threat that six million more may assimilate. That it may take a generation or two for the impact of the new school to be felt, and that only then will there appear the new Maimonides to state the case comprehensively and effectively should not discourage anyone. Maimonides, in his day, only accomplished what he did after several earlier generations of scholars had paved the way for him to build the complete edifice. This will happen again and Judaism will have met still another challenge for the continuing edification of Jews and all mankind.

Chapter Four

FERMENT IN ORTHODOXY

Every Establishment has its rebels, its mavericks. The Orthodox Jewish community, in America and in Israel, is no exception. This may come as a surprise to many who are wont to think of Orthodoxy as monolithic, and of its rebels as simply non-Orthodox. There are also rebels within the camp—rebels who may even be more religiously committed than leaders of the Establishment, but nonetheless severe, unrelenting critics of those in control of the institutions that presumably speak for Orthodoxy. They deserve our attention; they may be the "wave of the future."

In my life I have already beheld the emergence of two such groups. The first to appear opposes the participation of Orthodox rabbis and synagogues in the inevitable process of acculturation to the American scene. They frown upon decorous religious services, beautiful edifices and sermons in the Protestant tradition. They still regard the cooperation of Orthodox Jews with the non-Orthodox as a breach of Jewish Law; they are hardly enamored of Zionism and are certainly not zealous with regard to spoken Hebrew. Even in their attire and personal appearance they frequently seek distinctiveness. In their writings they deride the "modern Orthodox" as "assimilationists" who have become contaminated by winds of modern doctrine.

Their number increased in America with the new immigration that preceded and followed World War II and a few years ago at least one institution of higher Jewish learning on the American scene experienced an internal crisis because of their militancy. Their concern for America is minimal; the needs of the military chaplaincy do not move them; contacts with the non-Jewish world are shunned; and, generally, they crave isolation and insulation to the greatest extent possible.

The second, and more recent, group is quite different, but nonetheless anti-Establishment. This group consists of men who are very much at home with Jews and non-Jews, and very much the masters of Western culture. But here and abroad they are critical of the Establishment principally because the Establishment does not fully grasp the needs of contemporary man and does not respond to them with an authentic voice. They are critical of the Establishment because it is content to make kosher food available and expedite Sabbath observance, while on pressing social, economic and political issues it has virtually naught to say.

What is even worse, the Establishment makes the observance of rituals the hallmark of ultimate virtue and ignores the importance of ethical behavior in its appraisal of men and institutions. These rebels are especially critical of Jewish education—not excluding the day schools and the higher yeshivot—for the total irrelevance of most of the materials being taught. Indeed, they are scholars who cherish learning for learning's sake—Torah lishmah—but they regard learning that does not edify the inner man as a potential instrument for self-aggrandizement and for nothing more.

In Israel this group is expressing itself in a number of publications sponsored by pious university students and the members of religious collectives. There the Establishment consists of the religious political parties, the Chief Rabbinate and the yeshivot. In America the group has not yet succeeded in establishing its own organ; its initial effort in this direction was abortive. And the Establishment consists of the rabbinic and synagogue bodies, of which they them-

374

selves are members, and the yeshivot, including Yeshiva University, on whose faculties they often serve.

What they are saying merits our attention, for while their impatience may be a symptom of their youthfulness, their complaints are constructive and when properly confronted can enrich Jews and Judaism.

First, they want Judaism to reclaim its prophetic spirit. They cherish the Halachah, all of it, and its historic role in insuring our identity as a people and our commitment to its messianic vision. But they affirm that contemporary custodians of the Halachah, our "doctors of the Law," are not coping with the world in which we live. In Israel, to begin with, the rabbis rarely resolve basic issues. With only a few notable exceptions, they are as evasive as they can possibly be.

They are evasive not only in areas where the Law may require liberalization but even in areas where the Law requires enforcement with bold strictness. Thus, for example, the practice of usury in Israel is rampant and the rabbinate does nothing about this heinous sin which many of the most observant commit with no feelings of guilt whatever. The rabbinate also seems to be reconciled to the obsolescence of the institution of the Sabbatical year, during which the land is not to be tilled, as they resort year after year to legal fictions to subvert it. Many religiously committed individuals want to see more done to revive this institution and the other Biblical mandates whose social, economic and philosophical implications are so revolutionary.

They also complain that the rabbinate is meagerly knowledgeable in the area of the psychology of religion and unforgivably slow to exploit the resources of Judaism for the enrichment of religious experience. They want the insights of our ancestral legal heritage to be brought to bear on the legislation of Israel's Knesset where the representatives of the religious parties sit principally to safeguard their hegemony over very limited areas of public and private life.

But their murmuring is especially bitter in matters of educational philosophy and programming. They want the leaders of the faith to meet the challenges of modern anthropology and archaeology, the scientific criticism of the Bible and behavioral sciences. Even with regard to secondary school education, they have fault to find. From the collectives they send their best students to yeshivot on the secondary and somewhat higher level only to discover that the returning students have lost their interest in Talmud because it is taught with no eye whatever to its relevance to the modern State of Israel and the dilemma of modern man.

These are intellectuals who love the tradition and also love the new State and all that it portends for the ultimate redemption of Jews and all mankind. But they bemoan the failure of giant spirits to appear to make Zion a place from which Torah might still go forth to all the world.

Their counterparts in the United States are no less concerned or articulate. One of them recently suggested, at a national conference on Jewish education, that the age of Bar Mitzvah be advanced to 16 even if it meant that Jewish education begin at age 13. This was an appeal to get Jewish thought out of the nursery and kindergarten level and make it address itself to the teen-ager and his real problems in the jet and nuclear age. But he and his colleagues want more.

They want Jewish thought, and especially Jewish Law, to address itself to all the concerns of mature, modern men. They do not have the answers but they are asking good questions and they want their seniors and peers at least to admit that the questions merit earnest consideration. They want less attention to the irrelevant and more attention to the relevant in Talmudic studies. They want more emphasis in Jewish education on the molding of Jewish personality than on the mastery of skills in Judaica and the acquisition of more Jewish information. They speak in the idiom of the social psychologist and modern philosopher but their commitment is profoundly, heroically Orthodox.

Because they are modern and Western in outlook, they

are not as dogmatic or authoritarian in their contributions to Jewish thought or their rationalizations of Jewish practice. Indeed, they are distressed that we are not sufficiently aware of the damage we do the psyches of children even in the day schools when, in Jewish studies, our teachers are dogmatic and authoritarian while in general studies teachers stress the need for the open mind, the open society and a modicum of relativism in every quest. How does one achieve a happy balance between these two antithetical approaches? And how does one prevent adolescents from rejecting their Jewishness in the conflict of the two?

Several of these Orthodox intellectuals have been involved in teaching students at Yeshiva College and Stern College for Women at Yeshiva University. Among their students are many who acquired an interest in Judaism late in life. These are a challenge and a treat. Their sincerity and commitment are almost legendary and their teachers come to realize that perhaps like youth, Jewish education in America is being wasted on the very young. We might do better to concentrate on those who come seeking Jewish identity in their late teens. An authoritarian approach with such students will not avail and teachers, of necessity, must explore new avenues to make Judaism the answer to a genuine quest. Their experience will make for significant developments in the preparation of teaching materials and techniques for more mature Jews.

Both groups of rebels—the "isolationists" and the critical intellectuals—are making a real contribution to Jews and Judaism and are to be credited with much of the recent renascence of Orthodoxy in Israel and America—though my own identification and sympathies are with the second group. The former is extremist in character and as such makes manifest many of the ugly features that we are wont to associate with all groups that are extremist in orientation. Nonetheless, they are giving expression to strong Jewish identification and this has been contagious. Many Jewish youth cherish it and, as a result, their own ties with their people are strengthened. Moreover, it is always healthful for centrist, moderate groups to have fringe groups to the right and to the left that they may better fix for themselves the point that is the center.

But the second group is the darling of the intellectuals and understandably so. They are open-minded and rarely dogmatic. They are also creative and visionary. Consequently, they cherish communication on every level. They are not all averse to dialogue with the non-Jewish intelligentsia—Christian, Buddhist and secular. Moreover, they believe that Jewish intellectuals should communicate with each other outside the frame of established institutional lines. They already arranged and conducted a retreat of Jewish theologians—Reform, Conservative and Orthodox.

It is their feeling that in all the groups there are to be found many who share the same quest and that despite the diversity of commitments, Jewish thought can only be enriched by the exchange of ideas. To be among this group of Orthodox individuals is a spiritual delight. They combine in their outlook and performance the fervor of Hasidim, the critical reason of Mitnagdim and the ethical sensitivity of the Musar (Ethical) movement. Orthodox youth in the colleges clamor for them as speakers. With their lectures they excite the intellect, with their Hasidic songs and dances they fan the sparks of Jewish identity, and with their awareness of the modern scene and its problems they deepen ethical insight.

Have they no weaknesses? Yes, at least two. They cannot organize, lest they become an Establishment themselves. Thus they must remain goads and gadflies to stimulate others but never an organized party or pressure group. Second, they may become impatient and the bitterness that comes from frustration may replace their wholesome outlook and zestful deportment for the greater glory of God, Torah and Israel.

Chapter Five

A PLEA FOR INVOLVEMENT

Involvement or Non-Involvement in Social Issues

Within a span of fewer than forty years, the people of
the United States of America have experienced at least three
major revolutions—economic, social, and sexual. A fourth
may be even more cataclysmic—chemical manipulation of
the human personality. Jews and Judaism have been, and
will continue to be, affected by the resulting changes whose
impact will hardly be avoided even by those of our co-
religionists who succeed in completely ghettoizing themselves. For all those, however, who do not seek withdrawal
from modern, integrated society, there is no alternative but
to reckon with the changes as they occur and to become involved either in resistance to them or their control. Non-
involvement is no longer conceivable as a live option for
those who are committed to the Hirschian ideal of *"Torah
im Derech Eretz"*—of living in two civilizations by either
synthesizing them or assigning to each specific areas of
one's thought and action.

The economic revolution, which began in the thirties,
transformed the United States into a welfare state. Security
and abundance for everyone were the goals, and Jews pros-
pered as never before in Jewish history. That prosperity
contributed immeasurably to the establishment of the State
of Israel. It also made possible the construction of magnifi-

379

cent synagogues, a network of day schools on the elementary and secondary levels, the proliferation of yeshivos, and the fantastic expansion of Yeshiva University—the mother of all yeshivos on American soil. However, with prosperity also came greater social mobility for Jews, more intermarriage and assimilation, weaker ties with one's fellow-Jews, and less interdependence among them. Consequently, the younger heirs of Jewish fortunes feel less inclined to be philanthropic and support Jewish causes. But the American Jewish community is aware of what it has gained and lost because of the economic revolution and is taking steps to strengthen the gains and mitigate the losses. No one has said, "Let Jews become poor. Let Jews seek only subsistence. Poverty is good for the soul and Jews are more likely to remain loyal to Torah if they are not subjected to the trial of affluence." Even the Hasidic Jews take the fullest possible advantage of the welfare state and want it to expand to more areas rather than have it cut back. Perhaps it is because they, too, are human. Perhaps also they recognize that it is a mandate of Torah that poverty shall be no more. In the economic revolution, therefore, Jews rejoice and become involved.

They have not come to terms as fully with the social revolution in the sixties which is achieving, on the one hand, equality for all Americans—irrespective of color and ethnic origin, and, on the other hand, so much freedom for the individual that he can, with growing impunity, even defy established authority and refuse to obey laws which he regards as a threat to his equality or which order him to participate in wars waged by policy-makers of the state. In this revolution, orthodox Jews have been less involved than non-orthodox Jews. This is most unfortunate.

The Salvation of All Jews

Judaism requires that a committed Jew concern himself not only with his own personal salvation, but also with the salvation of all Jews as well as all mankind. One's obligations to one's family may be more numerous than one's obligations to all mankind. However, obligations there are to all, and it is unfortunate that today it is precisely among orthodox Jews that one senses a hesitancy to become involved in the problems of humanity, and even the problems of total Jewish survival. This is an intolerable attitude that must be branded for what it is—a form of self-centeredness under the guise of religiosity and divine approval. Those who espouse it also threaten the future of their own commitment.

The Halachah teaches us that even if a Jew has performed a mitzvah of the Torah—such as blowing the shofar or taking the four species—his performance is incomplete until every living Jew has also performed it. This postulate is not only homilectical; it has important Halachic consequences. Yet, too often I encounter brilliant students of Talmud in our yeshivos who, because they so want to advance in their own studies, resent being bothered to help weaker fellow students. They do not want to waste their time assisting a less gifted peer in the same room or in the same dormitory. Something ugly happened to them in their educational process. Teachers may have communicated to them an obsessive sense of their own elitism so that all they crave is the esteem of their equals or superiors. Frequently, the teachers themselves teach on a level that ignores the standard of achievement of even the average, not to mention the slow, student. And thus a vicious cycle is perpetuated. The drive to excellence, and, ultimately, renown, nurtures a preoccupation with self that is immoral and a violation of Torah mandates, and then there follows the alienation of many of our most learned Jews from the needs and concerns of people, Jewish and non-Jewish. This accounts for the fact that too few yeshiva students and graduates are today articulate and active participants in every phase of social action for Jewish and human survival. This also accounts for the fact that so many of them shun the pulpit rabbinate, and even as laymen in their respective communities are not active leaders in synagogues and day

381

schools. If the most learned among us are self-centered, what may one expect from the less tutored?

Many have written about this unfortunate phenomenon. However, what has not been said often enough is that the excuses offered by the offenders are inadequate, and that, in addition, their preoccupation with their own personal salvation as committed Jews may place in jeopardy the very Judaism they think they are preserving.

The principal excuse offered is that so few Jews presently devote themselves to the study of the Torah that those who can do so must deploy their energies exclusively to that area. But does the study of Torah relieve any Jew of the obligation to perform all the other mitzvos? Perhaps the scholarly rabbi cannot be as active as the dedicated pastor in visiting the sick, comforting the bereaved, caring for the needy, and counseling the troubled, but is he exempt from "Maaseh" (practice) because he is engaged in "Midrash" (study)? The Torah scholar must even demonstrate how his study of Torah leads to benign performances so that others may crave the light and crown of Torah. Time must be found for every commandment. As the layman must fix times for Torah, so the scholar must find time for involvement with others.

Greater Responsibilities

The orthodox rabbi, too, may have greater responsibilities than his non-orthodox colleagues for *kashruth, mikveh,* and Sabbath observance. But he may not say that, therefore, he will permit the non-orthodox to speak for Judaism on all social issues, thus making it appear either that Halachah has no point of view on such matters, or that orthodox rabbis do not regard these issues as important as rituals or religious observances. We must allocate our time and our forces judiciously, but unrelenting involvement there must be.

I am not arguing for or against any particular program —whether it be "black power," civil disobedience, or peace

382

in Vietnam. If rabbis cannot agree as to whether the territories recently annexed should be retained by Israel, they may not agree as to whether they should support C.O.R.E. or the Birch Society. It is against non-involvement that I argue. Jews cannot be neutral in these issues. Whether or not we want it, the social revolution is affecting fellow Jews and all fellow humans, and to remain aloof is to be oblivious to the needs of both. Nor is it proper for Jews to resolve the issues exclusively in terms of their effect on Jewish interests; the welfare of all mankind is also a Jewish interest.

Recently, I presided over a debate as to whether Jews should become involved in social issues. After the affirmative and negative sides had been presented, my revered and learned father rose to cite the examples of Abraham, our first patriarch. At the threshold of our history, he became involved in a war, and not a defensive one (Gen. 14:14). Our prophets also addressed other nations in the name of God and the righteousness He expects from all His children (e.g., Isaiah, Jeremiah and others).

In a world that has so shrunk that war or unrest in any area affects all mankind, how can any Jew say that the social revolution in the United States is not his affair? As a matter of fact, when I first uttered these words at a Yeshiva University Rabbinic Alumni convention years ago, it may have been thought that Jews had an alternative not to become involved. The revolution has moved so rapidly that in some areas Jews are the principal targets of the revolutionaries' attack. It is to be hoped that Jews will not, therefore, misunderstand the revolution. Safeguard themselves and their interests they must, but they must also seek to accommodate their interests to the just demands of the heretofore oppressed. There are no black and white answers—only grays. However, involvement there must be, with a point of view and a program and a continuing readiness to revise positions and redeploy energies and resources for the greater welfare of both Jews and all mankind. We cannot accept the blessings of the economic revolution and ignore the claims of the social revolution which is its direct consequence. As eighty percent of the population was cared for by the economic revolution, the economic depression of the remaining twenty percent became more apparent and intolerable. And, as the "Establishment" became more and more acceptable to a majority, the discontented minority had to threaten, with every conceivable weapon, the existing power structure. I am only explaining the phenomenon and urging that no sane person can ignore it. Resist it, if you will, or control it, but how can anyone but an ostrich avoid involvement?

However, the danger inherent in the stance of non-involvement is greatest in connection with the sexual revolution, and a fourth revolution yet to come—the use of chemicals to dominate or liberate the will of man, thus creating a threat to the very nature of man as conceived by our religious heritage. Those who refuse to reckon with these challenges in order to find solutions to what they spell, may be able, by their inaction, to help "kill God" more than any atheist philosopher of the past.

The New Morality

While orthodox rabbis may still debate whether the pill method for planned parenthood is permissible for Jews committed to the Halachah, we are overlooking the fact that within a few years there will have been removed the one great deterrent to sexual promiscuity by married and unmarried alike—the fear of pregnancy. The "new" morality is here. It may be as ancient as paganism, but youth—Jewish youth no less than other youth—are enamored of it. The dread of bastardy is no more. Children will not pay for the sin of their parents—they simply won't come into existence, or, if conceived, will be aborted—in most cases, lawfully. What are the educational as well as legal steps that we can take to preserve what we hold to be not only Halachic norms, but norms necessary for man to fulfill his divine image? Can a minority of traditionalists feel

384

safe because they train their daughters in their own schools? Can they shut off the ether about them and prevent contamination by television, movies, or the sensual attire of others not only on beaches but on the streets as well? Some Americans have accomplished it, but only by isolation in rural areas. Urban areas permit no such quarantine.

It is a pity that even the leadership of the yeshivos refuses to reckon with facts known to them. They prefer to assume that a yeshiva education makes one a saint and that yeshiva boys and girls are immune to the sexual revolution which has overtaken us. Panaceas I do not have, but I cannot close my mind to reality either. Perhaps a meeting of all those who care to become involved with the issue will yield a harvest of experience which will help to formulate approaches that will more effectively fulfill Halachic values and norms. But non-involvement—and a stance which says that we are simply against the new morality because it violates the mandates of Torah—is not adequate. If that is to be our stance, then we must recognize that the sanctions provided by the Torah no longer deter. Then new sanctions should be found or perhaps there are non-punitive techniques. Again, I am only arguing involvement in a major revolution—recognizing it for what it is and either doing something about it or declaring our helplessness in the face of it.

However, the fourth revolution threatens even more than our morality. It threatens our self-image. What could be more devastating!

Intellectual and moral excellence are the goals which Jews are to achieve. The highest excellence is the knowledge of God and complete submission to His will. However, our youth argue that they, too, want the vision of God which psychedelic drugs can induce. If computers can now do the work of the brain in so many areas which heretofore required the exercise of mind, why not, in this modern age, resort to artificial means of attaining mental states which Maimonides once deemed reserved for those who labor long and hard to become "prophets"? And if by the use of drugs men can be made even-tempered, generous, non-aggressive—even sexually, what is the need of so much indoctrination, and even ritual, to subdue man's will, when it can all be accomplished by chemistry?

What happens to freedom of will in Jewish theology? What happens to virtue itself when freedom of will is no more, and men are manipulated by pills?

What Jew, with an awareness of the four revolutions we are experiencing, can avoid involvement! Our house is on fire and those who would avoid involvement cannot hope that they will not burn simply because they decline to look at the flames.

But rabbis, especially, must look at and ponder the threats. The general literature on the subject is growing. It must be read and analyzed. And whether we decide to resist or control what impends, involvement there must be. We cannot assure the future of Jews or Judaism simply by looking backward. We must fathom our present situation and act with respect to three revolutions that already impinge upon us.

INDEX

A

Aaron, 135, 137, 138, 316
Abel, 50
Abraham, 5, 20, 124, 138, 178, 182, 183, 226, 247, 287, 288, 296, 297, 304, 312, 315, 383
  covenant with, 93
  encounter with God, 183
Abraham ben David, Rabbi, 175, 176, 273, 275
Adam, 50, 122, 123
Adler, 128
Adoption, 10, 114
Adultery 113, 114, 187, 258
Agency, 236
Agnostics, 153, 154, 331
Agudat ha-Admorim, 15
Agudat Yisrael, 14, 311, 347
Agudists, 312
Agus, Dr. Jacob B., 170
Albo, 274, 300
Albright, Professor William, 295, 370
Aliyah, 303
Amalek, 195
Amalekites, 278
America, 11, 198, 230, 266, 300, 334
American Council of Judaism, 178
Angels, 274
Annulment (of marriages), 213, 214, 242, 244, 251, 270
Arden, Enoch, 270
Aristotle, 184, 275

Aristotelian tradition, 121
Arizona, 100
Armed forces, 342
Art, creative, 52
Artificial insemination, 10, 107, 112
Asceticism, 82
Asheri, 213
Assimilation, 9, 83
Assyrians, 143
Atheists, 4, 5
Athenians, 184
Athens, ancient, 98
Augustine, 121, 141
Aurelius, 183
Austin, John, 40, 41, 43, 115, 225
Automobile, 53
Autonomy, 17
Autopsies, 89, 107
Avimelech, 172

B

Babylon, 295, 313, 337
Bachya, 246, 447
Bar Mitzvah, 57
Barth, Dr. Aron, 84
Bas Mitzvah, 57
Beethoven, 71
Belkin, Dr. Samuel, 205, 264, 347
Bell, Daniel, 183
Bergson, Henri, 179
Berlin, Rabbi Meyer (Bar-Ilan), 347
Betrothal, law of, 226-229, 237
Bikurim, 290, 296

389

Kook, Rabbi Abraham Isaac, 13, 264, 270, 307, 311
Kosher food, 271
Kotler, Rabbi Aaron, 264
Kuzari, 300

L

Laban, 172
Labor, 13, 49, 52
Lamentations, 295
Lamm, Norman, 103
Land, 182
  cultivation of, 61
  ownership of, 308
  title to, 307
Landau, Ezekiel, 256
Law, 8, 9, 12, 19, 24, 25, 27, 32, 34, 61, 84, 94, 153, 181, 203, 268
  divine, 47
  moral, 153
  observance of the, 94
  of the Sabbatical Year, 58
  oral, 24, 26, 27, 51, 61, 68, 70, 80, 88, 127, 128, 131, 187, 188, 190, 192, 194, 197, 207, 249, 260, 273, 352
  ritual, 26, 27
  written, 61, 84, 207
Lebovitz, Dr. Yeshayahu, 47
Legislatures, 13
Leket, 289
Levi, Eliezer, 327
Levi, tribe of, 128, 135
Leviticus, 44, 87, 109, 120, 175, 180, 190, 193, 247, 327
Liberty Bell, 290
Life, 163, 164, 190
Liebman, Charles S., 263
Logic, 174
Locke, J., 18
Lubavitscher Hasidim, 344
Lulab, 236
Lutheran, 358

M

Maccabean, 45
Machiavelli, 246
Machpela, cave of, 288
Maimon, Rabbi, 300, 312
Maimonides, 17, 46, 111, 130, 133, 144, 151, 175, 177, 207, 209, 210, 233, 260, 273, 275, 277, 299, 300, 302, 303, 326, 327, 371, 372
Maine, Sir Henry, 230
Malkizedek, 288
Marital Status, 232, 233, 234, 237
Marriage, 15, 124, 125, 226, 228, 232, 235, 236, 241, 242, 245, 270, 328
  by proxy, 235, 237
  civil, 241
  contract, 230
Martyrs, 118
Marx, Karl, 81, 361
Materialism, 152, 153
Matzos, 45, 66, 236, 329
Meat, eating of, 86
Medicine and Morals, 112
Medicine, practice of, 107
Meir, Rabbi, 248, 330
Mendelowitz, Rabbi Faivel, 344
Menopause, 111
Menstrual period, 91
Mesopotamia, 303
Messiah, 4, 6, 14, 274, 304, 328, 331, 334
Mevo ha-Talmud, 220
Mezuza, 294
Middle Ages, 42, 105, 115, 138, 141, 236, 241, 296, 298, 299, 304, 306, 317
Middle East, 300, 358
Midrash, 50, 267
Mikvehs, 384
Mill, John Stuart, 145
Mishnah, 80

Mishneh Torah, 46, 50
Mizrachi, 310, 347
Mizrachi Organization of America, 344
Mohammed, 299
Money, 56
Money lending, 268
Monogamy, 123
Monotheism, 365
Morality, 207, 208, 211, 212, 219, 217, 384
Moses, 8, 17, 20, 24, 66, 70, 135, 137, 149, 151, 181, 183, 188, 205, 276, 288, 295, 316, 352
Moslems, 21, 358
Mount Carmel, 249
Mount Sinai, 45, 71, 73, 129, 149, 177, 180, 182, 207, 366
Mourning, 42
Movement, 42
Murder, 85, 187, 254, 255, 259
Murphy v. *Waterfront Comm.*, 102
Musical Instruments, 272
Mussolini, 30

N

Nachman, Rabbi, 304
Nachmanides, 207, 277, 288, 302, 303, 326
National Council of Young Israel, 15
National Jewish Welfare Board, V11, 347
Naturalism, 151, 153, 154
Nature, 52, 53, 83
Nebuchadnezzar, King, 298
Negroes, 28, 357
Neturei Karta, 280
New York, 60
New York Board of Rabbis, 347
Newman, L., 76
Nissim, Chief Rabbi Yitzhak, 239, 269, 270, 307

Noah, 85, 172, 287
Noahide Laws, 131, 142, 143, 144, 195, 208, 209
Noam, 242
Numbers, 196
Nursing, 110, 111

O

Oath, the, 257, 259
Offerings, animal, 327, 328
Offspring, equality of, 126
Onan, 111, 112
Otto, Rudolph, 170
Ottoman, 14

P

Padan-Aram, 303
Paine, Thomas, 121, 167
Palestine, 300
Parochial schools, 345
Paschal Lamb, 66, 67, 70, 235
Passover, 30, 32, 56, 64, 67, 70, 72, 236, 297, 329
Patriarchs, 275, 276
Paul, 183, 367
Peah, 289
Penalties, 256
Penitent, 50
Pentateuch, 18, 98, 179, 273, 275, 276, 296
Pentecost, 69
Perjury, 257, 260
Persia, 295
Petrazhitsky, 34
Petuchowski, J. J., 172
Pharaohs, 67
Pharisees, 10, 24, 25, 27, 129, 137
Philanthrophy, 28
Philo, 128
Philosophy: An Introduction, 152
Philosophy of Purpose, 205
Phylacteries, 197, 236, 271, 329

Synagogues, 313, 314, 318-323, 326, 358
seating in, 272

T

Tabernacles, 45, 52, 59, 63, 72, 73, 75, 76, 236, 297
Talmud, 18, 35, 41, 55, 78, 81, 92, 102, 105, 106, 110, 134, 176, 178, 180, 186, 199, 204, 315, 317, 338, 346, 349
Talpioth, 57, 349
Tam, Rabbenu, 111
Target, 99
Taxation, 62, 106, 139, 141, 316
Teachers' Institute, 347
Tefilin, 175
Tehukat ha-Avodah, 212
Television, 57
Temple, destruction of, 297
service, 46, 47
restoration, 313
Theft, 187, 255, 256
Time, sanctity of, 330
Tithes, 105, 106, 289, 315
Torah, 6-8, 14, 32, 40, 21, 48, 58, 68-70, 73, 77, 81-83, 87, 88, 97, 98, 172, 173, 205, 206, 249, 250, 315, 353
Torah Umesorah, 344
Tosafists, 241, 250
Tosafot, 42, 213
Totalitarianism, 43
Toynbee, A., 183
Trading, 56
Tradition, 165, 166, 264-67, 365
Oral, 8, 25, 172
Written, 172
Traditionalists, 11
Truax v. Raich, 100
Truth, 21, 156, 159, 247
Tufts, 248
Turkey, 303

U

Unemployment insurance, 342
Union of Orthodox Jewish Congregations of America, 15, 343, 344, 348, 350, 354
Union of Orthodox Rabbis of the United States and Canada, 15, 345, 346, 347, 354
United Nations, 10, 63, 66, 96, 97, 99, 334
United States, 13-15, 62, 97, 101, 102, 107, 319, 342, 358, 376, 379
United States Supreme Court, 59, 100
U. S. v. Murdock, 102
United Synagogue of England, 15
Unity, 158
Universe, 164
University of London, 40
Usury, 375
Uziel, B. Z., 112

V

Vaad Hachinch Hacharedi, 344
Validity of Religious Experience, 158, 168
Vietnam, 21, 383
Virginity, 215

W

Wage contract, long term, 211
Washington, George, 342
Wealth, 13, 60
Weeks, festival of, 71, 72, 76, 77
Weinberg, Rabbi (of Montrieux), 242, 251
Western Political Thought, 183
Will, 31
Wise, S. S., 310